PRAISE FOR

"The journalist delved deep into archival material to find the connection between Mark Twain and a heroic San Francisco firefighter named Tom Sawyer, who became the model for one of Twain's most beloved characters."

—*SACRAMENTO BEE*

"A sizzling tale . . . [Graysmith] uncovers Mark Twain's friendship with the real-life Sawyer—a colorful figure in the city's early firefighting culture—and paints a detailed portrait of San Francisco, circa 1849–1866. It's jam-packed with notable residents whose long-ago importance lingers in the city's street names (Broderick, Brannan)—plus mustachioed hooligans and the Lightkeeper, an arsonist as mysterious as he was destructive."

—*SAN FRANCISCO BAY GUARDIAN*

"Thoroughly researched, written with verve and a storyteller's eye for detail and character, *Black Fire* is a rollicking tale, well told; it's safe to say that Mr. Samuel Clemens himself would have heartily approved."

—MIKE MEDAVOY, CHAIRMAN AND CHIEF EXECUTIVE OFFICER OF PHOENIX PICTURES

"Graysmith mined Gold Rush–era San Francisco and came up with 18 karats. . . . You can feel the heat and taste the ash on every page."

—MICHAEL CHERNUCHIN, EXECUTIVE PRODUCER OF *LAW & ORDER*

"Robert Graysmith has uncovered one of the most fascinating tales, both in the history of American literature and of the Old West."

—DAN GORDON, SCREENWRITER OF *THE HURRICANE*, *WYATT EARP*, AND *MURDER IN THE FIRST*

"A worthy first telling of an unknown but gripping story, *Black Fire* ignites the reader's fascination from the first page onward. The story of the real Tom Sawyer is as riveting a tale as the classic novel he inspired."

—DAVID ZUCKER, PRESIDENT OF TELEVISION AT
SCOTT FREE PRODUCTIONS AND EXECUTIVE PRODUCER OF *THE GOOD WIFE*

"Few nonfiction writers can match Robert Graysmith for capturing a city on the edge. Like he did in *Zodiac*, Graysmith paints a picture of San Francisco held siege by a mysterious criminal. I couldn't put it down."

—LARRY KARASZEWSKI, SCREENWRITER OF *ED WOOD*

"A compelling true story that reveals the legendary heroics of an American icon while unraveling an incredible mystery and giving life to the rise of California. Robert Graysmith deftly weaves an amazing historical narrative that will captivate and surprise readers."

—MICHAEL GOLDSTEIN, PRODUCER, LARKIN-GOLDSTEIN PRODUCTIONS

"I am in awe of the impeccable job [Graysmith] has done documenting this chapter in San Francisco's history . . . Graysmith brings to life this untold and fascinating story."

—RITA WILLIAMS, VETERAN TV REPORTER AND PEABODY-, EMMY-,
EDWARD R. MURROW-, AND ASSOCIATED PRESS-AWARD-WINNING JOURNALIST

"Mark Twain fanatics and firefighter-history buffs alike will flock to the tale of the real-life Tom Sawyer's adventures fighting fires in the Gold Rush–era city, depicted in remarkable detail by Graysmith . . . *Black Fire* captures the spirit of rugged adventure so beloved in Twain's work and so characteristic of the undaunted city built—time and time again—on the hopes of fortune-hunters."

—*BOOKLIST*

Black Fire

Also by Robert Graysmith

Zodiac

The Sleeping Lady

Auto Focus: The Murder of Bob Crane

Unabomber: A Desire to Kill

The Bell Tower

Zodiac Unmasked

Amerithrax: The Hunt for the Anthrax Killer

The Laughing Gorilla

The Girl in Alfred Hitchcock's Shower

THE TRUE STORY OF THE ORIGINAL TOM SAWYER—
AND OF THE MYSTERIOUS FIRES THAT BAPTIZED
GOLD RUSH–ERA SAN FRANCISCO

WRITTEN AND ILLUSTRATED BY ROBERT GRAYSMITH

Black Fire

B\D\W\Y
BROADWAY BOOKS • NEW YORK

Published in the United States by Broadway Books, an imprint of
the Crown Publishing Group, a division of Random House LLC,
a Penguin Random House Company, New York.
www.crownpublishing.com

BROADWAY BOOKS and its logo, B\D\W\Y,
are trademarks of Random House LLC.

Originally published in hardcover in the United States
by Crown Publishers, an imprint of the Crown Publishing Group,
a division of Random House LLC, New York, in 2012.

Library of Congress Cataloging-in-Publication Data
Graysmith, Robert.
  Black fire : the true story of the original Tom Sawyer—and of the mysterious fires
that baptized Gold Rush–era San Francisco / written and illustrated by Robert
Graysmith.
    p. cm.
  Includes bibliographical references.
1. Sawyer, Tom, 1832–1906. 2. San Francisco (Calif.)—Biography. 3. San Francisco
(Calif.)—History—19th century. 4. Adventure and adventurers—California—
San Francisco—Biography. 5. Firefighters—California—San Francisco—Biography.
6. Fires—California—San Francisco—History—19th century. 7. Arson—California—
San Francisco—History—19th century. 8. Twain, Mark, 1835–1910—Friends and
associates. 9. Sawyer, Tom (Fictitious character) 10. Twain, Mark, 1835–1910—Sources.
I. Title.
F869.S353S294 2012
979.4'04092—dc23
[B]
                        201200313

ISBN 978-0-307-72057-3
eISBN 978-0-307-72058-0

Printed in the United States of America

Book design by Elina D. Nudelman
*Illustrations by Robert Graysmith, except the historical images appearing on pages 78,
126, 179, 195, from the collection of Robert Graysmith*
Cover design by Christopher Brand
Cover illustration by Robert Graysmith

10 9 8 7 6 5 4 3 2 1

First Paperback Edition

IN MEMORY OF GAVIN

"You want to know how I come to figure in his books, do you?" Sawyer said. He turned on his stool, acknowledged the reporter, raised his brandy and took a sip. They were speaking of Twain, of course. "Well, as I said, we both was fond of telling stories and spinning yarns. Sam, he was mighty fond of children's doings and whenever he'd see any little fellers a-fighting on the street, he always stop and watch 'em and then he'd come up to the Blue Wing and describe the whole doings and then I'd try and beat his yarn by telling him of the antics I used to play when I was a kid and say, 'I don't believe there ever was such another little devil ever lived as I was.' Sam, he would listen to these pranks of mine with great interest and he'd occasionally take 'em down in his notebook. One day he says to me: 'I am going to put you between the covers of a book some of these days, Tom.' 'Go ahead, Sam,' I said, 'but don't disgrace my name.'"

—VIOLA RODGERS, INTERVIEW WITH TOM SAWYER,
SAN FRANCISCO CALL, October 23, 1898

CONTENTS

Part II: THE LIGHTKEEPER
September 17, 1850–June 22, 1851

Part III: STEAMING WITH TWAIN AND SAWYER
May 26, 1863–December 16, 1866

AUTHOR'S NOTE

Black Fire is the first book about Tom Sawyer, a bona fide San Francisco hero and poker-playing buddy of Mark Twain's, and his relationship with Twain, who, in 1863, was considering a first novel. In 1864, Twain began to envision a book of much wider scope as he heard more of Sawyer's incredible adventures a dozen years earlier in a landscape of burning roads, melting iron warehouses, mystery men and deadly gangs who extorted and ruled by fear. This is the true story of the volunteers; their band of boy firefighters, the torch boys; a U.S. senator; the World Heavyweight Champ; the most famous bruiser of the era; a lethal gunfighter; and fifty or sixty other misfits as they hunted a mysterious serial arsonist who, in 1849–51, would burn San Francisco to the ground six times in eighteen months. All the characters are real and their dialogue is based on letters, personal diaries, journals, memoirs, biographies, historical records, published newspaper interviews, public speeches, civil and criminal trials, illegal Vigilance Committee tribunals, transcripts and confessions, and original 1850–51 history volumes. In an 1895 interview Twain said he did not believe an author ever lived who had created a character, that characters are always drawn from someone the writer has known. "We mortals can't create, we can only copy," he said. He wanted Tom Sawyer to be the boy who carried on the nation's soul. In 1850, America was San Francisco.

—ROBERT GRAYSMITH
SAN FRANCISCO, CALIFORNIA, NOVEMBER 2011

Clockwise, from left: **Mark Twain:** *San Francisco Call* reporter in search of his first novel; **Tom Sawyer:** veteran volunteer fireman, customs inspector, and savior of ninety lives at sea; **Eliza "Lillie" Hitchcock:** a volunteer fire girl and potential subject of Twain's first novel; **U.S. Senator David C. Broderick:** chief of San Francisco's first volunteer fire company; **Bret Harte:** Mark Twain's writing partner and a rival for Lillie Hitchcock's favors

The Protagonists

Broderick's Crash Squad

Charles P. "Dutch Charley" Duane: the biggest, toughest brawler of the Gold Rush era; **Billy Mulligan:** a lethal, diminutive gunfighter with a chip on his shoulder; **James "Yankee" Sullivan:** former World Heavyweight Champ and the "Ugliest Man in San Francisco"

The Antagonists

Clockwise, from top left: **Sam Brannan:** the city's first millionaire and one of the bad old town's greediest men; **Davey Scannell:** "Prince of Rogues" and Sawyer's rival; **The Light-keeper:** an unknown serial arsonist who burns down San Francisco six times in eighteen months

# of Faithful Bully B'hoys

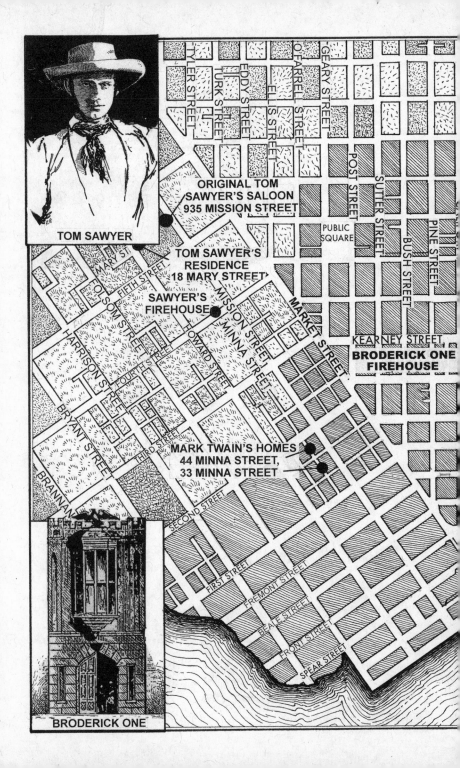

TOM SAWYER

ORIGINAL TOM
SAWYER'S SALOON
935 MISSION STREET

TOM SAWYER'S
RESIDENCE
18 MARY STREET

SAWYER'S
FIREHOUSE

KEARNEY STREET

BRODERICK ONE
FIREHOUSE

MARK TWAIN'S HOMES
44 MINNA STREET,
33 MINNA STREET

PUBLIC
SQUARE

BRODERICK ONE

LEAVENWORTH STREET

UNION STREET

JONES STREET

GREEN STREET

TAYLOR STREET

WASHINGTON STREET

PACIFIC STREET

JACKSON STREET

MASON STREET

BROADWAY

VALLEJO STREET

POWELL STREET

PUBLIC
SQUARE

STOCKTON STREET

LOMBARD STREET

CHESTNUT ST.

FILBERT STREET

"BAY" ST.

DUPONT STREET

GREENWICH STREET

**ORTSMOUTH
SQUARE**

STAHLE'S STEAMBATHS
NO. 722-724 MONTGOMERY
MONTGOMERY STREET

SANSOME STREET

ATTERY STREET

FRONT STREET

DAVIS STREET

RUMM ST

S·A·N F·R·A·N·C·I·S·C·O B·A·Y

MARK TWAIN

VOLUNTEER

GRAYSMITH

Black Fire

☞ An arsonist was loose in 1850 San Francisco. Whirlwinds of hot air spiraled around Tom Sawyer and the volunteer firefighters, then united to create a huge vortex. The giant ring rose above them. When directly overhead, the invisible ring of superheated air slowly began to turn clockwise. Gradually it took on the hue of the fire and became a golden ring. It spun faster until it created an updraft rising miles into the stratosphere. The center of the ring, hotter still, ate up all the oxygen to create a counterclockwise downdraft of sparks and lethal gases that was forced onto Sawyer and a ragtag group of boys, some as young as eight. As the inner ring rotated, it became a dark circle of smoke.

At the fire's center a hailstorm of burning embers flurried clockwise on the superheated wind. Burning coals rained down on the men. Sparks rose in the shifting gale. Highly disciplined soldiers and sailors, covered with soot, hauled kegs of black powder to buildings standing in the fire's path. Blasts more awful than the blaze shook the city and rose above the fire's monotonous roar. Terrified animals fled along the streets before the explosions. Houses leaped skyward. Sawyer held a moistened finger aloft. "The wind is altering its course," he called to the volunteers. "Yes, the gale's moving northward. We might be spared yet. The main district might not be lost entirely. The next hour will tell." But he knew the battle was hopeless.

Undeterred, the volunteers went on pulling down houses in the path of the fire to stay it. Tornadoes of flames and smoke columns walked alongside the haggard men, running clockwise and counterclockwise, creating additional whirlwinds that carried sparks miles away to start new fires. In the choking smoke the volunteers' breathing came in gasps as they rushed blindly searching for safety. Washington, Bush, and Sansome streets were thundering furnaces. The Lightkeeper, as some had named the firebug because he always struck when the Lightkeeper's Wind was rushing away from the encampment of ex-convicts on the slopes of Telegraph Hill, would burn San Francisco to the ground six times in eighteen months, the most disastrous and costly series of fires ever experienced by any major American metropolis. As Saw-yer fought the flames, he wondered what the Lightkeeper's motive was. Surely he must have one, if only to watch their hopeless battle against black fire, the most dangerous kind, produced when a heavy mix of fire gases under great pressure accumulate within a fire-involved structure and erupt at high velocity into boiling mushrooms of superheated black smoke and rapidly advance toward a hot, rich flashover. Firemen say it's "all the bad things come together at once."

The city's boundless hills, sand mountains, and valleys, its high, narrow streets filled with confusing echoes that carried for miles, made any fire impossible to find. During the volunteers' urgent missions in the twisting ravines, they dared not become lost. Thus, when darkness fell, Sawyer led his ragtag corps of torch boys ahead of their hand-drawn engines to light the way over the hazardously pitted, unlit, and fog-bound roadways. They carried fire to the fire, a very poetic occupation.

Sawyer studied the pumping and chopping firefighters of the com-pany called Broderick One around him. It took rugged brawlers to haul a one-ton water-filled engine up the steep hills of Gold Rush San Fran-cisco, including a senator, a lethal gunfighter, a master con man, the Ugliest Man in California, the World Heavyweight Champ, and fifty other street toughs and dandies, but it was left to Sawyer and his con-tingent of lightning-swift runners to unravel the Lightkeeper's identity. As if to aid the arsonist, the townsfolk slathered every jammed-together card house of oilcloth walls, white muslin floors, and canvas roofs with inflammable paint; they thrust blow pipes through tarred roofs and pumped cinders through defective flues.

The blaze rumbled westward and northeastward at the same time. The wind changed and filled the fire with oxygen. The fire's sound changed to that of a locomotive rumbling over broken tracks. Sawyer was amazed that smoke could roar. The torch boys led the men of Brod-erick One Company through shortcuts and down seldom-used alley-ways. The blaze swept toward them—a momentary darkening, then a gush of sparks followed by superheated air, dense gases, and a broad column of fire that shrouded everything with red.

There was no escape.

Mark Twain at 30 years

Mark Twain and Tom Sawyer steaming

PROLOGUE

It was the first time Tom Sawyer had ever seen Mark Twain looking glum. Sawyer studied the journalist—loose-jointed body; coarse tumble of fiery hair; long, black, lethal-looking cigar; and "soup-strainer" mustache. A rangy, lanky man, Twain did not really walk, but ambled and slouched his way through the muddy streets and back alleys of San Francisco. His normal dress was careless and disheveled. His clothes were unbrushed and freckled with tobacco, though at this moment he was nude, his chest a forest of matted hair, with one leg lolling from the arm of a chair. Twain's eyes glared like an eagle's beneath ranging, sopping brows.

On this rainy afternoon in June 1863, he was nursing a bad hangover inside Ed Stahle's fashionable Montgomery Street steam rooms halfway through what was intended to be a two-month visit to San Francisco that would stretch to three years. The sleepwalking and melancholic journalist regularly went to the Turkish baths to sweat out any dark thoughts of suicidal temptation, which were not uncommon. At the baths he played penny ante with the proprietor, Ed Stahle, and Sawyer, the recently appointed customs inspector, volunteer fireman, special policeman, and bona fide local hero.

In the clouds of boiling steam, Sawyer was mending his own wounds, though his were from a nearly fatal ordeal onboard a burning steamboat a decade earlier. In contrast to the lanky Twain, Sawyer, three years older, was a stocky, round-faced mesomorph. His sleepy blue eyes were comfortable to gaze into. His hair was a disordered haystack, a dark brown shock with sideburns. His chest was hairless and his body, smooth and well muscled, was without definition, though he could heft two men easily. In comparison to Twain's remarkable soup-strainer, his mustache and goatee were unimpressive. Sawyer was not completely nude; he wore a coat of smoke and soot that, as the three men played poker, the hot steam gradually washed away. Beneath their bare feet coursed an ancient secret tunnel and under that a huge raft upon which the massive four-story granite building floated. Two doors down was Hotaling's distillery, two doors up was the old gold-weighing station and a block away was the bloodstained ground of "Murderer's Corner," where men were hanged.

In early May, Twain had departed Virginia City for a two-month visit to San Francisco to visit Bill Briggs, the handsome brother of John Briggs, a close friend in Hannibal, and Neil Moss, a former classmate. Twain habitually passed hours at Stahle's posh ground-floor barber-shop and basement steam baths on Montgomery Street, a thoroughfare he likened to "just like being on Main Street in Hannibal and meet-ing the old familiar faces." The extensive chunk of granite known as the Montgomery Block dominated the southeast corner of Montgomery and Washington streets, numbers 722 and 724 Montgomery Street. It had been a Gold Rush tobacco warehouse, the Melodean Theatre, and now the Turkish bath where Twain parboiled with fireman Sawyer and Stahle, another good friend. Twain studied his cards and hefted a bottle of dark beer. It was cold and sweaty in his palm. He took a swig. A few glistening droplets caught in his horseshoe mustache and he left them there. He slumped as he played poker, smoking one of the Wheeling "long nines," which reportedly could kill at thirty yards. He had become addicted to them while a cub pilot on the Mississippi. Puffing, he con-tributed his own clouds to the roiling steam. Twain bought the long, disgusting licorice-flavored ropes by the basketful for a dime and by the barrel for four dollars (including the barrel). For his guests he bought the long nines in disreputable, square pasteboard boxes of two hun-dred. He awoke two or three times a night to smoke. He held his cigar poised in the air, took a few heroic whiffs, and scattered the vapor with a long sweep of his arm.

Twain had acquired a taste for steam baths at Moritz's Bath House in Virginia City and, while laboring under bronchitis and a serious cold, at the recently discovered mineral waters of Steamboat Springs, eight miles northwest on the Geiger Grade, the road between Virginia City and Steamboat Springs, a distance of seven miles. Over the first of a long line of nine beautiful steam columns, Nevadans had constructed a large house to bathe in. Twain likened the jets of hot white steam emitted from fissures in the earth to a steamboat's escape pipes. They made a boiling, surging noise exactly as a steamboat did. He enjoyed placing eggs in his handkerchief to dip them in the springs, soft-boiling them in two minutes or hard-boiling in four, depending upon his mood.

Sawyer luxuriated in the hot mist and surveyed his cards, murky in the haze. The pasteboards were damp from the sweat running down the players' arms, but the fresh bottles of German beer Stahle had had sent in were cold. In his thirty-two years Sawyer had been a torch boy in New York for Columbia Hook and Ladder Company Number Fourteen, and in San Francisco he had run before the engines and battled fire for Broderick One, the city's first volunteer fire company, under Chief David Broderick, the first fire chief. Twain, who held strong opinions on steamers, perked up when Sawyer mentioned he had toiled as a steamboat engineer plying the Mexican sea trade. The journalist had cautioned any bold boy who dreamed of shipping as a steamer fireman. "Such a job," he would say knowingly with a waggle of his finger, "has its little drawbacks." In Stahle's boiling steam room he pointed out the suffocating temperature of the furnace room where the engineer stands in a narrow space between two rows of furnaces that "glare like the fires of hell . . . he shovels coal for four hours at a stretch in an unvarying temperature of 148 degrees Fahrenheit! Steamer firemen do not live [on average] over five years!"

Sawyer had survived twice that long because he was a fireman in every sense of the word. He extinguished fires and stoked fires to fury; he knew furnaces and every aspect of perfect combustion intimately. "The stronger the draught, the thicker the fire should be," he explained, his face lighting up in the clouds of steam as he warmed to his topic. "If the fire's thickness is kept even and no hollow places are allowed to form in it, the furnace temperature gradually increases until at a certain breadth the fuel reaches a state of brilliant white incandescence." Sawyer could tell temperature by the coal's color to within a few degrees. Dull red meant 1290 degrees Fahrenheit, cherry red indicated 1470 degrees, deep orange meant the temperature exceeded 2000 degrees, and white signaled a blaze of 2370 degrees. Dazzling white meant the temperature was climbing beyond the limits of the iron boiler and had to be damped down.

Before Sawyer abandoned the sea for good, he had made a brief attempt at making a fortune in the gold mines with John W. Mackay, who did strike it big but not until much later. When bankruptcy threatened

Twain two decades later, he, too, sought Mackay's aid. By then the bonanza king was flush. An unusual number of sailors had a thirst for
prospecting and had been unusually lucky in their pursuit. Dame Fortune failed to smile upon Sawyer and he had gone back to steamship
engineering as fast as he could. When he returned to San Francisco in
1859, he became a special patrolman on land and was appointed Fire
Corporation yard keeper.

Though Sawyer never realized his dream of becoming the foreman of Knickerbocker Five, he had achieved an equally lofty position.
He had held literally the highest office in the city as a fire bell ringer
in the City Hall Tower, elevated forty yards above the mayor. In 1862,
because of his long experience fighting fire, he was elected as a delegate
under William C. Cox to the Liberty Hose Number Two, a volunteer fire
company he had helped organize a year earlier. In February 1863, he
replaced John D. Rice as Liberty Hose's foreman. Sawyer knew every
byway in San Francisco, every steep hill and twisting canyon.

Burly Ed Stahle, once a strong adherent of the rebellious and
bloodthirsty vigilantes, had lived with his family on the top floor of the
Montgomery Block since the building was erected more than a decade
earlier. Before that he had owned the baths across the way. He was living there when James King of William (King of William was so named to
set himself off from the eight other James Kings residing in his native
Georgetown, District of Columbia), the self-righteous, muckraking editor of the *Daily Evening Bulletin*, was gunned down out front. The shooter
was James P. Casey, a former volunteer firefighter with a criminal past
in the Tombs of New York. King, brought inside to die, was laid out on
Stahle's counter. In life, King's huge head, perhaps heavy from so much
brain, lolled to one side as he walked. As he lay dying, it lolled over the
edge of the beer-stained table. When King died in Buffett's store, room
297 of the Montgomery Block, the Vigilance Committee lynched Casey
and set the city aflame. Stahle still held strong opinions. He was vig-
orously opposed to a number of his patrons, especially the prominent
lawyers and judges who were not promoters of the law and order side.
"Many were the heated arguments almost to the danger point that arose
in bath and barber's chair," local author Pauline Jacobson wrote of him.

"When I first set foot in San Francisco in February 1850," Sawyer continued in the clouds of steam, "I wanted to be an engineer on a
steamer [Twain grunted in disapproval], but got sidetracked perform-
ing the honest business of fighting fire and training a gang of ragtag

adolescent boys to lead the engines with their torches. The city desperately needed Volunteers then and runners like I had been in New York City even more."

Sawyer's ninety lifesaving acts of courage had taken place onboard a burning steamboat, of which Twain had a particular horror—the kind of dread that awakened the journalist at night and set him shaking in clouds of cigar smoke. For that reason, he listened, sweat rolling down his brow, to Sawyer's story of fire and explosion onboard the steamboat *Independence*, in which nearly two hundred died from hideous scalds. The steamer, launched in New York on Christmas Day, 1850, did not reach San Francisco Bay until September 17, 1851. Blasting its whistle, laying a wide trail of foam and thrashing its paddles with abandon, the *Independence* glided toward Long Wharf, an extension of Clay and Commercial streets between Howison's Pier and the Clay Street Wharf. Pent steam was screaming through the gauge cocks. The cloud of white steam hanging above it was normal. In such noncondensing engines as those on the *Independence*, the exhaust steam escapes into the air like a Virginia City hot spring.

At the wheel swaggered a real-life pirate, the fabulous Captain Ned Wakeman. He had stolen a New York paddle-wheel steamer on the Hudson River from right under the sheriff's nose and sailed it around Cape Horn, the southernmost headland of South America. The giant's jet-black hair and whiskers gleamed in the morning light. Twain later sailed with Wakeman, who became a great friend, and described him as burly, hairy, sunburned, and "tattooed from head to foot like a Feejee islander." He conceded that Wakeman told yarns as well as he did, an incredible admission from a writer who liked his readers to think that all his ideas sprang fully grown from his fertile mind. Twain, as Sawyer reported later, took ideas from anywhere he might find them and claimed them as his own. He especially admired the pirate's animated gesture, quaint phraseology, and complete and uninhibited defiance of grammar. Wakeman lifted his huge hand—bells jangled, wheels stopped and then reversed, churning the water to foam as the *Independence* docked.

On October 4, 1851, when the *Independence* returned to San Francisco for a second time, Sawyer was on hand to sign aboard as a fireman. At 8:00 A.M., R. J. Vanderwater, the San Francisco agent for Cornelius Vanderbilt, lowered the wages of the crew and the stewards. Refusing to sail under diminished pay, the crew carted their sea chests ashore and dumped them at Vanderwater's feet. An hour later, Wakeman, who also deemed the agent's step improper, stepped onto the pier, his huge belly preceding him. Glowering with suppressed rage, "an earthquake without the noise," he had belted a bowie knife and a brace of pistols outside his jacket. Seventy-five disgruntled *Independence* passengers trailed behind this elemental force, demanding their money back. Four hours later, Vanderwater, cowed by Wakeman's fury and the loss of so many dollars, agreed to retain the rate of wages. Most of the crew and passengers returned to the *Independence,* and at 1:00 P.M., Sawyer, who could now fill a vacancy in the engineering department, sailed with them.

On February 16, 1853, the sea was running high on the *Independence*'s upward trip from San Juan del Sur, the Pacific terminus of the route across Nicaragua, via Realjo and Acapulco to San Francisco. The two-decked wooden side-wheel steamer, part of the newly organized Vanderbilt Nicaragua Line, was more than six hundred tons in weight and two hundred feet long. Its walking-beam engine, including cylinder, valve gear, beam, and cranks, was slung in graceful trunnions at the top of an A-shaped gallows frame. Below, in the engine room, Sawyer was toiling and dripping with sweat as the *Independence* steamed off the south point of Isla Santa Margarita, one of two barrier islands at the entrances into Magdalena Bay. Sawyer's shift had started at midnight alongside the firemen (Jackson, DeMott, Orr, Banks, Jones) and the coal pushers (Byrne, Gale, Merrill, Cormick, Herron, and Glenn). The firemen's mess boy, Harris, was in bed asleep. At 1:00 A.M., the ship, having been set inshore by the current, made the mainland to the east. Captain F. L. Sampson altered her course to southwest. An hour later he made the island of Margarita (then "south point at bearing W. by 8. per compass," he wrote in his log) and changed course to west southwest. "I intended to give the point a berth of three miles," he said later, "but owing to a haze over the land I was deceived in the distance." There was no haze and this was a lie. Sampson was not her regular captain. Captain T. D. Lucas, who had replaced Captain Wakeman as commander of the *Independence* a year earlier and whom Sawyer knew and respected, would have known better and steered farther away.

At 4:00 P.M., the end of Sawyer's engine room shift, he staggered on deck to get some fresh air. He had no appetite for breakfast. His mouth was dry as cotton. At daybreak the sea was smooth enough for him to spy breakers a long way off. The sight made him nervous. The Vanderbilt Line, known among angry passengers as Vanderbilt's Death Line, had suffered a string of recent accidents. On July 6, it had lost the *Union*, run aground on the lower California peninsula. Because the crew and passengers had celebrated the Fourth so heartily the night of July 5, no deck watch had been maintained. On August 17, the north-bound *Pioneer*, an 1,800-ton screw-driven Vanderbilt Line steamer, was run aground with a full load of passengers on a beach in San Simeon's Bay and abandoned. Shortly afterward, the *North America* went ashore at Acapulco in bright daylight and excellent visibility.

With these tragedies in mind Sawyer kept a watchful eye on the breakers and the much too visible shore. Those rocks had been laid down upon the chart with specific warnings in red to keep away from the point's strong currents, high rocks, and sandy islands. Some passengers who had turned out to give the crew a chance to wash the decks observed the rocks, too. "We're running dead on," they called up to the wheelhouse. "Mind your own business," Captain Sampson snapped and dismissed the high, craggy rocks as gray whales that migrate to California every winter. Sawyer knew reefs when he saw them. A sunken reef extended from the southern point of the island for about a mile offshore.

At 5:15 A.M., in a smooth sea, the *Independence* struck the high reef, shuddered like a leaf, and caught up against layers of jagged rocks. "Don't be afraid," Sampson told the passengers on deck. "You'll all get to shore safely." The *Independence*, which in spite of its newness had not been well maintained, could accommodate 250 persons comfortably and 350 unsafely. There were 359 passengers plus 56 crewmen on-board—415 altogether. Sampson barked the order to back off the rocks. Reversing engines is a complicated process in which the valves must be manipulated by hand by the engineer. Chief Engineer Jason Collins raised the hooks from their cranks until the rocker shaft hung free and then, using a six-foot-long iron bar to turn a shaft at the floor-plate level, he opened an exhaust valve. As the big piston reached the end of its stroke, there was a roar of steam. Collins stepped forward, threw the iron bar in the opposite position, and reversed the pressure from one side of the piston to the other side. "Up bar!" he cried as the hooks dropped perfectly onto the cranks. The *Independence* was backed off, but its hold was rapidly filling.

"I knew I would have to beach her to keep her from sinking," Sampson said. "I got a sail over the bow [under it] to try and stop the leak." He asked Collins to give him about five minutes' warning before water was high enough to put out the boilers so he could set a gang of men bailing at each hatchway. Sampson put the helm hard aport and ran the ship close in along the western side of the island for about four miles before he located a small cove on the southwest side. He pointed the ship head on toward the sand to beach it. In the raging surf the vessel swung around broadside, toward the beach.

Sawyer raced below and dropped into two feet of water. Through a huge rent, the sea was filling up in the *Independence*'s overheated boilers below the waterline, cooling them rapidly. Collins and his men were fighting to keep steam up. After the coal bunkers flooded, the men began tossing slats from the stateroom berths into the furnaces. Sawyer realized the blower channels were flooded and heard Collins cry, "The blowers are useless!" Loss of the blowers drove the flames furiously out the furnace doors and ignited the woodwork in the fire room and around the smokestack. When flames blocked the ladders to the engine room, the "black gang" cut their way inside with axes. Wielding an ax, Sawyer helped them. Flames broke out from the chimneys and burst from the engine room into the kitchen, killing the cooks and pantryman, and then erupted through the dead light fore and aft, spreading rapidly throughout the ship. Sawyer saw that two coal passers and a seaman were dead and ran back on deck to help the passengers evacuate. Men had begun pumping water from the sea and battling the blaze with hoses. "It's useless to do more," Collins cried.

Three lifeboats had been hoisted and craned, but among all three there was not one tholepin. Two such pins, forming an oarlock in the gunwale of the boat, act as a fulcrum for the oar. With his jackknife Captain Steele (a passenger) frantically began carving wood into working pins for at least one boat. Steam and flames were blasting up from the hatch and ventilators around the smoke stack. "The scene was perfectly horrible," Sampson said later. "Men, women and children, screeching, crying and drowning." According to passengers, "The captain seemed to lose his presence of mind and now the crew paid no attention to his contradictory commands." The badly wounded, some covered with hideous burns, flesh scalded to the bone, rolled on deck gasping.

Collins and James L. Freeborn, the purser, panicked, jumped overboard, and in the sea lost consciousness and sank. Seeing their distress, Sawyer, a powerful swimmer, dove into the water, swam down, caught both men by their hair, and pulled them to the surface. As they clung to his back, he swam for the shore a hundred yards away, a feat of amazing strength and stamina. The breakers were running heavier and the rocks were like razors. Depositing Freeborn and Collins on the beach, Sawyer swam back to the burning steamer. He made a number of round-trips, swimming to shore with a passenger or two on his back each time.

Finally the single repaired boat was lowered, and women, including a passenger named Mrs. Bolle and her two children, and many men, including the ship's surgeon, who would be needed on land, packed in and were rowed to shore. Those left behind were distraught: Spouses embraced, parents embraced children, and mothers threw their infants into the breakers rather than have them burn. Mrs. Howard and her three infants were lost; Mrs. T. Robinson and her three children drowned. General Ezra Drown, whose wife, Eliza, was drowned, described women clambering down the sides of the ship, "clinging with death-like tenacity to the ropes, rigging and larboard wheel." Mrs. Ayers, wife of the owner of the Commercial Hotel in San Francisco, threw her child to passenger John Greenback in the water below, then jumped. A protruding beam caught her skirt and she swung piteously over the waves until flames burned her dress away and she dropped. Wealthy men offered their fortunes to be saved. Others clung to spars, hatch covers, tables, trunks, coops, and planks, anything that would float, and tried to reach shore by kicking their feet. Their frantic movements attracted the attention of sharks, drawn to the area by whalers who frequented the islands and left whale carcasses behind.

At last the other two lifeboats were repaired and Thomas Herren, the steward, launched the second boat of passengers. Exhausted, Sawyer returned in a longboat to the flaming vessel, pulling hard for more passengers in spite of his badly burned forearms. And Sawyer had an idea. Though crippled, he got a group of passengers into life preservers, then towed them ashore all at once and went back for more. One father got his son to shore, but as he was wading through the heavy surf crashing on the beach, he looked back to his beloved wife. Before his eyes she was dashed overboard by "mad, unthinking men jumping upon her and driving her to the bottom." An hour later the ship was a perfect sheet of flame. The smokestack fell with a crash, raising sparks. The promenade deck tumbled. Chief Engineer Collins, recovering on the beach in the midst of two hundred people, some in the water, saw Sampson clinging to the bow as flames swept aft. Coal

Passer Beaumont, near the fore rigging, jumped into a rowboat leaving with two deckhands. Sampson swam to the boat, where he was picked up with others who were afloat.

On the beach, Sawyer realized their situation was dire: They were marooned on a lone, barren, and stony island off the coast of Baja California Sur with no food, shelter, or water. In the blazing sun, all were quickly overcome with a raging thirst. They found some water in rock fissures and, using a spoon, caught some brackish fluid. As the flames subsided that evening, the steamer burned to the water's edge and lay broadside. At midnight the mates and crew made a trip to the wreck and salvaged some fruit, pork, and salt beef. Sampson saw a steamer down the coast and launched a boat with two men and attempted to cross the heavy surf, but his boat was swamped and an oar, broken. He got to shore again, but was too exhausted to make another attempt.

The second day the beach was littered with corpses. Sawyer helped bury them above the high-water mark, but the howling wind constantly uncovered them. Using salvaged boilers and copper pots, Collins fashioned a crude distillery to condense fresh water and procured a pint of potable water every seven minutes. Next they salvaged some spars and an old sail washed ashore, and as the sun sank, made a tent for the women and children. They endured a night of looting and pillaging as the castaways fought over the corpses for their valuables and clothing. "That [Captain Sampson] was insane no one will say, would to God we could," General Drown raged. "That the act was deliberate and intentional, we believe can and will be successfully established." Drown estimated that 117 passengers, including 15 crew, had been drowned, burned to death, devoured, or driven out to sea. Collins estimated a total of 175 had been lost. Another passenger, James R. Willoughby, cursed his luck. He had engaged passage on the steamer *Northern Light* on January 20 just so he could rush aboard the *Independence* at the last minute and now was sorry he had made the ship. While Sampson went looking for help at the northern end of the island, a few passengers formed their own search party. On February 18, they located and signaled four whalers at anchor on the other side of the island. In the late afternoon they were taken aboard and fed and bathed. The whalers, though, would remain at anchor for two more weeks and delay the passengers' return to San Francisco.

The *Golden Gate* had last seen the *Independence* in the Gulf of

California. In San Francisco, relatives, concerned because the vessel was overdue, conjectured that it might have broken a shaft and put in to Guaymas or La Paz. Four days later the shipwreck survivors were spotted by the whaler *Meteor,* under Captain Jeffries, then the vessels *Omega, James Maury,* and the bark *Clement,* under Captain Lane, who had been at work in the Bay of Magdalena. Lane sent water and food back to them, and a small schooner was procured to take Captain Sampson, Sawyer, and many passengers and crewmen back to San Francisco. Ironically, just a few months earlier, the *Independence* had reached San Francisco carrying some of the 150 shipwrecked passengers off the ill-fated *North America.* Some of the *Independence* survivors found other ways home. Captain Wakemen passed them onboard the *New Orleans* on his way out of the Gate down to the Marquesas and Tahiti. On March 16, survivor James Willoughby got to San Francisco on the whaling bark *Victor* with no hat, luggage, or money. He did not need them. The magic of San Francisco worked a spell upon its citizens and imparted the feeling that in this city they could do anything simply by putting their minds to it. Willoughby went on to become a founder of the town of Ventura, a breeder of shorthorn cattle, and was among Ventura County's landowners with the largest spreads.

On Wednesday, March 30, the *Daily Alta California* learned that some *Independence* survivors had arrived on the *Meteor,* which was anchored fifty miles outside of the Heads. The next day at 6:00 A.M. the newspaper put out an extra: "Terrible Catastrophe!! Total Loss of the Steamship *Independence* and 125 Lives Lost!" and sent its reporters out into the stream to interview Sampson and Dr. Torbett, the ship's surgeon. Boatloads of survivors disembarked at Long Wharf: "Arrival of Passengers Saved," the paper headlined on April 1. Ultimately, Sawyer was officially credited with saving ninety lives at sea, among them twenty-six people he had personally plucked from the water by diving in after them and swimming them on his back to the beach.

Twain, floating in boiling clouds of steam at Stahle's steam baths, had been riveted by Sawyer's story. "Tom was a glittering hero once more—the pet of the old, the envy of the young," he wrote in the *Adventures of Tom Sawyer* years later. "His name even went into immortal print, for the village paper magnified him." He had not yet heard of Sawyer's amazing land adventures against six city-destroying fires and the hunt for the man who burned down San Francisco six times in only a year and a half. He would. Like Twain's fictional character and Twain himself, Sawyer liked to arrange the course of history to bring honor to himself.

Twain took a breath of the healing steam and raised his bet. Gradually he relaxed in the steam, his blood vessels dilated, his pores opened, and his blood pressure lowered slowly in the pleasant atmosphere. His pulse became regular, but his mind was aflame with the story he had heard. What a novel it would make. What a man this Sawyer was. Fire was in his veins. While he was in San Francisco, Twain intended to see more of him. Sawyer had more tales that also had the benefit of being true. "I pride myself on being a member of the first volunteer fire company ever formed in California," he began. "It was called Broderick One . . ."

PART I

THE MAN
WHO BURNED
DOWN
SAN FRANCISCO

December 24, 1849–September 16, 1850

Before [the engines] raced the most important members of the company—the torch boys holding their torches high as they ran, so that the way could be seen through the unlighted streets.

—Richard H. Dillon, *Embarcadero*

San Francisco's fire problems stemmed from its overabundance of regularly formed groups of desperadoes, who would as readily burn the city, murder, rob and steal, as eat.

—David D. Dana, *San Franciscan*

Liberty Hose had a young adventurer—a sailor and master firefighter whose name Tom Sawyer is said to have given Mark Twain the name for his masterpiece.

—Samuel Dickson, *Tales of San Francisco*

When the different fires took place . . . bands of plunderers issued to help themselves to whatever money or valuables lay in their way. With these they retreated to their dens, and defied detection or apprehension. Many of these fires were believed to have been raised by incendiaries, solely for the opportunity which they afforded for plundering. Persons were repeatedly seen in the act of kindling loose inflammable material in outhouses and secret places; while the subsequent confessions of convicted criminals left no doubt of the fact, that not only had frequent attempts been made to fire the city, but that some of these had unfortunately been successful. Fire, however, was only one means of obtaining their ends.

—Frank Soule, *The Annals of San Francisco*

David C. Broderick

CHAPTER ONE

Broderick and the Christmas Eve Catastrophe

Tom Sawyer had known from the beginning that the fierce competition between the volunteer companies would eventually destroy them all. In 1844, when he was twelve, his job as a torch boy for Columbia Hook and Ladder Company Number Fourteen, an outstanding company of New York fire volunteers, had brought him face-to-face with the deadly consequences of such bitter rivalry. During a race between Number Five Engine and Fourteen Engine through Chambers Street to reach a fire first, one of Fourteen's runners fell, and their 4,200-pound double-deck Philadelphia-style engine passed over him, catching him in the back with the kingbolt. As the boy lay broken and dying on the pavement, he raised his head and called out, "Go on, Fourteen!" His last words became the rallying cry of Sawyer's company as they worked that night with the stroke pump. The pump with handles fixed on either end required seven men on each set of brakes, bars by which hand-pumped fire engines are operated. Exhausted by night's end, they did not mind. The backbreaking labor helped them forget their sorrow.

"There's always a crowd of boys," one observer said, "victims of poverty and pinching and eager to earn some pennies, who vie with each other to run before the engines and hold aloft the torches that light the way." As a boy, Sawyer's occupations had been varied. Born in Brooklyn on January 1, 1832, he had worked in a bakery and shucked oysters in

Sam Brannan

Washington Market until his fingers were bleeding. But running with the engines was his passion. At age nine he had been a signal boy for the immortal Cornelius Ruderson's Hudson Number One and vividly recalled their firehouse in a lane (now Barclay Street) running down to the North River. It exhilarated him to race before the heavy engine to lead the way with a lantern on a pole over his shoulder. One engine company, Number Fifteen, had two teams of runners, the Fly-By-Nights and the Old Maid's Boys, who could beat any other company to a fire. Sawyer's Number Fourteen, known as the Wide Awake, had only fourteen men, who were pampered lavishly by their sponsors with well-furnished parlors and well-appointed bunks in an engine house under the protective wing of St. Paul's Chapel. Being a volunteer was a badge of honor and made a man somebody. Such men who risked their lives for no pay were celebrities. Some were impersonated on stage in a series of plays.

Fourteen's new neighbor and greatest rival was Howard Engine Company Thirty-four, named after Harry Howard, an orphan fire-fighter. They had relocated their firehouse on Amos Street to Greenwich Village at the northwest corner of Hudson and Christopher streets, just southwest of Washington Square. Thirty-four's greatest volunteer was David Colbert Broderick, a gifted stone quarrier and man among men. He was darkly handsome, compact and muscular. His startling blue eyes were hidden under thick dark brows. The long line of a knife scar trailed along Broderick's cheek. The raised scar displayed itself boldly whenever he experienced strong emotion. For that reason, he had cultivated a dark reddish beard to hide the imperfection. It was a Dutch beard with the upper and lower lip clean-shaven. He had gotten the wound not in a war but during a battle with a Manhattan volunteer fire company. "There was a natural human competition between our New York companies to turn out the quickest," Broderick said. Engine Company Twenty-six's battles with Company Two and Company One Hundred and Nineteen were already legendary. Broderick's chief rival in a competing unit, Protection Company Number Five, was Davey Scannell.

Because of the tremendous opportunities for political advancement afforded by being affiliated with a firehouse, the number of New York fire companies rocketed to sixty-four volunteer units with sixteen hundred blue-stockinged, exceedingly fit municipal workers constantly on call. Men fought to arm themselves with hooks and leather buckets, to callous their hands on pump and ax handles—to pump, chop, and scorch—anything to defeat a big blaze. Such huge numbers created a system so complex that a chief engineer, responsible for the care and operation of the fire engine, was appointed.

"We had a natural inclination to be first at the scene." Broderick continued. "Who wouldn't want to be first to extinguish the flames? First! God help us. We had to be first!" He pounded his fist. "But this competitive urge took a violent turn. Soon it was common for Company Number Thirty-four, my squad, the Red Rovers (named after the Cooper sea tale), to fight pitched battles (we called these 'scrimmages') for the honor of being first to put out a blaze while buildings burned to the ground. Guns and knives were frowned on, so we fought with the tools of our trade—hose butts, half spanners [hose couplers], blunderbusses, pipes [nozzles], wrenches, pry bars, ax handles . . . anything handy." A champion of weaker men, he was a first-rate bare-knuckle boxer, with the sloping shoulders of a powerful fighter toughened by a hundred street battles. "Now my strategy back in New York was to settle the conflict as fast as I could," Broderick said. "I would pick out the biggest guy the other company had to offer and take him on one to one—that's how I got this"—he ran the tip of his index finger along the long, thin line trailing under his beard. "I usually got beat by powerhouses like Mose Cutter, but I rallied my men each time." Broderick lost to the strongest the other companies had to offer. His enemies grew to respect him for standing up to them and never giving up.

Even to those who knew him best, Broderick remained a strange, extraordinary lone man who was rarely happy, often gloomy. Even in his youth he wore a savage scowl upon his face. Sawyer suspected the tough Irishman never smiled because he was in mourning. "He has no family left anywhere in the wide world," he said. Broderick, born February 4, 1820, in Washington, D.C., was the son of an immigrant father, a gifted stonemason and ornamental worker in marble. His father had carved the huge marble columns and capitals for the east front of the Capitol Building and the Senate Chamber and finished the interior decorative work in 1834. Broderick's family moved to New York, where his father became superintendent of a marble yard. His father, of feeble constitution, died two years later from his extreme labors. When Broderick's mother passed away in 1843, he cared for his younger brother. A year later his brother died in a construction site explosion when a bombshell in Duval's Foundry Yard accidentally burst.

He grew up in the roughest quarter of New York City, the notorious lower Manhattan slum the Sixth Ward, which contained the Five Points District. For five years he served an apprenticeship to a stonecutter in a yard at Washington and Barron streets. He called it one of the most laborious mechanical trades pursued by man, "an occupation that from its nature devotes its followers to thought, but debars him from conversation. I am the son of an artisan and have been a machine . . . I am not proud of this. I am sorry it is true. I would that I could have enjoyed the pleasure of life in my boyhood days, but they were denied to me, to my sorrow." He cut stone with a toothless, water-and-sand-driven, soft-iron gang saw in fifteen quarries on the East Side and on the East Aspetuck River. On tougher jobs, he used a saw-toothed implement with diamonds brazed into a blade that could slice through anything. With the help of well-placed charges of gunpowder, he carved huge blocks from the quarries. While serving at a minor post at the U.S. Custom House in New York City, Broderick joined Number Thirty-four on Gouverneur Street, where he worked their side-stroke, piano-style engine (so named because of the shape of its water box). This early pumper had seven-inch cylinders, a five-inch stroke, and a gooseneck—a swivel-jointed tube in the discharge pipe that let him accurately direct a jet of water. When Broderick, widely admired for his leadership, was promoted on May 13, 1844, his new helmet emblem, shaped like a detective's badge, was inscribed with the words "Foreman," "34," and "D. C. B." arranged in a neat rectangle.

"Goldilocks," one of the Red Rovers' young runners, was so brightly golden haired that Broderick joked, "We'll never need boys with signal lights when he is forefront at the rope."

Under Broderick, the Red Rovers challenged Sawyer's Fourteen to a "washing." To lose at a washing was one of the worst catastrophes that could befall a volunteer fireman. To play water on a fire, the engines had to line up from the source of water to the fire, one engine pumping water into another, and so on down the line. If, in the process of transferring the water, one engine could not handle the water pumped into it by the preceding machine, it was "washed" and, in the eyes of the members of other companies, disgraced. The battle between Fourteen and the Red Rovers took place at night in Mackerville, one of the roughest districts in New York City and a common battleground for the "fightingest" Irish. It was a place of squatters, tin can mansions, and shanties around Fourteenth Street and Avenue A and Avenue B. Sawyer's foreman, Venn, coaxed, cursed, and coddled his men for hours. A cry of "She's up to the rabbits! She's over!" came ringing through the cheers of the Red Rovers. They were victorious over Fourteen's machines. Fourteen was so stunned, some men cried as they lay on the ground exhausted. The "Mackereville washing" was one of the most exciting contests of the day.

"Although his origin was lowly," it was said of Broderick, "he felt stir within himself the forces of a strong nature. Though his associations were debased, he was not bound down by them and continued to rise year by year on the shoulders of the electors of the Ninth Ward." He was lifted to fame by his intense personal magnetism, marvelous knowledge of men, and absolute integrity. "He learned how to work hard, handle men and get what he wanted. He was no orator, but a man made for action . . . a populist whose strength of character was only rivaled by its complexity."

In 1840, Broderick had been a ward heeler for Tammany Hall,

the corrupt political machine of William Marcy Tweed. "Boss" Tweed yearned to be foreman of a New York volunteer fire company in the Democratic Ninth Ward that extended to the Hudson River west of Washington Square (now Greenwich Village) and housed New York's three most popular fire companies. Tweed joined several units before becoming foreman of Big Six, whose seal was a growling tiger painted on the body panel of their pumper. Tweed knew any political boss who affiliated himself with a district firehouse as their benefactor acquired that unit's prestige and great influence it wielded in their community. By allying himself, he gained not only a block of local voters but also a gang of street toughs to intimidate any opposition. The volunteers, tangible symbols of his authority, cracked heads at political rallies and got out the vote for him. When Boss Tweed became New York's "King of Corruption," cartoonist Thomas Nast refashioned the tiger into a symbol of Tweed's corrupt organization: the infamous Tammany Tiger. He incited such public outrage that his scathing cartoons eventually brought Tweed down.

In 1845, the electors of the Sixth Ward in the Bowery tapped Broderick to receive the Democratic nomination for Congress. As a devout Irish Catholic, he believed he could "make more reputation by being an honest man instead of a rascal." If he was elected, he could make a difference, but he lost to a Whig.

Broderick was a man of contradictions. Though he didn't smoke, gamble, or drink, he ran a New York tavern, the Subterranean, at the corner of King and Hudson streets, which catered to Irish laborers. Behind the bar he wore rough workingman's clothes, the class with which he most identified, yet read the great works of philosophy and literature, especially the poetry of Shelley. At the request of Colonel Jonathan Drake Stevenson, who was raising a company of soldiers to fight in the Mexican War, Broderick sold his saloon, poured the remaining barrels of whiskey down the gutter, and on April 17, 1849, resigned from the Red Rovers. As a parting gift, his men presented him with a heavy-duty, double-cased gold pocket watch. He set out from Manhattan for San Francisco, but hostilities had ceased by the time Stevenson's men reached the Pacific Coast. The tortuous trip crossing Central America damaged Broderick's health and he arrived in San Francisco on June 13, penniless and sick. The first day he vowed: "I tell you, Sir, by God, that for one hour's seat in the Senate of the United States, I would roast before a slow fire in the Square! I'll go if I have to march over a thousand corpses and every corpse a friend!"

His friend, Fred Kohler, a forty-year-old jeweler, assayer, former alderman, and volunteer assistant engineer in New York, joined him in San Francisco. Broad, clean-shaven, with muttonchops and a long straight mouth, Kohler had the stolid demeanor of a Quaker. In the summer, Stevenson pointed out to Broderick and Kohler that although gold flowed in rivers from the mines, gold coins were virtually unattainable in the Bay Area. The only coins accepted in San Francisco as legal tender were English shillings, French francs, and Mexican double *reales*—all of the same value. It would be almost ten years before San Francisco would have a government assay office to buy raw gold or a mint to manufacture coin more convenient than cumbersome buckskin pouches of gold dust. Kohler, who was clever with his hands, melted up the gold dust an idled Colonel Stevenson had bought west for fourteen dollars an ounce and cast it in five-, ten-, and twenty-dollar slugs. He and Broderick profited by putting four dollars' worth of gold into a five-dollar piece and eight dollars' worth into a ten-dollar coin. The muscular Broderick sweated before the furnace, striking coins from gold ingots, and casting and filing the slightly debased coins. As the first to coin money locally, as well as assay and stamp gold bars in their Clay Street office, they made enough by minting for Moffat and Company to retire for life. By Christmas Eve, 1849, Sawyer, who had followed Broderick to the goldfields, had been at sea for about two-thirds of his estimated five-month voyage to San Francisco. His ship, the *Splendid*, was battling the high waves and storms of Cape Horn. Sawyer was eager to become rich in the diggings and expected to reach the city by mid-February.

In San Francisco, Broderick awakened before dawn on December 24, 1849. He was not lonely. He had been such a beloved and charismatic figure in Manhattan that many of his fellow firefighters and political toughs had trailed him to San Francisco. Lying in bed, he considered the rains that had begun in early November and poured without cease throughout December. The early-morning stillness made him contemplative. He was independently wealthy, so what was he to do now? He limped to the window, wheezing and still recovering from the illness he'd contracted in Central America that had kept him from the mines and serving his friend Stevenson. Pulling aside the muslin curtain, he saw that the rain had momentarily stopped and the wind had faded away. The lull was a godsend.

Northeast of San Francisco, four-fifths of Sacramento still lay underwater, permitting a steamer to shuttle up and down its streets and enable passengers to enter their second-story City Hotel rooms by window. The fifty inches of icy rain and shotgun blasts of black hail that had soaked and pummeled San Francisco all winter had not dispelled the fitful dreams of its citizens. They tossed in their beds inside combustible homes, heads filled with nightmares of what would happen when the lifesaving downpour halted. They reposed in front of their fires listening to the faint clacking of sea coals and snakelike hiss of paraffin wicks. They watched the clear glass of their lamp chimneys blacken and, instead of being warmed, feared the worst. They dreaded the high winds off the bay that would dry the soaked wood to flammability. And with no water wells or flame-fighting equipment or the inclination to buy any, everyone knew that San Francisco would burn. Four years earlier in Pittsburgh there had been a disastrous dawn fire, but that had come after a dry winter, six weeks without rain. San Francisco's spring would be much different, but the results would be the same.

From his window, Broderick made out the end of the road where fog mounded in heaps and a prickly forest of masts towered. These nearly a thousand abandoned vessels had transported hundreds of thousands of gold seekers who in turn had made the ships orphans. Broderick's hands on the sill were the callused hands of a stonecutter, the practiced hands of a rough-and-tumble politician and consummate barroom brawler. During the night the ex-firefighter had slumbered fitfully, feeling all around him the thin boards of cloth-walled homes shaking in the rising winds. How strange the windy season passed and how tightly it had stretched his nerves. Broderick knew the danger San Francisco faced even if most of its citizens did not want to know. As in most man-made disasters, there had been indications of the tragedy to come. Someone had burned the Shades Hotel in January. On June 14, 1849, two weeks after Broderick first set foot in San Francisco, someone had torched the *Philadelphia* at dockside. A series of fires had gotten people to thinking, but no action was taken. Thinking was hard, and a little frightening. As Christmas approached, people forgot to even think. Instead they emptied Nathan Spear and William Hinckley's shelves of overpriced gifts, bathed in freshwater at three dollars a barrel, and curled up before their fires to shiver.

None were willing to take the least nominal steps toward preventing the tragedy they so feared, and which Broderick, from his experience, knew was inevitable. Instead, they pressed their noses against their windows and watched black water flow down the muddy streets to the shallow Yerba Buena Cove, a horseshoe-shaped bite in the western shore filled with abandoned ships. Bells rang low across the water. The harbor—chill, barren, desolate—fronted the instant city of San Francisco that was a world cut off from civilization. Bitter December cold, gloom, and disappointment were all about him. At this breaking dawn, the day before Christmas, 1849, Broderick thought his terrible thoughts.

He watched the road outside come to life and heard the calling of ducks and geese and tradesmen tramping sleepily through the deep mud to Portsmouth Square. Three sides of the Square were taken up by the devil: gambling dens and thrown-together hotels of dry pine with flammable canvas roofs, muslin floors, and oilpaper walls and bands who played music full blast but were silent now. Only on the fourth and upper side of the Square had God taken a small toehold in a small adobe building where the Reverend William Taylor preached in thunder that "the way of the transgressor is hard" and that a great calamity was surely to befall the great tinderbox called San Francisco. Reverend Mr. Taylor was rarely wrong.

"The [building] material is all of combustibles," a citizen complained to his friends back east. "No fire engines; no hooks or ladders; and in fact no water (except in very deep wells) available where it might be most required. Is it not enough to make a very prudent man tremble?" This canny resident warned that fire, once begun at the windward side, would be certain to burn the whole of the boomtown to ash in an instant.

The Christmas Eve fire at first appeared as the light of a candle in the second-floor window of Dennison's Exchange, one of thirty gambling dens in the Square and one of nearly a thousand in town. Dennison's stood dead center in the fledgling city on the east side at the corner of Kearny and Washington streets. From roof to ground, this "Genie of all catastrophe" was ignitability personified—ceilinged with painted cotton fabric and roofed with asphalt, or road tar. Even the paintings on its unbleached canvas walls were executed in oil. Throughout October and November, the wagering palace had sat, plump as an oil-soaked rag, ready to burst into flame at the touch of a match.

At 5:45 A.M., when the fledgling blaze was first noticed, a mild sort of alarm was disseminated along the saloons, most of them already preparing to reopen in five hours. Virtually no wind stirred, which in itself was unusual and fortuitous because the greatest threat to the city would have been an aggressive wind off the sea fanning the flames. At first the fire crawled as the halfhearted alarm ambled lazily along the Square. The news was met by silence at the City Hotel on the southwest corner of Clay and Kearny streets, the large adobe general merchandise store on the southeast corner, and the Crockett Building on the northeast corner. By day these were busy hubs. Crockett's gambling rooms and saloon had closed at near dawn and its brocaded gamblers had staggered home. It was silent, too, at the St. Francis Hotel on the southwest corner of Clay and Dupont. All the guests were asleep. The only sign of activity was between Clay and Sacramento streets. A handful of early-rising vegetable merchants and wine sellers setting up their stalls heard the whispered alarm and, yawning, absently took up the cry and passed it on as if in conversation. "Notice how prettily the fire curls along the beams," one remarked lazily as he put his crate down in the mud. "The Haley House and Bella Union are on fire, too," another added matter-of-factly.

Dogs began to yelp and the tiny fire bell *finally* rang out. At his window Broderick started at its first tinkle and observed ropy black smoke curling upward. This indicated a fresh fire. From its color he could estimate its temperature, and from experience knew what such a hot fire could do. Breathlessly he dragged on his trousers, pulled on his high boots, clapped his hat on his head, and rushed out in his shirtsleeves. The instant Broderick reached the Square, he began shouting, "Form a bucket brigade!" Fortunately, in those days everything to the east of Montgomery Street was underwater. Cove waters lapped between Washington and Clay streets, which ran from the northwest and southeast sides of the Square and rose halfway to Kearny on Jackson. So few buckets were available that the brigade had to use canvas sacks, boxes, and any container that held water. Broderick used his hat.

By 6:30 A.M. the blaze had changed its hue from yellow to blue as it fed upon casks of grog, rum, brandy, and Monongahela whiskey. The colorful blaze hypnotized onlookers who had so little to amuse them in the drudgery of their daily lives. "Well, I'll be damned," said one. "If that ain't pretty—Bengal lights [the San Francisco name for fireworks]." Charmed by the turquoise-green colors of now-blazing pharmacies, they inhaled chemical smoke as if enjoying a good cigar. By now the crowd had grown to a dispassionate audience of five thousand. Pleased at a little entertainment, they idly observed the betting halls being consumed: "Serves them right . . . lost a poke there . . . O.K. with me if Dennison's burns." The mob had a disquieting tendency to be cruel when it did not concern them and to find amusement in the misfortune of others.

In contrast to the detached spectators, the owner of an imperiled property dropped to his knees. "Help me!" he said, clasping his hands together and rocking backward and forward in the mire. "Have some mercy." After a hasty conference the spectators said, "We'll want wages." "I'll pay fifty cents a bucket to every man who fetches water to save my building," the owner implored. Just as flames began licking at the rear of his building, bidding between bystanders and proprietor reached an agreed-upon wage of a dollar per bucket. He saved his property, but it cost him several thousand dollars.

"Ooh!" said the crowd, still unconcerned. Smiles flashed in the eerie morning light. The unpaid audience continued to take a sabbatical from reason. There was not a breath of wind, so why worry? Wind was not necessary. Cotton-papered houses across the street in proximity to the scorching heat flared up spontaneously. The El Dorado, a huge canvas tent that rented for $40,000 a year, burst into flames. Burning beams and frames from the United States Coffee House crashed at their feet. Suddenly the Square, which lay on the slant side of a hill, was hot as a brick oven. Next door to the United States Restaurant was the Parker House, the first considerable house in the city. A regular two-story home with two stores, a saloon, and an entire second floor given over to gambling tables, it rented for an astonishing $150,000 a year.

Twenty yards away, Robert Smith Lammot was dressing for work when he gazed out his window. The Parker House was belching clouds of rough-textured smoke. Flames were surging wildly around every crack. Clouds of smoke were boiling from both ends. Inside, piles of gold and silver coins melted into slag. Lammot, frantically gathering up his valuables, then recalled a dreadful fact and rushed to his window. "Stored powder!" he shouted to the crowd below. "The Parker House has dozens of barrels of gunpowder in its basement! Run for your lives." *That* got a reaction.

Under showers of sparks, the mob transformed itself into an elemental force, a panicky human stampede more terrible than the fire. As the thousands scattered, the stored powder in the Parker House basement detonated, shattering the building and setting off munitions in nearby basements. A few citizens, suddenly in the middle of a battle-field with cannon on both sides, made halfhearted passes at the flames with canvas sacks and blankets. Others slathered walls with mud.

E. A. Upton, onboard one of the abandoned ships in the cove, saw the flames and rowed to shore. As he dropped onto the sandy beach, he realized he had pulled on the wrong boots. By then the fire was spread-ing rapidly down the Square. Upton remembered his stored trunks at the Merchants Exchange Hotel and frantically hobbled up Montgomery Street to hire a drayman. The road, a foot deep in mud, was over the hubs of most carts. For eight dollars he persuaded a ferryman to convey his trunks to the wharf and for another three dollars to row them out to his ship. Young John McCrackan, a Connecticut lawyer and artist who also lived inside the Ghost Fleet, joined Upton on the dunes. Together they ran toward the Square.

"The streets," McCrackan recalled, "were perfectly heaping with all kinds and descriptions of goods besides gold and silver which was melted up." The exploding Parker House had one benefit. It reminded Broderick how to slow the fire. During his marble-mining days on New York's East Side, he had carved blocks from a quarry with well-placed charges of gunpowder and used that technique fighting fire. "We must pull down and blow up a line of houses," he ordered. "If we throw kegs of powder into three or four of the burning buildings, we might isolate the blaze and pull the rest down." The impact would either smother the flames or leave the fire nothing to burn. He selected several wine stores along Washington Street, but before demolishing them allowed people to help themselves. When the proprietor of one store refused to have his emporium blown up, Broderick hauled him out by his collar, tossed him onto a heap of bricks, and exploded the adobe building. Still limping, Upton was passed by two men carrying a man hurt in an explosion. "Almost every store that was burned contained more or less powder and liquor," he said, "and explosions were taking place every moment, some of which were tremendous." A powerful north wind built, a freshening gale that sent sparks dancing and carried the blaze to three hundred houses. Feverish men axed the ground timbers of homes in the fire path and toppled them on their sides by pulling on ropes fastened to their roofs. Each time a building collapsed, flaming debris propelled down the side away from the fire torched neighboring structures. Slipping from one roof to another, the fire created its own bucket brigade of flame all the way down to the cove.

All morning the conflagration raged along the new fingerlike wharves as merchants lugged their safes and sacks of gold dust to the Maguire building at the end of Long Wharf. The blaze bridged the cove waters and burned the hulls of ships anchored off the beach. Thousands living in the Ghost Fleet plunged over the sides and swam for safety. A few fortunate ships, with the help of a light southerly turn of the wind, reached an anchorage just west of Clarke's Point. From there passengers thrashed and waded through a mile of waist-deep mud to reach unburned land and safety. At 11:00 A.M., Upton, chafed by his oversize boots, limped in agony to the beach. He rowed to his ship to soak his blistered feet. If a high wind freshened, two-thirds of the city would be burned. At least, he thought, this, the first big fire in San Francisco history, might persuade the Council to finally establish a fire department. At four o'clock in the afternoon, Upton, barefoot now, climbed back on deck. The wind had died. The fire might still be licking and leaping, but his ship's thermometer read seventy-four degrees, as if it were a mild and pleasant day. Three hours later, flames and smoke were still curling when the fire abruptly went out. Ships at sea clearly saw the red chimney of flame collapse upon itself and die.

"And by God, they've stayed the fire by resorting to powder and blowing the buildings up," McCrackan said, though during a blast two men had been killed and dozens had received broken limbs and burns. Surely, with such strong winds and paperlike dwellings resting on shifting sand, clay, and sucking mud, there would be more and greater fires, but San Franciscans had failed to comprehend the solution before their eyes. The fire only truly halted when it butted up against an unfinished brick building. Stunned, murmuring prayers, and covered with soot that made them scarcely recognizable to one another, harried men and women dug through the ruins, salvaged what they could, and cried in each other's arms. Broderick could not accurately estimate the tremendous loss of life. Fleeing mobs had trampled and kneaded bodies into the ooze. Corpses lay crushed under fallen buildings. As if shocked into silence, the winds over San Francisco scarcely stirred. For days an umbrella of ash hung unmoving above the city. John H. Brown speculated that Dennison's had been fired to avenge a racial affront committed against a black man by a southerner, Thomas Bartell, who ran the gambling house's saloon. No proof of his allegation existed. There were plenty of arson suspects.

At the height of the fire, seventy members of the Ducks, "ruffianly larrikins," ticket-of-leave men from British penal settlements, had been arrested for looting. After the fire, the Hounds, a gang of idled army renegades from Colonel Stevenson's regiment, terrorized the poor ranging through the blackened rubble and kicked apart promising heaps of debris as they searched for coins. What they had no use for they destroyed. Whoever got in their way they beat. Broderick suspected a member of one of the two gangs had instigated the arson. He pointed out how well organized and well timed the attacks had been. The Ducks and Hounds had been ready and waiting to strike. Somewhere there was a fire fiend who had set the Christmas Eve fire. There had to be. Broderick would bet his life on it. A month earlier the *Alta* had flat-out said there were arsonists in the city and demanded an increase in manpower to apprehend them. At least a night watch should be formed. The Council, responsive to their pleas, resolved to increase the police force by fifty men.

During the five hours the fire raged, it had consumed $1.5 million worth of ships, piers, and buildings—290 structures and the earliest vestiges of the city known as Yerba Buena until 1847. The one-story adobe Custom House, La Casa Grande, the oldest building in the city, survived. It was relatively fireproof. San Francisco lost all its buildings on both sides of Kearny Street between Washington and Clay streets, but they would be completely rebuilt by spring. If San Francisco's citizens were lazy when it came to forming a fire department, they set about rebuilding with awesome zeal. The Square's planked streets were still steaming as men galloped onto the surrounding mud-pit streets and leaped from their horses. Wagons carted fresh lumber down from the hills. Sailors ripped planks from the decks of the abandoned Ghost Fleet ships to incorporate into presumably haunted houses. At each site, men cleared rubbish in a minute. Within an hour, amid a racket of axes, saws, and hammers, men had raised the frames of three houses, nailed still-smoldering lumber into place, and hammered warm nails into scorched timbers. Their smoking hammers described graceful arcs in the cool air.

Tirelessly the men labored on. No sooner had they raised a block of new frameworks than a terrible gale from the sea sent them crashing into the mud. Indefatigably they lifted the timbers and stood them again. Down the beams went again, only to be thrown back up. Broderick walked the ruins looking for clues. The highly vaunted new metal houses had failed miserably and lay as misshapen grotesques, iron ovens that had baked everything inside. The uncompleted brick house that had stopped the spread of the fire interested him the most. The ex-fireman examined it for some time and even went away with one of the bricks.

No one else took heed of the indestructible building, but labored only on buildings identical to those that had burned: slight frame structures with split clapboard exteriors nailed on and interiors of simple unbleached cotton cloth, stretched smooth, with ceilings of bleached cloth that sagged in the middle. For partitions, a frame was raised, cloth and paper were applied to both sides, and a gap of air was left between. A private dwelling took two days to construct. A hotel took four days to erect and a church six days. Within the time it took to raise a church, six large houses had been roofed, weatherproofed, and completed, with four others almost done. "Beat that in the East if you can!" roared one worker, slapping his thigh as another dwelling shot up from the smoking mud—the Boomtown way.

A month earlier Captain Cole had arrived with twenty-five kits for wooden houses, numbered in sections for easy assembly. The prefabricated houses from New England were prepainted white and trimmed green. Thousands more of these prefab wooden sectionals—hospitals, churches, even bowling alleys—were at that moment being shipped west from Baltimore, Philadelphia, London, and Hamburg. Tasmania and China exported to the Bay Area portable ready-mades with mortised joints for effortless construction. Darkness fell, but the blackened figures rising from the mud were already smiling. "I have now only a $1.50 in my pocket," one optimist said, "but I do not care, for before many days are over, I will have a $150." Nothing could keep the greatest go-ahead city down. Singing and whistling, the laborers worked through the night as the fog came in and made them look like ghosts.

The morning after, Christmas Day, a few planked streets were still smoking. The cracked mud around them was still baking. When Broderick, wheezing, trudged to the blackened ruins, he saw that except for Delmonico's, the Square had simply vanished. In the fire's wake, land sharks cruised the ashes with papers and pens raised above their heads like fins. Tirelessly they crested the blackened hills seeking opportunities to buy gambling dens of their own. The time was ripe. A dozen new wagering concerns were already flourishing out of small tents. The more established gamblers saw money being lost and clamored for their burned gambling parlors to be rebuilt immediately. Dennison was arguing with Mr. Cornwall, the contractor. "I want my Exchange returned to action within two weeks," he bellowed.

"An impossibility, Mr. Dennison," Cornwall replied, surveying the gutted ground floor and furrowing his brow. Dennison whipped out $15,000 and flung it to the builder, who contracted immediately to raise the new building within fifteen days or forfeit $500 for each day past the deadline. Real San Franciscans like Dennison understood greed. It, too, was the San Francisco way. While the Parker House was still burning, its perpetually unlucky owner, Tom Maguire, was busily signing contracts to raise a new two-story building in its place. A ruddy man, top-heavy with an oiled mustache and white hair, Maguire, in the midst of such devastation, was impeccably dressed. A huge diamond was pinned in his scarf and a massive watch chain crossed his carpet vest. The former New York City hack driver turned saloonkeeper turned impresario wanted his new palace prepared by French designers and fitted out in Oriental splendor with glass pillars and mirrors that climbed to golden ceilings. Workers swiftly laid the Parker House's new basement floor timbers and arranged the building to be constructed in brick sections. Maguire expected speed and perfection. When glass panes arrived cut in sections too small for his new windows, he refused to alter his designs and instead ordered specially cut glass shipped express from Hawaii.

The El Dorado and the United States Coffee House had been decimated. The Mazourka, the Arcade, the Ward House, the Fontine House, the Alhambra, and the Aguila de Oro, in or near the Square, were badly damaged. The owners of the Bella Union, El Dorado, California Exchange, Empire, and Verandah shouted as they saw new gambling dens getting the jump on them. "Cut whatever corners necessary," they cried, watching their competitors' steady progress, "get us back in operation again!" The righteous in town, such as Edward Gilbert, the newspaper editor, would not miss the obliterated gambling dens. "Had that been the motive behind the city-destroying arson?" Broderick wondered. "Was it a way to be rid of the dens, along with squalid rows of shacks?" He saw the entire City Council—Steuart, Price, Ellis, Turk, Davis, Harris, Simmons, Harrison, Green, and Brannan—assembled in a corner of the Square and walked over, still wheezing. He concealed his discomfort.

The same iron resolution that had made him a king among men was at work. He would have to be at his most persuasive if he was to prevent another inferno.

Sam Brannan, the city's first millionaire and one of the good old town's greediest men, was such a cross between a constable and a cattle thief that one could not tell where one began and the other left off. Brannan, who had salted the city streets with flecks of gold from a quinine bottle to drum up sales for his mining supplies stores, was sitting on a barrel whittling a block of soft pine with his bowie knife. Nine months earlier he and hide merchant William Howard had transported the first thirty complete frame houses from the East. Dawn light revealed that their prefabs, advertised as "noncombustible houses," had proved amazingly combustible. The alcalde, colonial mayor John White Geary, was there, too. Geary, appointed postmaster by President James Polk a year earlier, had brought the first U.S. mail to San Francisco by steamer from the East. Everyone else had been drawn to California because James Wilson Marshall saw something glittering in his sawmill tailrace on the American River on the western slopes of the Sierra Nevada. Word got out and the world rushed in.

Chastened by the ruins, the eleven businessmen-politicians ceased talking as the acknowledged hero of the Christmas Eve fire began to speak. Broderick's Manhattan unit of volunteer firefighters had faced a similar disaster in July 1844 when three hundred buildings burned. "Why were no buildings blown up?" New York critics had asked then. "A few kegs of gunpowder judiciously ignited at 5:00 A.M. or 6:00 P.M. would have saved millions." The result was the formation of the New York Police Fire Patrol, forty volunteer smoke eaters called the Red Heads after their red leather fire caps who mastered the blasting technique in shifts at night. "Three hundred more buildings burned up on the same spot a year later," Broderick told the Council. "That's when we lost Old Number Twenty-two, a silver engine decorated with oil paintings. She could throw a stream of water six stories high. By God, she was 'The King of All Fire Engines.'"

"The King of All Fire Engines," Brannan said, wrapping his tongue around the words, trying them on for size. Yes, he liked the sound of that. It might be a way for him to humiliate Broderick, whose power was growing. A ragged scarecrow standing in the shadow of a twisted metal building inched closer. He might have been from Sydney Town, which the Ducks ruled, but unless he spoke and betrayed an Australian accent there was no way to tell. He just as easily could have been a Hound. "San Francisco has to change its habits or even greater calamities lie ahead. These workers"—Broderick swept out his arm toward the devastation—"are constructing new buildings from the scorched wood of yesterday's fire on the same spot and in the same careless way that has already caused us so much misery." He paused. "The ocean winds make the smallest fire unstoppable, so we can begin by examining what we don't have. We have no fire department, equipment, nor fire or building codes. What do we have? We have oilcloth, canvas, and cotton-batting shacks and clapboard warehouses. It boils down to three missing essentials: men, equipment, and water."

"Last May," the alcalde explained, clearing his throat, "the board appropriated money to begin digging a well and a reservoir. We passed a law that required townsfolk to keep leather buckets of sand in their kitchens to put out home fires." Geary's eyes strayed to the upper side of the Square where, until a day ago, he had dwelled in a modest room.

"And what came of this 'law'?" Brannan said. "Nothing!" He returned to his carving. A considerable pile of wood shavings lay at his feet.

"Alcalde," Broderick said, "the few cisterns we have in San Francisco are empty at low tide." In New York City the Great Croton Aqueduct brought water swarming with tadpoles to a reservoir at Fifth Avenue and Forty-second Street, where a crude pipeline of iron pipes nine to twelve inches in diameter carried water to hydrants plugged with cork. "After water, our next requirement is men. Fighting fire is backbreaking, man-killing labor, so we need fifty to sixty men—tough men—for each engine. When the alarm sounds, a man has to drop everything, run to the firehouse, and haul a two-thousand-pound engine over steep hills by rope and then pump for his life. Every municipality of importance has a chief engineer who coordinates the armies of competing fire companies. In New York, ours had a team of assistants and watchmen to run the essentials. We paid him twelve hundred dollars a year." Geary winced as if shot by a musket ball. The Boomtown, packed with instant millionaires, was curiously without funds. "San Francisco is flat busted," the alcalde said. In August, when he was sworn in, he disclosed that they were without a dollar in the public treasury, without a single police officer or watchman, and had no means for confining a prisoner for an hour.

"In short," Broderick said, "you are without a single requisite necessary for the promotion of prosperity, for the protection of property, or for the maintenance of order." The last prerequisite was equipment. "We lacked equipment in New York, though not so much as San Francisco does. Only forty-nine of our units were engine companies. Of those, only nine were hook and ladder and of those, only six were hose companies. Alcalde, what do we have on hand in the way of water wagons?"

Two weeks earlier the first fire engine in the city had arrived on the S.S. *Magdalen*. "We've got Number Forty-nine, which we call the Martin Van Buren, after the president," he said. The eighth U.S. president had used the hand-drawn engine to wet down the lawns and irrigate his fields on his New York estates before William Free brought the engine around the Horn to pump water at his gold mines. "Some engine!" Brannan said. "Twenty-years old. A toy machine." "We have another," Geary said, "an inefficient hand-drawn engine—the Oahu, a private water wagon brought from England by Starkey Janion & Company [a British importing firm]. It's well worn by years of service in Honolulu, in the Sandwich Islands."

"Put in an order for two engines," Broderick said. "Side strokers from New York for Volunteer Company Number One and Company Number Two."

"I can prevail upon Bill Howard to buy an engine for a Volunteer Company Number Three," Brannan said. The Mormon leader owned more real estate than anyone in town and could have bought twenty engines if he had been so inclined, but he allowed his wealthy partner to do the honors. "We'll still need ladders, pumps, and men trained in their use."

"And hoses," Broderick said.

"No hoses. No water. No buckets to put water in," Brannan said.

"Some salvageable merchandise still lies in the devastation," Geary noted. "Have the new police chief station men around the burned district to protect the property of the sufferers." Broderick suggested that they afford immediate medical aid to the few people who had exerted themselves during the fire and been injured. Geary nodded and resolved that the citizens meet in the Square on Wednesday at noon to organize fire companies. "So ruled," said them all, even Sam Brannan. The eavesdropping scarecrow lost himself among the charred rubble as the councilmen retired. Late that afternoon, under a heavy canopy of smoke, the most illustrious citizens in town appropriated $800 to buy hoses, buckets, ropes, hooks, axes, ladders, and Ed Otis's wagon. Otis suggested they call the new volunteer department the Independent

Unpaid Ax Company. The official names of the three volunteer groups became the San Francisco (or Eureka) Company, the Protection Company, and Engine Company Number One, which, because it was the first to organize, became Independent One. The next day the Council appointed Fred Kohler as the volunteers' temporary chief engineer at a salary of $6,000 per year, to be paid monthly from the city treasury, and increased by $1,200 within six months if he should be reelected. Kohler insisted Independent One be renamed the Empire because the unit was composed solely of men from New York, "the Empire State." Because the enormously popular Broderick had been so instrumental in establishing the first volunteer unit and was its first foreman, the majority celebrated the first volunteer unit as Broderick Engine Company Number One, ultimately renamed Broderick One.

On February 5, 1850, the Council ordered Kohler to obtain three engines. He was to superintend the organization of the volunteers, examine all engines, hose, and apparatus that the city might acquire, manage the construction of engine houses and cisterns, protect all engines and apparatus placed in the houses of private companies, and have the authority to blow up any buildings he deemed necessary for the suppression of fire.

CHAPTER TWO

Sawyer

On February 17, 1850, shortly after the striking of a single match burned San Francisco to the ground, the *Splendid*, a 392-ton mining company ship under the command of Captain Bayliss, anchored in the stream with Tom Sawyer aboard. The *Spendid* had sailed from New York on September 17, 1849, and taken 139 days by way of Cape Horn, St. Catherine's, and Valparaiso to reach the city of gold. Sawyer, who had just turned eighteen a month earlier, and sixty-five other passengers were rowed ashore for $3.00 apiece. Dressed in a hickory shirt and corduroy trousers, he sat at the bow and added up his worldly goods. It did not take long. The mud-caked and scarred boots on his feet and $11.50 in his pockets were the only items of value he owned. His immediate plan was to seek gold and then to enter steam shipping, running as a coal pusher or fireman between San Francisco and the San Juan and Panama ports or perhaps on one of the river steamers to Sacramento. Unfortunately, San Francisco Bay was jammed with an abandoned fleet of Gold Rush ships that clogged all shipping. In 1850 alone, thirty-six thousand people would arrive by sea. Those vessels that reached the bay were deserted at once by gold-crazed crews and left jammed with cargo and rotting in the harbor. Yerba Buena Cove was so shallow that bigger ships could not approach the shore to pick up passengers or tie up to unload. The loss of all the piers in the Christmas Eve fire had made unloading difficult. Things were no better along the

Tom Sawyer

San Juan route, where shipping was in disarray and rioting mobs at
Panama City, the last stop before continuing on to San Francisco, were
fighting for passage to the Golden Gate. Onboard these arriving ships
cholera was rampant. Things were worse in the goldfields. An unabated
violent rain, a very warm rain, had melted the snow so that the river
overflowed the rich diggings, submerged the goldfields, and washed out
the miners, thus mining and engineering were temporarily out of the
question for Sawyer. He learned about the first city-destroying fire not
long after he reached shore.

    An arsonist was at work in the City of Wood, an arid tinderbox of
kindling and matchwood, of brittle buildings and a few juiceless trees.
Fear was everywhere and no one knew what to do. Sawyer surveyed
the devastation. San Franciscans were enthusiastically rebuilding the
city on the exact site of the cataclysmic Christmas Eve fire and inad-

vertently making it ready for the next burning. A valiant, experienced runner with long legs and a keen sense of direction, Sawyer decided to use his experience to help organize packs of boys, some as young as seven or eight, to run ahead of the engines to light the way. If there was a vacancy, Sawyer could work the pump with the new volunteers and occasionally be a fire engineer on the river traffic, which was composed of smaller and lighter boats able to escape the shallow cove.

"Right at the beginning," Sawyer said, "I temporarily put aside my dreams of being an engineer and sought out San Francisco's first fire chief, Broderick, whom I knew from our battles in New York. I would be a signal boy, as I had been in New York, running ahead of the engine to light the way with a signal light of polished metal so that the volunteers could find the fire in the confusing streets and avoid any obstacles in their path." He quickly learned that in San Francisco they used flaming torches, not lamps. Signal boys were nicknamed torch boys or runners. Just as the volunteers bestowed pet names on their engines, San Franciscans dubbed the new fire-eaters Salamanders, implying they could survive a blaze and rise from the ashes like the fabled amphibian. They called a volunteer who tore shingles from a burning house with an ax to gain access a shingle eater.

On Sunday, Sawyer went to see Broderick at the new engine house on the south side of Kearny, between Sacramento and California streets. He found a fine brick building with the word *One* carved into its facade. How romantic it appeared in the dim light of February. The lamps had been lit. The smoky air quivered in anticipation. Evening was falling. A giddy, raucous laughter and whirl of discordant music spilled into the street. The powerful New York volunteers known as Broderick One were busy cleaning their huge engine. Old hose carts and used pumps cluttered the firehouse ground floor. Compared to the rest of rugged San Francisco, it was the most attractive, well-constructed, fireproof structure in town. Even more remarkable was how fast they had erected it, in San Francisco style: three days for a house, six for an engine house. When its entrance doors were open, like barn doors, the arched opening looked like the spreading of an angel's wings. Sawyer felt he was returning to paradise, though the men inside were not angels by any stretch of the imagination.

Broderick welcomed him as a temporary "bunker" because he had no place to live. "My men are rough men with rough pasts," he warned, "hard as flint and possessed of lightning tempers." A town formed as hastily as San Francisco was as inflammable as its inhabitants' tem-pers, and these men were walking tinderboxes. Broderick had known them from his New York firefighting days. They had either sailed west-ward with him or followed him on their own, slavish in their devo-tion. They sprang from every class and included merchants, soldiers, laborers, and bankers, but no greater gang of rogues existed—deadly gunslingers, gamblers, professional blacklegs, barroom brawlers, and a world heavyweight champion known as the Ugliest Man in Califor-nia. All were political shoulder strikers, electioneering ruffians who protected the ballot box as poll watchers for Broderick. A couple were murderers. "Broderick has certainly allied himself with a lively set of rogues," Sawyer thought. Though of dubious character (many had served time in prison), they loved to fight fire and would lay down their lives for Broderick. That was their saving grace, though almost all of them, like diminutive gunfighter Billy Mulligan, were destined to meet tragic ends: murdered, hanged, or deported. Broderick needed his roughnecks, street ruffians, ex-boxers, and gunslingers to make the political and civic changes needed if San Francisco was to survive the arsonist some called the Lightkeeper because he struck only when the Lightkeeper's Wind was blowing from the north and signal men on Telegraph Hill were lighting their warning fires against the dense fog. In the process his men might steal a little from rich thieves like Bran-nan, break a jaw or two, or rig an election or three or four to increase Broderick's political clout, but was it not all for the greater good? For most volunteers firefighting was secondary to political expediency. They all had other jobs except for Sawyer, who was waiting for an en-gineering berth on a steamer.

Broderick's men—rugged, leathered, and weather-bleached—had been rushing about all day, shouting, joking, spitting, cursing, rough-housing, and fighting—mostly fighting. Five had been heavyweight box-ers. All walked with a light swinging step, defiant and jaunty, much like gamecocks. Saints or devils, the volunteers were worthy of their pride. Their dress, as befitting such a dangerous occupation, was loose, careless, lively—and even sexy. A few wore high collars and fancy deco-rated vests, but most wore the current New York–style uniform: tight blue-black trousers or leggings, thigh-length black cowhide boots, red double-breasted flannel shirts with black buttons, and black ties. Some wore wide leather belts, but a third wore colorful suspenders in the style of New York Company Twenty-four. These gallowses, fastened in back by a leather clasp in the shape of an eagle's head, permitted them more speed in dressing.

Sawyer walked to the center of the engine house to study the barely functioning manual pumper under the lantern light. It was an offspring of an ancient line of "reg'lar highbred little steppers" and "light musical snuffboxes" of steel rods and brass supports that had emerged full born from the Continental Eagle in Old Maiden Lane. East Coast volunteers endowed their engines with fanciful names. Manhattan's Engine Three called theirs Old Brass Backs because brass covered most of its pumping mechanism. Another named their double-decker end-stroke engine the Valiant. In that tradition Broderick One called their pumper the Mankiller, after a similar hand pumper owned by New York's Exempt Fire Company.

Sunday was the time allotted for repairing the pumper and equipment—high maintenance that Broderick and every wise chief demanded of his men. The rogues swarmed around the water carrier, bearing down on the nickel and brass pipes and silver fittings, rubbing and polishing them to brilliance. They scrubbed the signal lights and lamps, filled them with oil, charged the torches with fuel, and ground, cleaned, and oiled the bills, hooks, pikes, and axes until they gleamed in the flickering light. The yellow, red, and gold side-stroke engine was very heavy, hard to pull, and harder to pump. Its rear wheels were taller than Sawyer, but its front wheels were small and pivoted, an innovation that enabled the Mankiller to turn corners on a dime. All other types of engines except the Hunnemans had to be lifted up to wheel around corners.

The Mankiller possessed another clever feature: a ricklike set of double brakes by which twenty men or thirty men on each side manually moved the brakes up and down to operate the pump. When not in operation, these suction bars could be swung up over the top and locked into place with two large brass pipes called squirrel tails. When in operation, these brakes could swiftly be lowered from the folded position to the breast-high pumping position. The cross arms of the Mankiller's pumping mechanism were slotted so the leverage could be altered without changing the length of the stroke. The hand engine operated at sixty strokes per minute (a stroke is a full up-and-down motion of the brakes) or could be sped up to double the tempo. The Mankiller's two nine-and-one-half-inch cylinders were fitted with air-discharging valves (a nine-inch stroke could produce a steady single or double stream of water). At normal pace a man could last only about ten minutes. As the rate of pumping increased, the time a man could pump lessened. The Mankiller was truly a killer of men. Fully manned and working for two minutes by the muscle power of forty volunteers, horizontal distances of between 150 feet and 196 feet could be achieved. If this old, reconditioned New York side stroker was so impressive, then what must "the King of All Fire Engines," which Broderick recalled with such admiration, have been like?

Sawyer's first job was to wash the leather apron covering the hose wheel and dress the cowhide casings and covers as others adjusted the brakes and greased the wheels. As he washed the coil of rope fastened to the Mankiller's stern to control its operation when Broderick One hauled the pumper to a blaze, Volunteer George Oakes rushed up. He drew the coil out to its length and ran his hand along it to shake off excess water. "After a blaze," Oakes ordered, drawing out the tail rope again and violently shaking it, "this is never put away wet. Nor are the drag ropes [thick cables used for pulling the engine to the fire]." Sawyer dried the ropes and then mended a bucket. As Oakes was rubbing down the silver pipes and pump handles, he smiled and asked, "Did you know that frost makes flames green?" Sawyer shook his head.

When the immaculate hose spanners, half spanners, and wrenches were put in place and the toolbox repolished, they were done. Sawyer smelled dinner cooking on the second floor and ascended behind the others into a true paradise. His breath caught in his throat at such magnificence. A huge engine might clutter the ground floor, but the upper floors were the most majestic in San Francisco. Grateful benefactors had converted the rooms into handsomely fitted-up clubrooms with billiard tables, card rooms, bars, parlors, and fine libraries. Such luxury was acceptable to a public who granted every luxury a frontier town could bestow on the men who kept the city alive when the citizens did not want to be bothered.

The Council expected the unpaid men to buy their uniforms, equipment, and engines out of their own pockets. Eventually they would offer a little financial assistance, but not before granting themselves hefty raises. The intangible rewards for the firefighters, though, were tremendous: lavish events, fashionable balls, and magnificent parades in full-dress uniform. Membership in the volunteers made a man someone in San Francisco, exempt by statute from jury duty and after five years in the unit exempt for life. Fire service was a badge of distinction equal to a gold medal. In the East, Pittsburgh's Valiant Engine Company was so popular they charged volunteers to join. Politics and firefighting had been linked from the nation's earliest days. Benjamin Franklin, father of the fire service, started the Union Fire Company in Philadelphia, the first volunteer group in America. George Washington was an enthusiastic firefighter and James Buchanan was a volunteer. Any politician who aspired to public office required the backing of at least one firehouse. Broderick realized Broderick One might pave his way to the State Senate. Kohler had his doubts. His partner was a work in progress.

San Francisco was not a city, but a ship crewed by adventurers, opportunists, and thieves. In a city teeming with blown-in-the-bottle scoundrels, a "bad man" was only slightly a scoundrel. Among the forty-niners, frontier men, and fortune hunters, there had finally arrived real heroes—the volunteers. But these heroes needed torch boys. Broderick felt a sense of urgency. Even now, the arsonist was plotting their destruction. The chief asked among the fleetest, most agile children living in the city and on the outskirts if they were interested in becoming torch boys. One such boy headed downhill to meet with him. A few leafless trees stood quivering in the morning mist. The grass was wet— where there was grass—and the hard mud around tufts incised with the tracks of rats. The boy exhaled a puff of white and gazed out over the sand hills of Contra Costa across the bay. It was like looking at the same mountainous, monotonous dunes of downtown San Francisco. A few cozy homes had tucked themselves into live oak thickets across the bay. Sturdy boats and barges glided off Yerba Buena Island, trailing white wakes in the black water. White gulls circled over Alcatraz Island. The boy counted line upon line of wharves under construction stretching from the shallows into deeper water where bigger ships could safely unload. The cove, a mile across, covered 336 acres, but near shore it was shallow as a teacup. The winter storm had washed gold down from the mountains into the streams, but there were more valuable things than gold. Lumber, brushwood, and tree limbs were more precious than any commodity except freshwater. The only uncontaminated, drinkable water in San Francisco was a single well on the western slope. Thirsty San Franciscans had to import drinking water in bottles from Sausalito or buy from water-cart men who sold barrels on the street or door-to-door for three dollars.

The boy saw Broderick in the big plate window of the Occidental Restaurant on Washington Street, where he was eating a steak butchered from a thousand-pound bear. In a town where cabbages might sell for $3 a head, tea and coffee for $400 a barrel, and a butcher knife for $30, grizzly meat was a bargain—$1 a pound. Fat on a bear's back stood three inches deep, but the meat was red, nutritious, juicy, and as sweet as a grilled pork chop. The boy and Broderick talked as they ate. When they finished, Broderick pushed back his chair and they went out onto the street. No vestige of the Christmas Eve blaze remained now. The city had swiftly rebuilt itself. Builders had thrown together any covering to make a house: wood, leather, canvas, frame, Chinese (paper), zinc, and iron. The same cursory construction went into the roads. Chests of tea, bags of coffee, and boxes of rice and beans were strewn in the mud. Stones, bricks, wood, lime, sand, bottles and boots, crockery and rags, dead dogs and cats, and enormous rats, of which the city was particularly rich, clogged the most frequented arteries. By day the up-and-down streets were dangerous. By night they were deadly.

Midblock, Broderick found himself trapped ankle deep in mud. "Why does a city of millionaires keep its roads in such disrepair," he moaned. "Surely, planking could be gotten from somewhere?" He conjectured that the roads were kept in such poor condition because the townsfolk put all their energy into the accumulation of gold. Nearby a street inspector and his two assistants balanced on planks as they carted buckets of sand and armloads of chaparral to fill in a quicksand pit. "It's a hopeless job," Broderick said. "By tonight, the mud pools will be wider and deep as ever." Broderick and the boy had gone only a few steps before they stubbed their toes on a protruding bundle of mill saws. Uneven planks encased in jagged sheets of zinc cut into Broderick's boots. New boots, like oiled clothing, were hard to come by. The interminable rainy season left local stores so understocked that one advertised knee-high boots at $96 an *ounce*. "Let's cross to Kearny here," he said. "There won't be a safe passage to the opposite side for another three blocks." Only three makeshift walks existed in town: the upper side of Kearny Street between Sacramento and Clay in front of Barrett & Sherwood's jewelry store, part of the west side of Montgomery between Clay and Washington, and Montgomery Street in the section by Burgoyne and Company's bank.

As they crossed, Broderick looked both ways. Recently a man was knocked off his horse on Kearny Street merely for undertaking to ride over a fellow who had no horse. To secure a foothold, folks ruffled the slippery battleground with iron and wooden hoops, tons of wine sieves, barrel tops, and discarded shirts and trousers. Dozens of men, horses, and wagons black with mud churned and beat the swamp until it was thick glue. Heavily laden wagons pulled by reliable London drays inched along. A pile of casks and barrels blocked a sidewalk that was only a rutted dent. People, like dancers, moved a step at a time along a bridge of bottles, drinking as they went and providing empties for future stepping-stones. Comically dignified men tiptoed to the other side of Market Street only to plunge full face into the morass before they reached it. "Pick, jump, stride, and totter," a citizen groused, "and we got something that no doubt looks somewhat like a street on a map, but is not recognizable in its natural form although they call it a street. All we succeed in is getting stuck."

Each segment of the planked Kearny Street sidewalk was different. There was a stretch of packing cases, window shutters, and a mosaic of sides and ends covered with tin. In front of Hanlon's Saloon, forty kegs had been hammered into the mud as a makeshift sidewalk that ended so abruptly unwary pedestrians plunged full length into the mud. "The narrow Kearny Street sidewalk is fearfully and wonderfully made," Broderick said. They turned onto the south side of Clay Street between Montgomery and Kearny where the city had laid its first sidewalk—stringers and springy barrel staves. The Montgomery Street sidewalk from Clay to Jackson Street was the oddest of all: two blocks made from pianos. "The fill was composed of heavy crates, big machinery tied together, and discarded cook stoves," Broderick said. "When the stoves sank, the city plugged the holes with a shipload of damaged pianos, then layered over blades twined together to make a loose crust that lack the gravity to sink further." Some streets were partially planked or had rugged cobblestones, but mostly it was mud and more mud. When the rains stopped, prevailing winds whipped the dunes over the roads. Then it was sand and more sand. "I wanted you to see firsthand," Broderick said, "that the unlit streets offer a blackness deeper than a moonless country road. On the most star-filled night you might make out the outline of a man next to you, but never his features. Fog conceals obstructions dumped in our streets everyday. On the way to fires there are nails, stones, and abandoned wagons for firefighters to trip over. You could be sucked under by quicksand or tumble headlong into surprise pits." Packs of feral pigs, "white wings," rooting in garbage along every route could be fierce. "We can't afford to get lost in the numerous hills and mazelike streets. We need fleet boys to light the way to the fire at night and carry torches ahead of the engines." The torch boys would call out hazards, potholes, abandoned wagons, and crates along the quicksandlike streets, choose the best route, and take the volunteers speedily and safely to the blaze and back. "It's a very romantic occupation for young lads to carry fire to the fire. Each will attach himself to his favorite firehouse as they are organized and receive room and board." The boys would be busy. The Lightkeeper was ready to burn down San Francisco again.

<hr />

The dense forest of rolling masts in the darkness all around the Lightkeeper had been compared to Le Havre and Marseille. From the waterfront he heard the groaning of nearly a thousand ships straining at their cables, the endless flapping of sails and scrape of anchor chains dragged about by currents. Hulls thumped together as he picked his way along the waterfront. He watched every step and listened to the creak of every board. He was wise to be wary. Passengers who had passed safely over all the dangers of the vast ocean drowned like dogs— on *land*. The wooden quays were dangerous and the worn, fire-damaged boards, easily broken. At night residents of the waterfront routinely heard the splash of heavy bodies plunging through holes into the water. These fatalities were most prevalent at ten o'clock at night, when river steamboats down from Marysville, Stockton, and Sacramento landed at Long Wharf, which was unlighted and full of gaps. Neighbors were used to fishing floating bodies out of the bay as part of their morning chores. In just four months of 1850, sixty people had plunged to their deaths through the yawing pitfalls. The number might be inflated. Jim Cunningham, the city coroner, was paid by the inquest. Thus, in the dead of night he would sometimes take a drowned corpse and dump him through the rotted planks to be fished up and autopsied again. He was once paid for six inquests on the same individual.

In early 1850, nighttime robberies were so common, powerful men kept to the center of unlit streets. They checked their concealed pistols and knives at the doors of theaters and restaurants as commonly as gentlemen might check their top hats at the Paris Opera, slipping bowie knives from their boot tops, removing derringers from vest pockets, and shaking daggers from their sleeves. Any man claiming to be unarmed was met by a startled look of incredulity and promptly searched. Criminals had the city by the throat. Edward Gilbert wanted something done. A Mexican War veteran, he had arrived in San Francisco three years earlier to become the hot-tempered senior editor of the *Daily Alta California*. His editors fought duels on a regular basis. So did Gilbert, who was infamous for challenging, then backing out, a gambit that would eventually get him killed. His sarcastic diatribe against crime read: "We doubt if there is spirit enough among our people to even reprimand one of these throat-slashers, were he caught in the act of strangling a child or setting fire to church. . . . We look with apparent satisfaction upon the sprightly attempts of the recruits of penaldom to illuminate our city free gratis."

Editor John Nugent in the *Daily Herald* saw no remedy for midday crime "but the strong arms and stout souls of the citizens themselves." He suggested that the citizens organize a band of three hundred regulators to treat a few thieves to "Lynch law" and make their fellows more careful about future depredations. "The floodgates of crime have been opened," another editor roared, "and thieves and vagabonds can do as they please and it makes me damn mad. Someone should do something, anything, *or burn the place down!*"

"Burn the place down!" the Lightkeeper agreed. "Now there's an idea!"

He moved along the pier, biding his time. At his waist he carried a small lantern. The arsonist felt some sympathy for the rabid editors. Reliably reporting on an unreliable police force must be tedious work. The new department was composed of so many ex-bandits and active bandits' pals that it must be difficult to tell the cops from the crooks. The cops made sure, for a wink and old times sake, that no punishments ever fell upon their chums. If that failed, the corrupt courts set them free for the proper monetary consideration. One could not count on juries, either. Some men made a comfortable living as jurors whose vote was for sale. Should the Lightkeeper be captured, though his existence was barely suspected except by the wisest, the chances of his conviction were slim. He looked around. The waterfront was dangerous, but then so was he.

Deeper inland Broderick One's new ragtag band of torch boys, bunkers and ragamuffins, veered off the main street onto another road, their torches carving a sharp line in the night. The echoes in the ravines were confusing. The city was filled with baffling sounds that carried for miles. Searching for a burning house ahead, the runners saw not a spark. Many buildings were hidden in pitch-black canyons or behind hills. San Francisco was small, but its high cramped streets, endless dunes, and sand mountains made any fire invisible. They were also learning that the going was tough. No level roads existed except for Washington Street.

Washington Allen Bartlett, the first alcalde, ordered Jasper O'Farrell to lay out the city following the natural hilly terrain. The Council over-ruled his plan and insisted on a gridiron layout to give the most profits upon subdivision. O'Farrell complied, with one deviation. Market Street would intersect the grid at a right angle striking out from the waterfront to the Mission District, dividing San Francisco to this day. The model of the extended city was two sections of right-angle grids with streets running north/south and east/west above Market Street, and north-east/northwest and southeast/southwest below. Thus, San Francisco streets plunge forward as if they were on a flat plane, racing over moun-tains as if they were not there at all—straight ahead, straight ahead—Onward!—the San Francisco way.

Above the roar of his forge, Othello the blacksmith heard splash-ing in the frigid blackness that was Montgomery Street. Someone was plunging through the thick mud toward his shop. He judiciously inter-spersed his blows by taps upon the anvil, always shifting his iron. He heated his tire to a bright red and deluged the rim in a water barrel to prevent it from being burned up. A cloud of steam rose. He pumped his bellows until the coals glowed white and began pounding. Iron-struck sparks flew over his leather apron, burning holes everywhere but his bare black arms and hands. "The flames know me," he thought. "The flames are my friends." He smiled, his face reddish brown against the fire and his teeth dazzling white. He wiped his glistening brow and walked to a barn door–like opening onto the thoroughfare to listen to the rhythmic *slap, slap, slap* of bare feet. He wondered how anyone dared tread at night, much less sprint, through the numerous unlit pits and obstacles of the potholed quagmire of streets. He heard the babble of many voices, the clank and creak of heavy machinery. An army was advancing upon him. A light brighter than the sooty glow of the nearby saloon danced erratically in the distance. Then a panting Olympian runner, a boy with a torch, broke abruptly through the mist, trailing a column of smoke. Nervously, Othello remembered the mysterious fire that had recently burned all of San Francisco. The city, quickly rebuilt, was plump and ready again for burning.

In March a gang of rugged firemen had dragged a bell weighing several hundred pounds into the belfry on Brenham Place—as if the simple act of hanging it would solve the problem of fires. The bell, cast by the Hooper Foundry of Troy, New York, was the first erected in California and had rung first for the burning of the steamers *Santa Clara* and *Hartford* at the end of Long Wharf. Now Othello could hear the new bell toll again—sharp, staccato taps like the pounding of his hammer. The order of the taps designated the district where the fire was and summoned the volunteers. Jumping into harness, dozens of men had raced to their firehouses to haul the heavy water rigs to the fire. At his door Othello saw a boy with upheld torch running as if to set the city ablaze again. Another set of running feet and another barefoot boy with canvas pants rolled to the knee, dashed out of the fog. Smoke from the first torch still floated in the air. The light revealed his double-breasted red flannel shirt with two vertical rows of brass buttons, a white leather belt, and ragged corduroy trousers. Chin uplifted, breath whistling, legs pumping in a blur, he hooted and called and lifted his torch to illuminate as much road as possible. The fate of an entire city was in their hands. There was always a crowd of ragged boys eager to run before the engines and hold aloft the torches that lit the way. Sawyer's eyes darted over the mud road, searching so intently he overlooked Othello, who towered as big as his smithy, whose arms were as massive as his anvil and who was backlit by his blazing furnace. Another blacksmith in town, John A. Steele, really was a giant. Sawyer would have overlooked him, too, so intent was he on missing anything in the roadbed that might hinder the progress of the volunteers. He heard the rumble of their mighty water engine keeping pace behind him. As the runners sprinted they shouted warnings back to the firefighters. Sawyer's moving torch revealed an iron stove blocking the intersecting road ahead. It had not been there that morning. "Stove leeward!"

"Crate in the road!" he called next. His warning was still ringing when a group of calloused street toughs, breathing heavily, trudged into view dragging a primitive two-thousand-pound engine with a hose reel fitted into a wrought-iron ring up the incline. Pumping brakes on each side of the four-wheel jumper, folded up on the way to a fire, gave the impression of a hay wagon with high-posted sides. As red-shirted "Bully Boys" swerved to avoid the half-submerged stove, there came the squeal of hand brakes and audible curses of sweating men gasping for breath. The large back wheels turned twice in the mud, found traction, and the odd relay race was on again.

Sawyer hoped to attach himself as a volunteer to a company still being formed: Big Six, made up totally of Baltimoreans who had hung the new bell. He might make a start there as a pumper or runner. If no bunks or torches were available with the Monumentals, he could sprint for one of the other developing units, such as Knickerbocker Five. Each would need a contingent of young boys and teens to light the way and each was violently competitive to be first. The lead boy, usually quickest, chose the fastest route. The strange rushing, lurching parade of men, heavy silver machine, curious neighbors in night dress, barking dogs, crowds of yelling boys and blazing torches, progressed. The massive wheels of the heavy manual pumper cut ribbons in the mud. The motto "Onward!" rang out. Sawyer's heart beat rapidly. "Onward!" Behind, the volunteers chanted, a counterpoint to the thudding of boots, slapping of feet, and rasping breath. Chief Broderick lifted the silver trumpet at his belt. Its clear bellow alerted the people ahead. That single note gave them hope, though not much. "The fire engines the city possesses," people knew, "are of no more use than an old maid's teapot."

As sixty hard-drinking roughhousers, heaving and chanting, rocked to and fro at the handles of the hand-pumper and extinguished two small brush fires, they knew another city-destroying blaze must happen as surely as the sun now rising over the flimsy structures. Charlie Robinson, most famous of all San Francisco torch boys, nearly broke his neck on such a treacherous street. Born in East Monmouth, Maine, he had grown up in a two-story gabled frame house at Number Nine Calhoun Street on Windmill Hill. Perched on a white picket fence across from the house where Hudson, the coffee and tea merchant, ground his spices, Charlie drew fine views of the bay. At age seven, he took painting lessons from the artist Charles C. Nahl. Threats of criminal reprisals forced Charlie's father, Doc Robinson, a theatrical producer-playwright, to flee San Francisco. He left Charlie and his mother without any means of support, so the boy began running for Big Six. Torch boys might attach themselves to their favorite firehouse, but when there was a fire, they observed strict neutrality. "If no torches were to be had in the Monumental's house," Charlie said, "I would run for St. Francisco Hook and Ladder [on Dupont Avenue], Germans, or for Lafayette Hose, the Frenchies." One night he ran for Vigilant Engine Number Nine out of their two-story fireproof brick firehouse on Stockton Street. He and a band of torch boys lighted the way for Nine's New York side lever and searched for nails on the board road. "There was a night fire in North Beach," he recalled. "Three of us were running with the engines. The first boy darted ahead and suddenly we saw his light disappear. I was next." In the next instant Charlie's torch flew out of his hand, the pockmarked ground whirled around him, and he was swallowed up. He felt blindly in the blackness. Mud and water were on both sides of him. The other boy lay under him, motionless yet breathing. His brand, balanced high above, cast down enough light for him to evaluate their predicament. They were lying at the bottom of an enormous pit. Another boy fell on top of them. "When the men with the engine saw two lights disappear and then a third, they knew something must have happened. A big hole that none of us knew about had been dug that day right in the middle of the street." Charlie heard the volunteers swearing, a piercing screech of metal, and the double squeal of brakes. If that gleaming two-thousand-pound water engine should plunge into the hole on top of them . . . He braced himself. A sudden lurch and the tips of hobnailed boots peeked over the edge. His chief's hand shot down and pulled the boys up. "Let's get going," he said and they did.

"The arsonist hadn't struck since the end of January," Sawyer recalled. "We were all on edge in those days and still woefully unprepared." The *Alta* wrote, "One of the most desperate scoundrels of England who have been serving the Queen set a fire above Washington Street." Three other small fires followed, but none got out of hand. Everyone knew the inexperienced volunteer fire companies had no equipment and excelled more at socializing than putting out city-destroying fires. "Pride comes before the fall," and pride was about all the three fledgling companies had. The arsonist counted on that.

At sunset the northwest wind, which had been blowing furiously through gullies and rushing down hills since breakfast, faltered. At ebb tide it died away completely. A deadly chill set in. According to locals the abandoned ships in the shallow cove were so saturated with ghosts their planks and sails were haunted. As proof they told the story of a runaway vessel from the fleet that rode the night fog at the Golden Gate and of a sloop lost in the towering reeds and swamp grass of the east shore frantically trying to find her way, bumping and banging, and howling away with her whistle. These orphaned vessels gave Sawyer an idea.

At 9:00 P.M., he walked toward this graveyard of ships, or as the Spaniards called it, Graveyard Harbor. Because the city had no streetlights, he measured his steps by the light of canvas houses made so transparent by interior lamps they became dwellings of solid light as so many Japanese lanterns illuminating paper houses also shed their light far into the cove. Fog-wet cobbles shone. Finn's Alley, the roughest region of a rough town, overflowed with red-eyed ex-convicts who had drifted down from Spyglass Hill and Sydney Town, the enclave of ex-convicts to the north. Sawyer negotiated an area people avoided in daylight and never visited at night. Shadows were cast on the walls of tents. Men in slouch hats slouched in saloon doorways. Shouts, clapping, and laughter drowned out bands of pumping concertinas. Monte tables were piled with bags of dust, double eagles, and doubloons, the losses and wins from monte, trondo, faro, roulette, poker, *rouge et noir,* and vingt-et-un. "Make your bets, Gents," a croupier yelled. Gamblers with drooping mustaches, wide felt hats, diamond shirt studs, and Prince Albert coats hooked their thumbs in brocade waistcoats. Sawyer rushed by the bright saloons. Ahead, the black silhouettes of ships' masts peeked over low rooftops where Montgomery Street delineated the water's edge toward its northern end. He reached Long Wharf. By day it teemed with industry, its planks rattling under the iron wheels of carriages, handcarts, porters, and drays. By day the mock auction houses, shanties, commission houses, saloons, and gambling establishments lining both sides of the pier and the frame warehouses on piles trembled. But by night Long Wharf was a silent, forlorn place, stretching a half mile into the fog of the shallow cove. The pier led him far out into the fleet moored and forgotten there. The city officially estimated that ten thousand people lived on these hulks. "In a city like this, where whole streets are built up in a week and whole squares swept away in an hour—where the floating population numbers hundreds, large portions of the fixed inhabitants live in places which cannot be described with any accuracy." Many were deserters, refugees, fugitives, mutineers, or ex-convicts and murderers hiding out from roving bands of increasingly put-upon citizens. The residents also included gamblers who had welshed on bets, thieves planning their next robbery, and respectable citizens waiting to find homes on dry land. They would have a long wait. On shore a tiny room, if available, rented for $150 per month.

Those vessels closest to Long Wharf had been transformed into lucrative ship warehouses and ship stores, ship restaurants, ship saloons, and a waterborne city hall. Ship houses and ship hotels stood shoulder to shoulder with land buildings as men began filling in the cove with sand. San Francisco embraced this waterborne metropolis as it built slowly outward to the landlocked fleet. As they cannibalized their cordage, spars, and planks, a third of the wood-scarce city would ultimately be constructed from these spectral ships. Because the finest steamers, clippers, and whalers brought only a fraction of their worth at sea, workers had begun hauling the abandoned vessels ashore.

The arsonist was abroad tonight, too. His wind, the Lightkeeper's Wind, had failed him. He rowed into the Ghost Fleet to make plans with a confederate. He always found the water city overwhelming. Hundreds of windjammers and square-riggers crowded two square miles of the bay, a lost armada dwarfing the navy of any country. San Francisco's population had swelled from two thousand to forty thousand within just seven months. Abandoned in the cove were 650 vessels and soon nearly a thousand, the greatest amount of deserted naval tonnage ever to clog a major harbor. Gold-fevered crews had instantly abandoned them in their mad quest for gold. The runaway sailors, officers, freight men, and passengers who had leaped over the side before anchors dropped had abandoned not only perfectly serviceable ships but also holds packed with unclaimed cargoes. In a city obsessed with riches, no worker would lift a hand unless paid wages more than the worth of the merchandise remaining onboard. Crewmen who had gotten $2 a day on their ships now commanded $30 on shore. Brigs, frigates, colliers, and windjammers, at the mercy of the receding or filling harbor, arched their sterns toward the Golden Gate or pointed their bows into the oncoming flow. Surrounded by half-sunken hulks and ensnarled by anchor chains and lines tangling upon themselves, so much penned-in tonnage could never be moved. The geography then was this: two groups of 250 vessels, jammed together and separated only by Howison's Wharf, Long Wharf, and the Clay Street Wharf. At the line dividing the two halves floated the Spanish brig *Euphemia*, a notorious prison ship that employed torture and forced labor. Her owner, Sam Brannan, had turned her into a regular Calcutta hole. A moan from her beaten and lashed men rolled across the choppy water. The Lightkeeper shivered and put his back to the oars. He did not wish to become one of those prisoners. Ahead he saw a ship lit by a single lantern, pulled hard, and soon reached the vessel. A rope ladder flew down and he ascended. Above he saw his secret partner.

Meanwhile, at the end of Long Wharf, Sawyer untied a skiff tethered to a piling and began rowing toward the stern silhouettes. Flocks of seabirds took wing like bats. He rowed into a covered passage between two rust-stained hulls created by fallen shrouds. He smelled tar, decaying wood, rusting iron, and rotting sail—the perfume of derelicts left to rot and sink. Pirates moored to the northeast hid out alongside genteel families. Treasure was hidden inside Graveyard Harbor, but Sawyer was after something more valuable. He planned to salvage what Broderick desperately needed: buckets, ropes, hooks, ladders, axes, and hoses. He was watchful. Huge ship storehouses such as the *Apollo* had watchmen to guard the riches and records of the city. Ahead, wavering lanterns sparkled. Smoke trailed from cooking fires. Figures on surrounding decks stood listening. Steps led up from the water to doors cut into the sides of ships. So few available lodgings existed on land that frigates in the Ghost Fleet had been drafted as ship hotels. Overcrowded, unwholesome staterooms with six berths each permitted the lodgers to sleep only between 12:00 P.M. and 4:00 A.M. Sawyer listened at these side doors for the gentle snore of sleepers, heard none, and climbed aboard a likely vessel. Wind whispered through tattered sails as he scrambled onto the deck. The frigate was canted at such an angle he had to mountain climb. Swiftly he discovered several lengths of hose. On the next abandoned hulk he ferreted out two axes, several long pieces of cracked hose, and ten leather buckets in good shape. Night was waning. This would be his last trip. Fog was drifting two feet over the water's surface as he reached a deserted whaling ship. Blubber hooks rang hollowly in the wind. The heavy-timbered ship, a cluttered superstructure of cranes and boats, had settled on the shallow bottom. Crates of cargo had swelled and stoves and prefab metal homes had burst through the hull.

Swinging up over the railing, he splashed across the deck to an entryway. Where the deck shone through, the boards were oily and rough. Paint was peeling off the spars and blocks. A deckhouse aft held useful tools. Cutting-in tackle, four large double blocks assembled in two falls, hung just below the maintop. Along the port side and aft on the starboard side, two long boats hung from davits. A squeaking noise alerted Sawyer. He lifted his lantern. Sharp discolored teeth and red eyes shone. A Danish black rat feasting on abandoned stores of cheese and rice peered back. Rats that had journeyed to San Francisco aboard vessels from every deepwater port scampered on the lacy catwalks between ships. On shore, huge aggressive rats ruled the muddy streets. Travelers tread on them in the dark. In the Square rats did at least $500 worth of damage a day and bit the ears, noses, and cheeks of sleeping men. In a single hour the rats massacred a shipload of cats shipped in from Southern California to eradicate them. The only local rat catcher was Tips, an English terrier belonging to *Alta* editor Gilbert, who refused to risk his pet.

Sawyer pried up a hatch cover. Cargo, seaweed, and a foot of oily water swirled below. He dropped down, waded in black water up to his waist into the darkened ribs of the ship, and brought up salvaged axes and long pieces of hose. He lifted himself onto the watery deck and crouched, shivering until he quit the vessel. Dawn was coloring the sky as he trundled a wheelbarrow to the firehouse on Kearny. Broderick was awake and fretting over his newly formed department's lack of equipment when he glimpsed Sawyer shaking with cold at the angel-wing doors. He ran down and swung open the doors. Buckets! Hose! Axes! He could hardly believe it. For the first time he believed they might stand a chance against the forces of treachery and indolence gathering against them—but only a slim chance.

Sawyer and some other torch boys spent the next three mornings repairing the recovered Pennock & Sellers hoses and building a rack of pegs to dry them. Hose was heavy (though Goodyear had come out with a light rubber hose eleven years earlier) and weighed about sixty pounds to each fifty-foot length, excluding couplings. The lengths of buffalo hide had been folded over to form a tube, the joints being riveted along the seams. Hose of any type was valuable and this kind was worth $1.25 a foot. Hose permitted the smoke eaters to work a safe distance from the flames and, by reversing the flow like a suction hose, eliminate the tedious task of hand-filling the pumper tubs. To lose a hose at a fire was to face a loss of honor.

Sawyer expertly pieced the cracked hose segments together with well-placed recovered rivets and with pride hung the last length of salvaged leather hose on its peg. "Just like 'leg of boot,'" said Broderick. In the noon light he examined the seams of the durable hose. "The best hose is pure oak-tanned leather," he said, turning it this way and that. "Just like the sewn leather hose we used in New York—double-riveted seams with twenty-two copper rivets of number eight wire." He counted them: "twenty-one . . . twenty-two." After Sawyer washed the repaired hoses, he rubbed them with "slush," a cheap preservative of beef tallow mixed with neat's-foot oil for leather hoses. The smelly concoction had to be applied before the hose was dry. A more supple hose allowed the engine to suction water easily.

He cleaned the tools, the nozzles and half spanners used to couple the hose; filled the salvaged buckets, mostly hand sewn of tanned sole leather; and examined them for leaks and patched some with pitch. New York fire buckets, on average, held two and a half to three gallons. Broderick One's buffalo-hide buckets were not nearly so capacious. The men spent the afternoon polishing pipes, pump handles, and trumpets, repairing slender ladders and narrow hoses, and sharpening axes with handles shaped like lazy S's. Oddly, their most important pieces of equipment were not the formidable axes, sharp and lethal, but the glazed, hand-sewn black fire helmets of quarter-inch-thick leather. They were indestructible, reinforced inside the crown by arches of tanned cowhide. A prodigious rear duckbill or beavertail brim kept water from running down their necks, protected them from falling debris, and shielded them from heat. If a volunteer lost his ax, his helmet was heavy enough to smash a window. The fire caps identified them, too: hook and ladder companies had red leather shields, engine companies had black with white numerals, and the chief's and assistant engineers' helmets were colored white. Men designated for house duty tied colored scarves around their helmets.

Their brass trumpets saved lives, too. Once, during a building fire, the second-floor planks broke under a volunteer and sent him plunging toward the flames below. At the last second he was caught by his long trumpet and suspended between floors. He was saved, but his back was black and blue for a month. During celebrations Broderick's men corked their trumpets and filled them with fine champagne. At small fires they attacked with hooks, sacks, mud, and bare hands, holding their greatest weapon, explosives, in reserve for a fire as huge as Christmas Eve's.

The times between alarms were dreary for the volunteers. After drills and equipment maintenance, they maintained the firehouse, practiced their singing (Sawyer had a beautiful singing voice), played cards, and shot billiards. Former gunfighters practiced quick draws and the ex-prizefighters boxed. The torch boys swept floors, scrubbed windows, polished the engine, washed dishes, scoured the kitchen, and peeled potatoes. When there was a shortage of official volunteers, Sawyer joined in the firefighting and never retreated, even when the fire's breath singed his only clothes.

Gloom hung over the city during the first months of 1850. Unemployment was high. Drowning on dry land was a distinct possibility. The uneasy landfill grew hungry during rainy weeks that stretched into wetter months. Water rushing beneath the streets created sinkholes, mud pits, and bogs. Montgomery Street was a mud plague of quick-sand. Drunken men were swallowed whole; half-drunk men were swal-lowed halfway. In January and February the bodies of three men were discovered under the mud in front of Everhart's Tailors. Any man who stumbled into a boggy sink at midnight, too tipsy to extricate himself, would be there in the morning, cursing, and had to be lassoed like a wild steer by strong men pulling from the safety of a planked sidewalk. No one faulted the victims. In bright daylight, sober, heavy-booted men got stuck as often. To avoid being pulled "eyeball deep," merchants fre-quently unloaded directly on the Montgomery Street waterfront. Sac-ramento Street, above Dupont, existed only as an impassable ravine and was not even "jackassable." A mule team, wildly snorting and still hitched to their wagon, disappeared into its quicksand and was never recovered. Teams were sucked under marshlike roads. Luckier steeds were hauled out by cables reeved to blocks lashed to the pillars of any standing building.

Sawyer wandered along Market, passing storefronts proclaiming "Crooks Sperm and Polar Oil," "Union Rooms," and "Eighteen-Carat Hash." With no pavement, he chose his steps carefully, ready to leap to safety at any moment. Volunteer George Oakes favored bottle steps as a way to get around the mud streets. "Some merchants hammer bottles neck down into the mud in front of their stores so their customers can cross the street on pretty little glass stepping-stones," he said. "Drink-ing here is such a passion that empty bottles are our greatest resource."

Meanwhile, Broderick's quiet search for the arsonist continued. He had a secret weapon: a way to discover the Lightkeeper's identity. He did not have much time.

The Mankiller

CHAPTER THREE

Sleeprunners and Flying Houses

One golden March day in 1850 followed another at the new firehouse as Broderick's volunteers threw balls; held grand dinners; presented stage musicals, plays, and chowder parties; and competed with the other companies to see who had the grandest furnishings. The new Sansome Hook and Ladder Company spent more than $5,000 for theirs. In the evening Broderick One's angel-wing doors were opened to the coolness. Sawyer, who had just turned eighteen, and Fred Kohler, Broderick's partner and chief engineer of all the volunteer companies, arms folded, leaned back on cane-bottomed chairs and observed the blue light that came so suddenly over the Gold Rush town. As summer approached, its soft evening light would seemingly last forever. These were fine times for the Brooklyn street boy—a warm bed, good friends, and heroes packed with foolhardy courage to admire. Best of all he had a puzzle to solve and a villain to catch. At that moment San Francisco was the most exciting and swiftest-moving city on earth. Every day on average thirty new houses were built, two murders committed, and one small fire set. Rugged, heavily armed men trudged past on Kearny Street—unkempt, unwashed young men—a fine hardy breed in heavy woolen shirts with rolled sleeves, sashes for belts, and trousers cut from canvas tents. Rugged mountain men and well-fed merchants passed together. Lynx-eyed gamblers in black broadcloth coats learned that their patent leather boots got just as caked with mud as the miners' plain boots. The arsonist, if Broderick was right, could be any of them, even someone Sawyer knew. One question dominated his mind: What was the arsonist's motive for burning down San Francisco? In the search for the Lightkeeper, Sawyer's attention focused on a gang called the Hounds. It happened that he and George Oakes met a particularly vicious band of them the following Sunday.

"Watch out," Oakes warned the boy. "The Hounds are barking!" When the Hounds barked, the town became meek. Like an army under command, the thugs struck hard and shot fast. Storekeepers never antagonized these masters of the plunge and knife who robbed and stabbed in daylight without the slightest provocation. One passerby returned an insult from a Hound. The thug tore his tongue out. Another accidentally brushed a Hound's shoulder. His ears were sliced off. One Sunday some citizens collided with their ragtag parade. The riot, which lasted all afternoon, left the innocents clubbed and bloody and the Hounds stronger and more feared than ever. At the head of the reconstructed Square, an arrogant group of men in grimy quasi-military dress entered the public space. Playing discordantly on a fife and drum, the Hounds marched, accompanying their makeshift parade with groans, hisses, catcalls, and yelps. Tramping directly into the center of the Square, they stopped waving their banners to shove a few folks from their path.

"Lieutenant" Sam Roberts, the "Hound Supreme," guided five of his men into a restaurant. Roberts, an illiterate brute in a tattered uniform of full regimentals with dirty gold braid, made sure his men ate and drank gratis. He sat down at a table and propped up his muddy boots. "Gin and Tonic! Gin and Tonic!" he jeered. The owner obeyed. He knew the Hounds often piled up restaurant furniture and set it afire before they left. At a shadowed table not far away, a tall thin man with greasy black hair sat listening. His hands were callused and scarred and his face pockmarked. His long coat hid a soot-stained, handmade copper lantern the size of a snuffbox at his belt. A crude opening had been cut into its side to create a small door. The interior was large enough for a single coal and some kindling. This man observed the Hounds wherever he could. It was easy. All day every Sunday, Hounds dressed in outrageous military costumes marched into every corner of the city.

"The Hounds are a semimilitary company of sixty to a hundred young thugs," Oakes explained to Sawyer. They sprang from the gangs of the Bowery and the Five Points at the intersection of Baxter, Park, and Worth streets, a "bull-baiting, rip-roaring hell" with its own "Den of

Thieves" and "Murderer's Alley." New York diarist Philip Hone wrote of
Five Points' child gangs as "swarms of ragged barefooted, un-breeched
little tatterdemalions." Many had been signal boys for the New York fire
companies. Too unlawful and unsavory to last, the Five Points' "Plug
Uglies" and "Dead Rabbits" from the Empire Club on Park Row had
come west with Broderick's mentor Colonel Jonathan Drake Stevenson
in March 1847. The Hounds were remnants of the 750 ragtag soldiers
in the First New York Volunteers that Stevenson commanded to secure
California during the Mexican War. Hostilities had ceased by the time
they reached the Pacific Coast, so in San Francisco they were idled
and ill content. Because sailors deserted every ship that arrived in the
cove, the city hired the ex-soldiers as peace officers, called them the
Regulators, and paid $25 a head for each runaway sailor they captured.
Finally, the Regulators became a greater evil than the lawbreakers they
had been hired to apprehend. They formed a ravening gang of sharpers
and gamblers, named themselves the Hounds, and set up headquarters
in a big tent they called the Shades, at the corner of Kearny and Commercial streets.

In the Square the intimidated restaurant owner served Roberts
and his men for free. He would endure. Soon there would be no Hounds.
In the meantime, it was wiser to let them take out their viciousness
on the town's minorities. Allegedly under orders from the former alcalde, T. M. Leavenworth, the Hounds set out to rid the town of Spanish
Americans. In the lee of Telegraph Hill lay Spanish Town, the Chileno
quarter. The Hounds, who lived at the base of the hill, launched mur-
derous raids on the villagers on the slopes above. The night of July 14 in
the year before, their self-appointed committee of justice perpetrated a
drunken racist attack on Little Chile. Beating, killing, and raping, they
stole a fortune in gold dust and set ablaze what they could not use. W. E.
Spofford organized 230 citizens into armed police squads and headed
toward the Shades, which was empty at the time. Roberts escaped, but
the search of a Stockton-bound steamer unearthed him in the hold hiding behind bags of sugar. In a single day Sam Brannan tried, convicted,
and deported twenty Hounds and sentenced the ringleaders, including
Roberts, to terms ranging from one to ten years at hard labor. Because
at the time the city had no jail to confine them, they were temporarily
lodged on the warship *Warren* in the cove, then released into the city.
Everyone knew the Hounds set fires for protection money. In the Square
the six thugs finally left and staggered down the street. The sound of

the fife and drum and their calls of "Woof! Woof! Woof!" faded into the distance. The thin man paid for his meal and strode in the direction of the waterfront. "Woof! Woof! Woof! indeed," thought the Lightkeeper.

When Sawyer returned to Broderick One, he heard terrible news. Recently an incumbent state legislator had been named to the California Supreme Court and left a vacant State Senate seat. Broderick, revered because of his heroic actions during the Christmas Eve fire, was overwhelmingly elected 50 to 1 to replace the departing senator. Broderick's dream had been realized, but now the chief's time would be divided between San Francisco and San Jose, the temporary state capital forty-nine miles to the south. Thus a strong leader and calming influence that might have prevented the next city-destroying fire would be absent.

Because there had been no major new fires, the movement to build well-equipped firehouses began to decline and the pursuit of daily business again took precedence over the city's survival. In short, the citizens forgot to be afraid and fell back upon their indolent ways—just what the Lightkeeper had been waiting for. The first real trouble came from the volunteers themselves, not the arsonist. As more fire units rapidly formed, the firefighters, having no fires to fight, felt their special niche in society slipping away and began to battle one another for dominance. Earlier the discord had been kept to the playing field where Broderick One, with little competition, had excelled in every field, especially marksmanship. Broderick, though only a middling-to-fair shot, had organized a crack musket company to compete for awards with the other departments. His rifle team, a military organization called the Empire Guards (after the Empire State), grew to 125 members. On field trips they competed publicly with their muskets for prizes in target shooting. They were still tops in pumping, singing, dancing, and organized bare-knuckle fisticuffs. Fighting was a way of life to the New Yorkers and battles at minor fire scenes became commonplace.

Senator Broderick returned from the capital to check with Kohler about the worsening conflict between the engine companies and cautioned him to defuse the situation. Unheeded, their discord could destroy everything they had worked for. But winning battles didn't establish the magnificence of any firehouse; its engine did. In this, Broderick One was not deficient, but hampered by the Mankiller's age. To them the old New York side-lever pumper's clean lines and graceful curves were beautiful. Their hearts leaped as the dilapidated machine rattled over newly planked streets peaked in the center to facilitate water runoff. It took all their skill to keep the engine on the straight and narrow. Beloved as their antique fire wagon was, it was not "the King of All Fire Engines" that Sam Brannan yearned to make his own. No one doubted any volunteer company possessing the invincible king would reign supreme. While no engine house could afford such a machine, Brannan could. With his deep pockets and crooked schemes, the man who had built a terrible floating prison, salted the muddy streets with gold, and fleeced the miners could buy anything he desired. And he desired everything.

Harsh winds whipped sand off an eighty-foot dune and into the streets. A storm provided the water to turn sand to mud. Ocean wind set clapboards banging, doors slamming, gates rattling, and shingles soaring over Sawyer's head. From the abandoned ships he heard squeaking blocks and yards and spars snapping. Feeling the first few drops, he ran onto a piazza running alongside a house. Two fashionably dressed women were huddled in conversation beneath the overhang as a downpour began. In the slanting rain, launches sped from the anchored ships to the rude, fire-damaged adobe near the lower end of the town, the Custom House. Men rowed for the Merchant's Exchange and gambling houses. Carriages and drays flew pell-mell. Teamsters in sugarloaf hats lashed their horses, only sinking deeper. Rolling wheels cut deep trenches in the mud. Across the street huddled "the Fountain Head Man," who kept a tray of horehound and peppermint candy tied around his neck. Another vender tried to keep his armload of China silk handkerchiefs dry. "Only half a dollar each," he hawked without hope.

The rain turned all of San Francisco into a slough of liquid mud, a bog that ruled their lives. It ranged from ankle deep to "off soundings," ensnared grown men up to their knees, and sucked down small boys. Sawyer rolled up his trousers and plunged on. The rain poured with little interruption until March 22, when it stopped altogether and the city dried to tinder overnight, ready for its next burning. During the following days strong winds and dust kept everyone dirty. Anyone who escaped the mudpits still became filthy in the hard labor that was everyone's lot. All their work was for nothing. Soon afterward the second great fire completely destroyed San Francisco.

Sawyer turned restlessly in his bunk and listened to the heart of the city beating—church bells chiming, the crack of a pistol, volunteers serenading a favorite actress at her hotel. In the shallow cove he heard rotted sails flapping. Out there somewhere was a man who could reduce it all to ruin. On Wednesday, May 1, 1850, voters formally elected John

White Geary as the city's first mayor and Malachi Fallon as the first city marshal (chief of police). Thursday was Steamer Day, that special twice-a-month time, approximately the first and fifteenth, when arriving steamers brought as many as sixty thousand letters and picked up eastbound letters to loved ones, business correspondence, and gold dust for shipment. On Steamer Day the post office lines were often three blocks long. It took a day and a night to give out all the letters. While waiting in line, men drank brandy toddies, juleps, and brandy straights or paid someone $50 to stand in for them. The sturdy post office, the former home of first citizen William Howard, was an improvement over the former Pike Street office, with its single delivery window. Howard, who had made a fortune in hides, moved to a small cottage which, as he added little colonnades and connected wings and extensions to increase its capacity, he converted into a weird maze. He took in borders, including the hasty but cowardly *Alta* editor Edward Gilbert, who raged against the lawlessness.

Sawyer observed that several ships had arrived with heavily insured merchandise identical to tons uncrated on the wharf last week. Should the city burn while the floating and landlocked warehouses bulged with a glut of unsold inventory, the merchants might profit instead of failing. Could some merchant have been behind the Christmas Eve fire? Some of the recent small fires had been arsons, but not all. The towns of Grass Valley, Columbia, and Sacramento had this week been nearly wiped out by blazes from natural causes. On the slopes along the San Francisco coast a cluster of redwood shacks had been dried by sea winds and spray. The makeshift frame two-by-fours, rough planked and unpainted, stretched in every direction. Brush surrounding them on the reddish cliffs made their ignitability inevitable. Inland, the same rising gales whipped the Square and dried the wood. The city by turns denied and braced itself against the threat of fire.

Sawyer recalled how Manhattan One back east had kept a small hand-drawn emergency conveyance in their Dutch Street headquarters. They stored this "pie wagon," which carried six buckets and four booms, under the roof. Promptly at 7:00 P.M. they lowered it to the street, where it remained until 5:00 A.M., when, like a weary little bird, it was hoisted up to its nest, ready to fly again. In San Francisco, Broderick One stood as ready, though its men were short-tempered, out of sorts, and yearning for action. They relied on a single lookout spotting for fires from a tower on the roof of the City Hall. The lookout's job, day and night, was to estimate the blaze's locality and tap out on his bell the number of the ward afire. All volunteers knew the eight ward numbers by heart and could pinpoint the fire from the audible code. This time they would need scant direction. The second city-destroying conflagration would explode on the exact site as the first. The volunteers knew the way. They were practically there.

At 2:00 A.M. on Saturday, May 4, they were asleep on an upper floor of the Broderick One engine house. Their only pajamas were red shirts and their only blankets were coats. The night was deathly still. Sawyer was asleep on the floor upstairs. Downstairs, Fred Kohler had dozed off watching dragons flicker in the hearth, a sheaf of reports on the Sacramento and Grass Valley fires clutched in his hand. The bunkers, those homeless volunteers and orphaned ragamuffins who slept in the engine house, had a great advantage in reaching the fire before the others. Crescent Ten, forming over on the north side off Pacific, had the greatest number of bunkers, thirty-nine sleeping at one time in its firehouse. At every engine house the lightest sleepers had the best opportunity for gaining a favored spot on the engine. Outside Broderick One the Lightkeeper's Wind rose, blowing fiercely from off the sea, away from Telegraph Hill and toward the Square. Inside the engine house everyone slept on.

Around 3:30 A.M. the Lightkeeper detached a scaled copper lantern, green as flames in a frost, from his belt, lifted it by its ring, and coaxed the live coal inside with his breath. His was a gentle breath, tinged with alcohol and flavored by beef and tobacco. He turned the lantern and angled the crude opening so the coal was exposed to the fullness of the gale coming out of the northwest. The coal needed a constant supply of air flowing underneath. The anthracite glowed brighter. Gently, softly, get it to a blue flame, watch for witnesses. His heart was pounding. In April the leader of the twenty-man gang he belonged to, English Jim Stuart, had gone up to the southern mines in Nevada County at Foster's Bar to hide out from the authorities. His absence had left the arsonist at loose ends and hankering for a big fire in May. Carefully he lifted the coal out with pliers, watched until the bed of chips began to smolder, and then left the building with a measured, confident step. The rising wind tore at his long coat as he vanished over the rise. He did not run. His smoldering fire gave him plenty of time.

He had kindled his fire inside a building erected on the same spot as Dennison's—the United States Gambling Exchange, a rickety three-story drinking and gambling den. Fanned by the high winds, the blaze was out of control before anyone noticed. At 4:00 A.M., the first clangs of the Monumental fire bell sounded, but the howling wind drowned them out. It seemed forever before Broderick One was alerted.

New York fire patrol houses had special chutes allowing drivers to slide from the upper floor down into the engine seats. The men of Broderick One had no chutes, but still made excellent time to the ground floor. Kohler claimed they could throw their boots out the window and get to the street before they landed. The first two volunteers down were entitled to hold the tongue, the front shaft that guided the four-wheeled water engine. "Give me the pipe," the first cried, "I'll hold her!" The pipe was a blunderbuss nozzle of copper-riveted leather with brass and bronze tips. The others were relegated to the pulling ropes. Dozens of athletic men, long trumpets slung over their shoulders, grouped four across to pick up the twin drag ropes.

Sawyer and six young boys and teens grabbed the prepared torches lining the firehouse wall like billiard cues and dashed into the street. Nonbunkers were still arriving. A few still had their uniforms tucked under their arms, but most were pulling on their red flannel shirts, black leggings, and white macintoshes on the run. The team began pulling the Mankiller, heaviest of all engines and filled with canvas buckets, ladder hooks, and a one-hose reel. "Hell for leather! Pull her along and jump her, fellows!" Kohler cried. All this manpower glided the engine toward the Square. It was only a short distance. The road was inky black. Even the air was black. This lasted only a moment before an appalling glare lit up the sky and they no longer needed torches to see.

Cursing, the haulers and draggers slogged through the mud. The boggiest part of the city was at the corner of Kearny and Clay streets, a block from the fire. Once, a horse had sunk to its neck in the mud and had to be shot. For burial, they pushed its head the rest of the way under. That bog separated Broderick One from Portsmouth Square. Ahead, the crowd heard their shouts and the tinkling of their bells as they broke free. Kohler bellowed through his trumpet, ordering the placement of the Mankiller in the right position to attack the burning buildings. With arm movements, George Oakes signaled to get the hose placed in its serpentine track and get the side tracks lowered. Using their long-handled spanners, the volunteers coupled the pipes, manned the brakes on each side, and began to pump. Kohler roared, "Stave her sides!" suggesting that the rapacity of strokes would cause the suction to draw the sides of the water carrier inward.

Thirty determined men on both sides of the Mankiller faced one another. Working at top speed, they could push 170 strokes per minute before they tore their fingers and wrenched their backs. With the Mankiller ten minutes of pumping was the best any man could do without rest. Rock—rock—steel bars forced up the water. A man leaped in to spell another and seized the handles without letting the high-speed rhythm of the pumping falter. Otherwise, the foot treadles might trap his leg, break his arm, or pinch off his fingers. The pipe holder grasped the squirting tube and aimed it at another roof that had just burst into flame. "Down on her, down on her, boys!" The Mankiller propelled a thin stream of water an amazing four or five stories high. As water pressure increased, it took all his strength to hold the pipe against the immense force. Sawyer had once seen a runaway pipe knock a firefighter down the street. Company Three's foreman arrived and shouted through his leather speaking tube: "Play away, Number Three!" Three quickly "absquatulated" [quit the scene] because the building behind them had burst into flames. They only saved their water cart by moving it to a safer spot. Within a few minutes, not only was the Exchange afire, so were the two large buildings on either side. Their frameworks were so light that strong winds threatened to carry them away, flames and all. Like most buildings in the Square, their walls were lined with cotton cloth and sealed with painted paper. The flames climbed to their roofs. Now more than 120 volunteers labored—climbing a few spindly ladders, putting down pipes, and filling leather buckets in a bucket brigade. Flaming shingles flew off as the wind carried the fire on its back to other blocks and tossed embers high into the sky.

All the Exchange's windows blew out. Venting fire crooked at Sawyer. Smoke pumped out the beams, yet no bystanders offered assistance, only stood and watched. Some smiled as flames stalked on "fiery legs" across the Square to a handsome four-story hall completed only a day earlier. Just the night before the same crowd had enjoyed a free champagne supper inside the new hall. The first floor, filled with beautifully painted wood paneling, provided a tasty appetizer for the flames. The ceiling fresco and expensive furniture served up the main course. Ten

minutes and the grand structure seemed doomed; in twenty its timbers were blazing heaps. Sawyer and his comrades were powerless even
though the fire had practically started on their doorstep.

Owners pleading for help ran headlong into the same indifferent
audience who had dispassionately watched the Christmas Eve fire. The
fire was not affecting them. Until it did they were uninterested. "What
can I do to get you to help," sobbed the proprietor of a burning store.
The spectators politely conferred among themselves. "We want three
dollars an hour for firefighting," they responded. "We want a dollar and
a half for a bucket of water and sixty dollars for a cartload of water."
Some merchants refused to pay, hauled their goods far from the blaze,
and stationed guards to watch them as waiting thieves swooped down.
The potential for being blown up also kept citizens from fighting the
fire. Every store had on its premises one or two kegs of black powder. At
intervals the kegs exploded with low *booms*.

On his black charger, new sheriff John "Coffee Jack" Hays galloped onto the scene. As his horse reared, the great Texas Ranger's long
brown hair blew out behind him and his twin Colt revolvers glinted in
the light. When he saw the *Pacific News* catching fire, he placed his dep-
uties on top of the building and organized a bucket-and-water-keg line.
"Coffee Jack demonstrated the fire could be stopped if the people would
only work," wrote one paper. As the fire spread rapidly in every direction
and again threatened the entire town, the mob asked, "Where is this
fire to be stayed?" Finally, bystanders began to help, but without proper
organization because so many tongues were spoken in San Francisco—
by the Dutch, French, Spanish, Jews, and Celestials (Chinese). It took
three men to rescue a dog from a burning store it stubbornly refused
to abandon. Its beautiful coat was burned to the consistency of coal.
The fire rocked back and forth to gain momentum and then split into
tiny whirlwinds that united into one huge tornado. The fire moved east,
silently circling the volunteers, who only noticed it when they felt its
heat through their backs and had to run for their lives. By 6:00 A.M. the
conflagration had leveled the blocks bounded by Kearny, Clay, Washington, and Montgomery streets to the east of Portsmouth Square. Captain
Vincente, a beloved waterfront figure, rushed several times into a burning building to save lives. On his third sortie inside, a wall of fire sprang
up. His friends waited out front. As minutes crawled by it was apparent
that the good captain would not return. The house collapsed and their
old friend was lost.

A torch boy noticed that bronze rivets had popped loose from a leaking leather hose and knelt to repair it. About twenty feet away Sawyer was plastering a building side with mud—the city offered an almost inexhaustible supply of muck. It seemed to be effective. In spite of the volunteers' efforts, the block went up in smoke in a few minutes. "Up to the bend," sang out Kohler, ordering a volunteer to gauge the depth of water in the fender box of the engine. He did so, and then paused to get his breath. The heat-dissolved carbon in the air was burning his lungs. Black saliva clung about his mouth. Sawyer leaned against a tumbled wall and tried to breathe too. He felt the hot bricks through his shirt. Suddenly an odd shadow crossed his path. It quivered in the flickering light. A flare had cast the long shadow of a man over the heated cobbles. Sawyer raised his eyes. A thin wheat stalk of a man was leaning at the opening to an alley. Backlit by fire at the opposite end, he seemed to have no features at all. Flames flickered eerily around his long coat. The stranger turned his collar up as if chilled. His eyes approximated worm holes bright with excitement. Smoke drifted across the figure. A shower of fireflies covered him. Sawyer turned to drag down a wall, and when he looked back, the alleyway was deserted. The stranger had vanished as utterly as if he had marched into the flames and become part of them.

The inferno reached a block facing the Square north and bounded by Kearny, Washington, Dupont, and Jackson streets. The wind not only spread the fire, but supplied it with oxygen. The hot, light air became superheated and rose to create its own wind that made the fuel burn hotter. Cold, heavier air rushed down to replace the heated air. This loop of gases and smoke, once set in motion, was impossible to stop until the fire triangle of fuel, oxygen, and heat was broken. This huge convection engine overrode the local wind patterns, broke poles in half, sent blazing brands whirling ahead for blocks, and made tornadoes of superheated smoke and flame. Company Three had attacked this area because its terrain offered some small promise of success, and Broderick One, seeing an opportunity, joined them and together they tore down every house on Dupont between Washington and Jackson streets. The fire was so loud the volunteers could hear neither themselves nor the cries of the victims. As the wind sent flames rushing uphill, the steeper terrain served as a funnel for the fire. The high winds pushed the wall of flame forward into the funnel and sent it roaring along.

"All the fire engines in America cannot stop a San Francisco conflagration," one pioneer observed. At a dry goods store Sawyer observed

smoke seeping out of its eaves and heard debris falling inside. No sooner
had he taken two steps back than fire suddenly blew out all the windows and knocked him on his back. Flames erupted through the roof in
a single red twist. As the smoke banked down Sawyer feared he might
suffocate. All around him a flaming sea surged with explosive violence.
He crawled for his life. All the volunteers lacked training. Who had experience in fighting an urban fire on such an incomprehensible scale as
this? Their worn-out engines failed one after another until only seventy
exhausted men and a hook and ladder company staffed by forty-five
more stood between San Francisco and total ruin. At the fire center
a hailstorm of burning embers flurried clockwise on the superheated
wind. Burning coals rained down. In the shifting gale, disciplined soldiers and sailors, covered with soot, hauled kegs of black powder to
buildings standing in the fire's path. Owners signed contracts for rebuilding their homes even as their homes, still standing, were targeted
for demolition. Blasts more awful than the blaze shook the city and
rose above the monotonous roar. Terrified animals fled along the streets
before the explosions. Houses leaped skyward. Soon not one structure
stood in the gutted block. By noon all three blocks north and west of
Portsmouth Square were smoking deserts. Finally, citizens formed a
ragged bucket brigade and slowly the tide began to turn in their favor.
The intensive blasting had paid off. The march of the half-mile-long
inferno was halted. Coughing, Sawyer and the volunteers returned to
Broderick One, baptized with soot. You could not tell them apart except
for the difference in their heights.

The next day there were still frequent explosions of powder, dull
rumbles like an earthquake below ground. Dunbar's Bank, rebuilt after
the Christmas Eve fire, tacked up a notice on its outside wall: "Open
as usual." The bank, a simple brick safe with fire ventilations, was just
large enough to admit three standing customers at a time. Remark-
ably, it stood alone at the center of a hundred yards of flattened ruins.
J. J. Bryant, who had been defeated at the polls by Coffee Jack Hays
in the race for sheriff, had better fortune this time. After the fire was
beaten, his hotel and gambling den, 150 feet above Kearny Street, was
the only house still standing in the entire city. Broderick got to the
scene in time to see flames still flickering on one block while lumber
was being hauled for a new house on another block. By evening, two
new frame buildings covered with canvas had been completed by the
light of dying flames. Fifty similar structures flew up. "Claptraps and

paper houses," Broderick said in disgust. He doubted anyone would be erecting expensive wood buildings soon. No one would insure them. Yet money was everywhere in the boomtown. Broderick had only to kick at the ashes to see a large quantity of melted gold glittering like a bright river under the charred ground. Try as he might, he could not find one long face among the crowds. Every man looked as if he would momentarily have more money or take on another blaze without a qualm. "What spirit!" he thought and let all the air leave his body at once. He coughed and steadied himself. The old Central American illness had attacked his fragile lungs again.

That night the Town Council convened in the ruins to tabulate the damage. Three-quarters of a mile of San Francisco had burned, sixteen blocks including ten blocks bounded by Pine, Jackson, Kearny, and Sansome streets and five more bounded by Sansome, Battery, Sacramento, and Broadway. The city lost three hundred buildings and fifteen hundred single dwellings, losses totaling around $4 million. Though the conflagration had started on the same ground as the Christmas Eve fire, it had burned three times as much area. "All but a few buildings out of three blocks were destroyed," a Council member commented, "and these blocks are the very heart of the city. The loss has been very much greater than can be estimated with any degree of certainty. We shall not recover from it for some time." He sat down hard in the ashes. A cloud of soot covered him. "It's folly to keep rebuilding the same blocks over and over," he moaned, but nobody listened. The townsfolk were busily rebuilding on the smoking earth of the burned-out area. Within ten days the industrious citizens had rebuilt more than half of the incinerated area—just as flammable as before and stretching along impassable, "jackassable" roads that made getting to fires impossible for the volunteers.

The Council ordered the digging of artesian wells with a capacity of three hundred thousand gallons. Portsmouth Square had been the flash point of both big fires, so they designated that a twelve-thousand-gallon cistern, a square wooden box of tar-soaked planks with caulked seams and flat wood covers, be installed there. Fifteen more were prepared, each holding nearly fifteen thousand gallons and sunk ten to fifteen feet underground. Next, the Council set heavy fines for noncompliance with the city's first building ordinances banning cotton-cloth buildings outright, ordered each homeowner to keep six leather buckets of water always available, and made it a crime not to render assistance

during a fire. Any person who refused to fight fire or assist in moving
goods to safety would be fined $100. Next, they ordered men into the
dead flotilla of deserted ships to find, as Sawyer had, buckets, lengths
of hose, and planking. All this belated activity only enraged the friends
of the late Captain Vincente, who stormed City Hall along with those demanding compensation for fighting the fire. When the Council refused
them all, a near riot broke out.

The following day, the mayor offered a $5,000 reward for the in-
cendiary's capture. The coordinates of the fire had now left everyone
convinced that the blazes were the work of an arsonist. Within a year
a claim would be made by a condemned Australian prisoner that the
Lightkeeper was an Australian brigand named Billy Shears. No one
could offer a motive for Shears to have set the fires and he had left
the area before more fires were set. Only merchants had benefited by
the fire. Sawyer turned his scrutiny on them. Before the blaze they had
enough surplus lumber to rebuild the city thirty times. Afterward lumber prices quadrupled. Rich merchants like Brannan enhanced their
social standing by contributing equipment, real estate, and funding to a
specific engine company. William Howard, a prosperous merchant, had
personally cosponsored Company Three, comprised entirely of Bosto-
nians. A commanding figure—six feet tall with full ruddy cheeks; sparkling eyes; and a soft, musical voice—his most recognizable mannerism
had been the habitual stroking of his full sandy beard in thought. Now
he was clean-shaven. Unquestionably, he was the town's first citizen.
He had arrived as a cabin boy on the sailing ship *California* and immediately had become a collection agent in charge of hides and tallow and
then formed the most active commercial firm in town with his partner,
Henry Mellus, to buy the Hudson's Bay Company's property.

Company Three, having failed at being Company Number One by
a few hours' delay in filing, was still fighting over its name. One faction wanted it to be called the Howard in honor of their benefactor's
generosity. The other remained loyal to the company's other angel, Sam
Brannan. For a while both rivals sabotaged each other. The drawn-out
battle ended only when the Brannan faction stole the company fire engine during the night and ran it into the bay. In the days it took for the
Howard faction to extract the pumper and the week it took to restore its
unsullied condition, both sides reached a truce. But the title that found
favor with the public was not the Howard, the Brannan, or the more formal Eureka. A fire and an explosion inspired Three's final name. Their

first engine house, an old warehouse belonging to the Stanford brothers at Pacific and Front streets, stood so close to the water that one day half of it plunged into the bay. Company Three stored their gunpowder in the remaining half. When five thousand cases of coal oil in the basement ignited, the oil curled in a burning stream along Battery Street. Flames ran back along the same stream and detonated their stored explosives. As a replacement, Howard built a lavish and elegant brick-and-stone-fronted building on Merchant Street between Montgomery and Sansome streets. The upper story became a lavishly furnished meeting room. In their new posh surroundings Three became more convivial, ostentatious, and social than Broderick One and Manhattan Two combined. They threw glittering balls for the two thousand women who had arrived in town in January and February. On gala nights they moved their fire apparatus into the street to allow room for dancing. As the most congenial volunteer unit, folks dubbed them Social Three. They had the city's finest singers in their glee club and their piano pumped music at all hours. Three's men were dressed in full regimentals when raven-haired Lola Montez debuted the "Spider Dance" at a benefit. Sam Brannan, having forgotten he was married both in San Francisco and Utah, was smitten with the fiery dancer, but had quarreled with her and refused to attend. Social Three filled their leather helmets with flowers, showered the stage with them, and elected Lola as an honorary member. After her performance they carried her home on their shoulders. When they gave a banquet at the American Exchange, their bill of fare alone, printed on the richest of dark blue silk in pure gold ink, cost $5,000. They drank more champagne than all the water they ever poured on a fire and, impatient to drink, did not wait to draw the corks, but knocked the tops off with their axes and drank while they beat out flames with wet sacks and brooms. With 537 local drinking houses to choose from, the jolly comrades overindulged at every opportunity.

Three months earlier, when the Council had enlarged the San Francisco police force to fifty men, Brannan had reported a deficiency of funds in the city coffers and cut the force back to thirty members. It was then that the Council decided to inexpensively thank the new fire departments by channeling their recent animosity toward one another into peaceful public displays and decided to launch the annual Volunteer Fireman's Day to show their gratitude to the men who had saved San Francisco. It would also give Broderick One, Manhattan Two, and Social something to occupy their time. The valiant volunteer companies could compete in a parade and calm their nerves while waiting for the city to burn again. Broderick agreed. He had earlier laid out a plan to confine competition among the three firehouses to the parade ground.

A recent Chicago parade had featured nine hundred firefighters carrying ornamental axes and elaborately engraved silver speaking trumpets while riding on stunning parade vehicles. When any firefighter died, his fellows deployed the company hose cart as a hearse and the entire city turned out to share their grief. The volunteers were not only heroes, but family members and an extension of the citizens themselves. The fledgling San Francisco companies kept two sets of uniforms—one for firefighting and a more ostentatious costume for ceremonial purposes. The volunteers pressed their dazzling full-dress uniforms and assembled a dazzling array of parade coats, belts, ties, suspenders, capes, gauntlets, shields, and decorative fire hats of felt and leather for the day. Coach and sign painters painted fire company names and heroic oil pictures on helmets and fire buckets. They depicted countless eagles, flags, and burning buildings on the sides and end panels of massive water wagons, a rolling, functional canvas for a magnificent parade. On parade day, the two-fisted fashion plates strode from their engine houses. "The chief interest . . . of the exhibition lay in the appearance of the men themselves," the *Annals* reported. "They were of every class in the community and were a fine athletic set of fellows." San Francisco might be the City of Gold, but silver dominated the volunteers' parade. The men wore silver watches, jewelry, and capes; and their chiefs blew silver trumpets, all except Brannan's personal company, Social Three. His volunteers, who cut dynamic figures in their formfitting black trousers and patent leather helmets, wore expensive gold jewelry and cloth-of-gold capes to their fires. Foreman Frank Whitney had a gold speaking trumpet, a priceless instrument he liked so much he megaphoned orders to men standing right next to him. "Their foreman was a figure of such worshipful splendor—an uncommon human being, that you would have thought he could have put out the world if it were burning," commented William Dean Howells, the realist author and critic.

Swaggering and full of confidence, the volunteer companies in blue leggings, leather hats, silver- and gold-trimmed capes and gleaming boots presented a heroic sight, their freshly trimmed beards set off by high collars and elaborately decorated vests. The chiefs were known by their white helmets with gold lettering and long white coats with enormous side pockets to hold their trumpets. In every way their getups outshone the militia in the same parade. With luminous silver ropes, the firemen drew three gleaming engines through the muddy streets. Supporters decked them with ribbons and wreaths, and draped the fire engines with banners and bouquets while brass bands played firemen's quadrilles and polkas.

As the opposing fire companies filed past one another, it was their practice to shout out slogans. Kohler, aware of the tense situation growing between rival units, ordered his men to keep a civil tongue. "No insult should be allowed to interrupt the good feeling and harmony among the three companies," he said. That would change soon enough, but during that first parade, amid the throng cheering from the ruins, goodwill ruled. Now at the sound of any alarm, all Boomtown poured from their combustible houses to cheer on their favorite volunteers as they would a favored sports team. San Francisco had swiftly taken the new volunteers to its heart. "Almost without exception the firemen here are gentlemen and almost every gentleman in town is a fireman," a local man wrote home. "I never saw any men work as well and as hard as they do at a fire, fearing nothing but failing to stop destruction." Each night that the torch boys ran, carrying torches high, scanning the roads for debris, detours, and obstacles, they never ran alone. When on calls, they heard, mixed with the labored breath of the firemen pulling the heavy engine, the panting of other boys who thrived on the excitement. Behind them, drawn by panic and calamity, the populace, in bedclothes, followed the engines en masse as if they were sleeprunners—wide-eyed, features fixed, and faces white as paper.

FIRE OF MAY 4, 1850

SAN FRANCISCO AFTER THE FIRE OF MAY 4, 1850

CHAPTER FOUR

Broderick's Rogues

Davey Scannell, a ferociously gluttonous "toss-pot of homeric capacity," performed some of his most Olympian gastronomic feats at the Parker House next door to the United States Restaurant. Obviously, though, Broderick's rogue reserved his greatest marathon eating sessions for the fashionable Occidental Hotel on Washington Street. The ground-floor restaurant faced Jones Alley and the Bank Exchange. Because Scannell's meals were so voluminous and time-consuming, Proprietor Sam Hall permanently reserved a huge round table in the front window for him to better showcase the spectacle. Huge crowds gathered on the street to applaud him and his trusted lieutenants, all of enormous physique, who always accompanied him.

Foremost among Scannell's gang of voracious eaters and fighters was Charles P. "Dutch Charley" Duane, a former gunfighter, bare-knuckle boxer, and wagonmaker who, after Ira Cole, became Broderick's closest friend. Broderick and Duane first met on April 14 when he was at Long Wharf to greet an old friend, Chris Lilly, arriving on the steamer *Tennessee*. Eight years earlier Lilly, a fight promoter and notorious pugilist, had killed Tom McCoy during a 119-round bout. Broderick noticed the big blond, cold-eyed, twenty-three-year-old New Yorker standing at Lilly's side. The man's superb physique was fashionably clad. He kept his trousers half tucked into high wrinkled boots and cinched at the

Charles P. "Dutch Charley" Duane

waist by a belt bristling with an assortment of knives and pistols. Dutch
Charley claimed to be a passenger but was really a stowaway.

Next to arrive at Scannell's table were the Parker House's own Sam

Hall, a heavyset man with huge shoulders; then heavily mustached Judge John W. Dwinelle, who weighed more than 250 pounds. Wheezing, Dwinelle squeezed his enormous paunch between the table and chair. Attorney William Patterson, who weighed nearly as much, slid into his seat more gracefully. Also seated was John Felton, a great civil lawyer who suffered from gout and who had a lunch of three dozen oysters (in season) and a quart bottle of champagne messengered to him at the Bank Exchange each noon. Alexander Campbell, a rail-thin man who favored English fashions, rushed in and took the last chair. He ate as much as the others but never gained an ounce.

On holidays, when court was not in session, Scannell and his cronies assembled by 10:00 A.M. and ate until early afternoon. If court happened to be in session, and Patterson or Felton had cases before Judge Dwinelle, they met at the Occidental around 4:00 or 5:00 P.M. On those days, the moment Judge Dwinelle joined them they began a four- to five-hour feast that ended in a drinking marathon at 10:00 P.M. In early morning Scannell and Hall had made the rounds of the Washington Street markets running up through Merchant Street and picked out the choicest cuts of beef from beer-fed steers. Toward the pier they ferreted out delicacies like cockscomb oysters (for six bits), sweetbreads, and very small shad (five dollars each) and had them trucked to the Occidental for preparation by their chefs. The menu listed every variety of local bounty. Scannell licked his lips; his finger moved slowly along the menu, caressing the items—ham, curried sausages, lamb and green peas, venison in wine sauce, cheese and prunes, and stewed kidney in champagne sauce. He came to Irish potatoes, sweet potatoes, squash, brandied peaches, rum omelets, and canned tins of exotic foods from back east. He made his choices. So did Dutch Charley. So did all the rest. They wouldn't necessarily finish it all, but it was great sport between fires because then they had all the time in the world.

That afternoon a gang of torch boys pressed their noses against the front window to watch. For the first hour, Scannell, napkin tucked under his chin, ate fowl—a partridge, a little quail, squab, wild goose, some snipe, a little curlew, and plover. His favorite was canvasback duck (fifty cents a brace). He was very particular about its preparation. The duck must be roasted exactly thirteen minutes and served underdone with blood oozing. He was as particular about his special punch, a conglomeration of sparkling burgundy, champagne, white and red wines in equal parts, and a quart of the finest cognac. Waiters with spotless white napkins over each arm hefted armloads of silver trays and covered dishes from the kitchen and ferried away dirty plates and glasses. Heated metal plates held quarter-inch-thick steaks; elaborate tankards contained beer and wine. Fruit and roasted nuts—filberts, chestnuts, hazelnuts, pine nuts, and black walnuts from Mount Tamalpais—showered onto the table. They exchanged fire stories as they ate. "Remember when Mrs. Wallace's kitchen stove set fire to the wall behind? She grabbed up her child and also snatched up a leg of lamb. She ran out of the house with the baby held by one leg and the leg of lamb cradled in her arm." The second hour Scannell and his men reserved for mutton. The masticating and grinding of jaws went on—faces flushed, beads of sweat dotting their foreheads, cheeks as rosy as uncooked sirloin. Their features held benign expressions, like cows, though they bickered throughout the courses. The third hour was crowded with dozens of oysters, smoked eels, and Point Reyes shellfish. Hall swayed in his seat. Patterson gripped the arms of his chair. The chewing and popping of corks was audible through the glass window. Dutch Charley's face grew redder. Perspiration clung to his upper lip. Even his gunsight eyes had lost their lethal coldness, but when he gazed at the muddy street outside, they flamed to malevolence again. He wiped his lips with the side of his hand, pushed back his chair, and heaved himself up. He had recognized a man tying up his horse outside who had turned in a false alarm. Charley shoved through the crowd on the street and advanced on the "false alarmer." Catching sight of a bull-like juggernaut rolling his way, the man tried to remount his horse, but Dutch Charley grasped his arm, broke it like a twig, shot a booted foot into his ribs, and ground his face into the mud. Spectators stood fixed in horror as Dutch Charley reentered the Occidental, coolly sat back down, and began eating with increased vigor. He had worked up an appetite.

A fourth hour saw the appearance of pork dishes—loin chops, curried sausages, more cured meats, and country-style ribs. Dutch Charley's cheeks were distended. The eating had slowed considerably. Some things he ate only a bite or two. The conversation had grown torpid. Heavy breathing filled in the gaps. No one was bickering now. During the fifth hour the crowd outside pressed against the steamy glass in expectation. The last of the dishes had gone, all but Scannell and Dutch Charley's plates. Scannell ate on, the only man who had not unbuttoned his vest or loosened his belt. Could he stuff much more into his belly than Duane without bursting? He could. When Scannell finished, the waiters were lighting the lanterns against the evening. Over the years he was never known to have faltered in any of the marathon sessions that took up so many hours of his day. Only the clang of a fire alarm could dislodge him. Then he kicked over his chair and hurried through the streets to his firehouse. Dutch Charley, having gotten his second wind, was eating again. Scannell found him the most interesting of Broderick's rogues. He had greatness inside him—if he could stay out of prison.

Born in Tipperary, Ireland, Dutch Charley as a boy had been called German Charley until he bested a Dutch boy in a fisticuffs match. The ladies had another nickname for him: "Handsome Charley." He captivated women of every age and station. The press labeled him and the rest of Broderick's rogues hired bullies, but Broderick's "forty-niners" (forty-nine shoulder strikers) were fanatically devoted to him and, according to Dutch Charley, "more like lovers than friends."

The waiting period between the great fires affected the most violent of Broderick's rogues most violently, especially the diminutive gunfighter Billy Mulligan, another New York crony of Broderick's. Lightning tempered, he was a fierce fighter, fiercer when drunk, and he was almost always drunk and spoiling for a showdown. When there was none, he seemed about to boil over. Troublesome, bandy-legged Mulligan was the quintessential gunfighter. His hands were scarred from fighting fire and his knuckles walnut size from fighting men. Yet those tortured, muscular hands could draw and fire a revolver with remarkable speed and deadly accuracy to protect the political interests and person of Broderick. Mulligan's voice was a deadly whisper, razor edged as wind hissing through an Iowa four-pointed barbed-steel fence. Like fast guns Ty Hardin and Billy the Kid, his deep-set eyes were a neutral, meditative gray. Slender and small, he weighed scarcely more than his huge twin guns. He claimed to weigh 140 pounds and stand five and a half feet tall. Broderick had never known him to weigh more than 120 or stand any higher than five feet. His stovepipe hat added to his stature, and for that reason and because of his sparse hair, he was never without it. Trim, of good form, wiry and sinewy, quick as a cat in his movements, Mulligan had the pluck of a bull terrier and boundless energy. He staged prizefights, gambled, claim-jumped in Tuolumne County, got into gun battles, and once sold the office of mayor for $28,000. He had boxed and won his share of barroom brawls, but was more famous for the dozens of notches on his pistol grip.

Though Irish born, like most of Broderick's men, Mulligan spent his youth in New York as an apprentice barrel maker, ward heeler, and gunman. When he was jailed in 1846, Warden Sutton of the Tombs, practically spitting in his fury and disgust, categorized Mulligan as "a professional blackleg" and "as desperate a character as could be found among the hoods of New York." The *New York Times* called Billy "the wild, tremendous, roaring, tearing, fighting Mulligan." He escaped to New Orleans, enlisted in the Louisiana Mounted Volunteers, and saw action in the Mexican War, where he earned the title of colonel for bravery. He arrived in San Francisco in 1848 and quickly became known as "a philosophic villain." On February 9, he had gotten into a shoot-out at a dance with young Billy Anderson. Both gunhawks unleashed a fusillade of eighteen slugs. The first dozen killed an old man in the street. The last six wounded a Mexican girl in the next room and shattered Anderson's knee. The seemingly minor injury turned out to be a fatal wound. Anderson died three weeks later. The first time an *Alta* reporter laid eyes on Mulligan was at the Bella Union when Billy confronted a much taller man, Bingham the actor, and said, "Stand straight up and take it, sir, or blast your soul to blazes I'll make a hole through you." Bingham took it. Like everyone else, he feared Mulligan too much to disobey him.

When Mulligan was wounded in the shoulder at Coyote Hill while dueling gunfighter Jimmy Douglass, he hobbled to the bar and raised his glass to the man who had just plugged him with a Colt Pocket Navy five-shooter at twelve paces. He called it a scratch shot. Mulligan had bet several adobes, fifty-dollar gold pieces, that neither of them would be hit, and he lost them. Douglass gave a blowout and the two enemies shook hands and toasted each other. "You mustn't think Jimmy can't shoot good because he shot so poor today," he said. "We'd both like to have done better, but somehow we couldn't, I'm sorry to say. We'll do better some other time, when we're in a better fix. Don't you think we will, Jimmy?" "We will that, Billy!" Jimmy replied and raised his glass.

Billy Mulligan was fiercely protective of Broderick. One Independence Day, they were at the Union Hotel bar celebrating when a local bully, Big Jim Campbell, began insulting Broderick. Mulligan, though elegantly attired for a fireman's ball, grasped Campbell's head with both hands, head-butted him into near unconsciousness, downed his drink and, covered in blood, returned home to fetch a fresh white shirt.

If Mulligan always was on edge, Dutch Charley was edgier. The blinding rages that came upon him frequently caused him to be jailed. Each time his friend Broderick used his political connections as a new state senator to bail him out. He needed such a tough battler. Though Dutch Charley had Whig tendencies, he had immediately attached himself to Broderick's Democratic political camp as a shoulder striker. Always up for a little "fist duty," he could deliver a thousand votes any election day by having Broderick's adherents vote three times in different sections of the town, a feat accomplished by herding voters from precinct to precinct and chasing away the opposition. He got into his most serious trouble when he attended a ball at the French Theater with a few members of the Lafayette Volunteer Company. He entered without a ticket, battering the attendant who stopped him. During the evening Amedee Fayolle, an actor and manager of the troupe, nudged Dutch Charley while he was dancing. When he tried to apologize, Dutch Charley went for him, but the Lafayette volunteers restrained him. At the end of the night Fayolle approached Dutch Charley again, but because he did not speak English only gestured instead. Dutch Charley took it the wrong way, jabbed him twice, knocked down his two friends when they intervened, and turned back to Fayolle to stomp his head. As Fayolle crawled to the door, he reached out for the knob. "The sonavbitch's got a pistol!" Dutch Charley cried and shot him in the back. The bullet lodged in the actor's abdomen and they rushed him to the French Hospital.

Placidly, Dutch Charley waited at the dance for the police. At the jail he took time out to help them beat a prisoner in the station house basement. No one thought to ask what an arrested man was doing assisting the police in obtaining a confession, but Dutch Charley, who held a grudge against the prisoner, was not put out at all. Broderick got him released on $15,000 bail. At his trial there was a hung jury. Broderick spent $50,000 to induce witnesses not to testify in the next trial, tucked some cash into Fayolle's breast pocket, and booked passage for him to France whether he wanted to go or not. With the prosecuting witness unavailable to testify, the case against Duane was dropped.

Dutch Charley visited Broderick in San Jose during a storm. After a hard ride, Dutch Charley arrived in San Jose about daybreak. He went to the hotel where Broderick was staying and found him seated in his room reading a paper. "I was wet through and through from the rain," Dutch Charley recalled, "and Broderick insisted on putting me to bed in his room and getting dry clothes for me. He would not hear of me attending to the business on which I had gone down there until I had taken a rest." With no visible means of support, he lived like a king on credit through the largesse of his benefactor, Broderick. A man of such lightning rages was unbeatable outside the ring due to a style of fighting learned in a lifetime of "bloody mills." While his foe was still speaking, Dutch Charley would deck him with an open hand or head butt, deliver a kick to the chest, and, the instant his victim was flat on the ground, leap up and down on him. With this method he was undefeated. Dutch Charley's fatal flaw was that he could not ignore an insult or perceived challenge. Any word might provoke his hair-trigger fury; anyone might become the target of his wrath. Odd things set him off. He once shot a dog that had bitten him, grabbed the officer who came to arrest him, choked him, and then stomped him in the stomach. Once he attacked a citizen because he was "quiet." Another time he thrashed a fat man because his belly shook while he was dancing.

At least he was honest. Manhattan Two elected the swindler Con Mooney as their foreman. Mooney had a penchant for barroom brawls. During one confrontation, someone shot off Con's third finger. "Now it's my turn to shoot," Mooney said, shaking off the blood. He paused. "Why don't you shoot?" a bystander asked. "You're a crack shot." "Oh, pshaw," Mooney said, tossing his gun to the saloon floor, "I don't want his life." Soon after, Tim McCarthy, the prizefighter, challenged him to a bare-knuckle fight—London prize-ring rules and to a finish. "It's all right with me," Mooney said, "but the stump of my finger would interfere with my every punch. If you give me time till I get this finger amputated," he said, "I'll fight you." "Con feared nobody and nothing," stated Barney Farley, his fight manager. In Virginia City, where he ran a saloon and billiard parlor with Joe Coburn, then the American heavyweight champion, Mooney's quiet appearance belied his gameness as one of the coolest and best firemen in the city. He never allowed his men to enter a fire scene without first going in himself to see if there was any danger. When he was not fighting fire, he conducted violent cock and dog fights at the Pony Express Saloon for $2,500 purses and held barbaric rat-baiting contests in a big room with rows of benches set around a pit full of rats. The frightened albino rats (blood showed better on white fur) tried to escape, but the smooth pit walls prevented them. When a pitter threw a ratter, a fierce dog trained to kill rats, into the pit, the audience wagered on how many rats it could kill in a fixed amount of time. Jenny Lind, an English bull terrier, once killed five hundred in an hour. Because Mooney lacked Broderick's moral fiber and political savvy, the likable nine-fingered volunteer would never rise higher than assistant chief. This remained his greatest disappointment.

Thirty years in the future Mooney would still be taking the suckers. When he noticed that San Franciscans were flocking to the seaside via the new Ocean Railway, he and his cronies offered various amusements at the beach and sold the bathers parcels of real estate. There were two drawbacks: Con didn't own the lots he sold and the parcels he unloaded were twenty feet under the Pacific Ocean. When the Council received too many complaints, they ripped down Mooney's shantytown at the beach, tore down his house and his confederates' homes for good measure, and closed down his illegal enterprises until he was forced to go straight. "I'll go along with it," he complained, "but honesty is against my better judgment." His sister brought in a good income as landlady of the unusual Niantic Hotel, originally a three-story vessel with masts sitting curiously on land among two- and three-story buildings. San Francisco was packed with grafters, thieves, get-rich-quick schemers, and political sharpsters like Mooney, though his thirst for graft paled beside that of Sam Brannan, who had robbed John Sutter, whose gold ore had ignited the Gold Rush. In a city of thieves only the volunteer firemen represented any heroes. But not all the firemen were heroes at Manhattan Two, nor even at Broderick One. Not by a long shot.

James "Yankee" Sullivan, political shoulder striker, former World Heavyweight Champ, and "the Ugliest Man in San Francisco," was the last of Broderick's principal rogues. One morning at Broderick One, George Oakes was arguing with another fireman, Kelly, assuring him that "Woolly Kearney is much uglier than Yankee Sullivan."

"Horse feathers!" Kelly replied. "Yankee's the homeliest looking mortal I ever saw in town—in California—for gosh sakes—in the world." He banged down his cup. "What do you think?" Oakes said, turning to Bob Cushing, later foreman of Engine Company Ten. "I never met Mr. Sullivan," Cushing said, "and am at a loss to compare him to Mr. Kearney because I never met him either." He got a chance the next day when Woolly showed up at the firehouse. Oakes had not exaggerated. Woolly's battered, flattened nose, gnarled as an oak root, twisted to every compass point; and at every corkscrew turn it became more hideous. "Say, Woolly," James O'Meara once said, "when you blow your nose, I can't understand why you don't blow the dratted thing off." "If Woolly looks this bad," Cushing thought, "what does Yankee Sullivan look like?" Woolly Kearney, like Broderick's other stalwarts, was a scoundrel, but a fearless scoundrel with stern stuff in his heart. In October, when a Placerville mob tried to lynch "Irish Dick" Cronin, he was the only one to stand up to them, though they hanged Irish Dick anyway. In February, Woolly fought a twenty-five-round bare-knuckle battle, a combined wrestling and punching match, against an Australian on Yerba Buena Island. Though thirty pounds lighter than his opponent, Woolly won the grueling fight and retired to take up running the Ripton House on Old Mission Road.

Cushing was on Montgomery Street checking on fire conditions when he observed a man jogging toward him along a short stretch of irregular planked sidewalk. His stovepipe hat was cocked over one eye and he was waving a shillelagh. Despite being obviously drunk, he darted effortlessly in and out of doorways and around posts, making a noise like a steam engine. "*Puff, puff, puff!*" he wheezed. "*Whiff, whiff, whiff!*" went his air punches. "He must be simpleminded," Cushing thought as the shadow boxer feinted past his ear and began circling and throwing phantom punches just above his head. "*Whiff, whiff, whiff!*" He estimated him at five feet ten and about 160. He had a round compact chest and the clean, well-turned shoulders of a seasoned athlete. His features were lost among a minefield of scars, red irregular bumps, blemishes, and calluses. His nose, a level lump carelessly thrown down between two cauliflower ears, was as flat as his smashed right cheek. One nostril was cut away, so every breath for him was a struggle. His thin, bluish lips were smashed and swollen to one side. Many of his teeth were missing. Ridges of gristle and broken cartilage surrounded two black eyes so slitlike he had to squint painfully just to see. He stopped dancing and wiped his forehead with a handkerchief painted with an American flag. "Hear it?" he wheezed and cocked one cauliflower ear filled with blood. "Bells, all going off at once—cheerin,' chimin' and tollin'—bells! There must be a fire nearby or a fight. I'm Yankee Sullivan. Heard of me?"

"The former heavyweight champ," Cushing said. "You're Woolly Kearney's friend." Yankee Sullivan, the first great bare-knuckle champ in the United States, had come to join the Gold Rush. Tough and fast, he hit hard with both fists. His real name was either Francis (or Frank) Murray or James Ambrose or Frank Martin. At this point could even he be sure? He had been born April 12 (or April 2), 1813 (or 1815), in County Cork, Ireland, or was it March 10, 1811, in Brandon, south of Cork? Twelve years earlier, convicted of burglary (or the accidental drunken killing of his wife, depending on which report you read), he had been sentenced to the island of Van Diemen's Land (now Tasmania). A year later he escaped the penal colony at Botany Bay and fled to the United States, where he adopted the name of James Sullivan and became a fighter. Irish and English immigrants had spread the more formal English style of boxing to the states by fighting for bets. Boxing was illegal in New York State, thus a fighter could not be paid in cash. If he won his match, he could be awarded a prize, usually a watch, which never left the premises. After the bout a "commissioner" would technically buy the prop watch from the winner for a fixed sum, usually $25 to $50. In September 1842, Sullivan, convicted as a fourth-degree accessory to manslaughter as a promoter of the Chris Lilly–Tom McCoy debacle, fled to London, where he fought in Limehouse under the name Liverpool Jack against Jack "Hammer" Lane. Yankee got his nickname because he always entered the ring with an American flag wrapped around his waist. After he returned to New York, he worked as a butcher, political strong-arm boy, and proprietor of a popular Bowery saloon, the Sawdust House, on Walker Street. There he became friendly with Tammany Hall committee members and firefighters Billy Mulligan and Dutch Charley Duane. Sullivan, like those brawlers, had a reputation as a street fighter prone to fight at a second's notice. He once staggered into a New York oyster bar at Park Place and Broadway where he spotted Tom "Young America" Hyer, his twenty-two-year-old rival. With only five formal fights, Hyer claimed he was the American champ. Hyer, broad chested, nearly five inches taller and twenty-five pounds heavier than Yankee, got him in a headlock. When a policeman arrived, Hyer was standing over the semiconscious Sullivan and placing a percussion cap upon the nipple of his pistol, ready to fire. After he was overwhelmed and arrested, the two enemies trained for weeks for a fierce grudge match.

On February 7, 1849, spectators caught steamboats to Rock Point, Maryland, on Stillpond Creek, the secret location of the championship fight. When police intervened, the fight was moved to Roach's Point, on the Chesapeake. Political ward bosses and volunteer fire companies provided most of the $10,000 prize money. Rounds were unlimited with no fixed time limit and only a half-minute rest between rounds. Snow was falling at 4:30 P.M. when Yankee, in emerald green and white, walked out of a farmhouse wrapped in an American flag to literally throw his hat in the ring. Hyer entered, tied his colors—red, white, and blue—to the ropes, and at sunset the fight began. Yankee was clotted with gore when Hyer caught him with a left and right to his face that was so devastating he could not return. Finally they hauled Yankee away unconscious to a Baltimore hospital and placed him in intensive care. The fight had lasted less than ten minutes. When Yankee left New York, 8 of the 163 passengers on the *South Carolina* were backers of David Broderick. In San Francisco, Yankee conferred with Dutch Charley, then set out to tour the mining country and stage boxing exhibitions with his friends Woolly Kearney, another Tammany acquaintance, and Billy Mulligan. When English pugilist George Thompson came west to prospect, Dutch Charley sent him up to a mine in El Dorado County while he arranged a fight. After only a few days Thompson sent down word he had a prizefight on hand. The Thompson–Big Jack Willis bout at the Brighton racetrack near Sacramento was the biggest fight of the Gold Rush period. "Naturally, I had the fight fixed," Dutch Charley said. "I wanted Thompson to win the fight." Thompson won and they equally divided $8,400.

Yankee, a sad, complex man, had heart. He was fearless, afraid only when he was sober. He was also filled with rambunctious good humor. He once brought his pet beer-drinking goat into the lobby of Lucky Baldwin's opulent hotel. And he was patriotic. Yankee's painted flag was not window dressing. The tough, scarred, and astonishingly ugly Irishman really loved America. Sober or drunk, he was most loyal to Broderick, who employed him, along with Dutch Charley, Billy Mulligan, and Woolly Kearney, as an electioneering ruffian to direct henchmen to vote repeatedly, stuff ballot boxes, bully the opposition, rough up citizens who protested, and destroy existing ballots. Broderick had learned the four lessons of Tammany Hall—patronage, bribery, perjury, and vote rigging—from Boss Tweed, another fireman. He placed as many of his ruffians on the public payroll as he could and subsidized the rest out of his own pocket. Broderick's method of running his machine was no secret. He put public offices up for sale—alderman, district attorney, judge, or assessor. "The job you want is worth so many thousand dollars a year in 'perquisites,'" he would say. "Give me half and I will see you are nominated and elected. I need the money to grease the wheels of the machine that will put you in office and keep you there."

Broderick needed his organization of repeat voters and ballot stuffers to get the votes to put his plans for change in motion. No one was better at this than Yankee. When he was elected head of the First Ward, the most corrupt precinct in San Francisco, Sullivan's name was not even on the ballot. As judge of elections, he controlled the ballot boxes and direct precinct voting. "Here, you," he would tell a voter, raising his huge fist and scrunching up his horrible face, "take a walk! You can't vote here." Once a man voted in Sullivan's precinct, but when election returns were published, the name of the man he had voted for did not appear on the list. Yankee had counted out all votes for that particular candidate.

Though Yankee pretended to be thickheaded, he had invented and perfected probably the most valuable creation in Gold Rush–era San Francisco: a rough pine box painted dark blue and measuring two feet by fourteen inches and a foot deep. In the middle was bored an auger hole big enough to receive slips of paper. Round the bottom ran a neatly fitted molding with two inner slides constituting a false bottom. A false side neatly fitted into a groove inside the real side and bottom. When closed, both inside and outside possessed the appearance of a plain box. But Yankee had engineered the key lock to the box to be sprung by a peculiar pressure on one side of the lid. This allowed him as election judge to insert a bundle of tickets bearing his candidate's name by drawing out the slide and filling the space between the true bottom and false one. The side space could be likewise stuffed. After Yankee shoved the slides back into place, he locked the box and gave the key to the inspector, who sealed the top aperture with wax. One Election Day morning, the agent of one of the candidates offered Yankee $500 to bring a majority for his man, the money to be paid after the election. Yankee declared himself incorruptible and tore up the phony returns. Another agent offered him $300 in cash to put his friend in, but he had once treated Yankee badly. "You shall not have the office at any price," Yankee said and instead sold the office to a man he liked for $100. He had his scruples.

In the East, officials and law enforcement authorities engaged in political favoritism to an even greater degree. As the street gangs who ran as protective escorts for New York City fire companies gained in prestige, their battles escalated from control of a neighborhood to riots at fire scenes and arson and murder. One Philadelphia gang, the Rats, took over the Southwark neighborhood after attaching itself to the Weccacoe Engine Company. Another gang, the Killers, infiltrated the Moyamensing Hose Company and became the most feared group in Philadelphia. They attacked the Shiffler Hose Company, captured their pumper, and dragged it to Moyamensing, where they hacked it to bits and handed the pieces to a crowd. They torched a hotel and tavern owned by a black family and then fought off the fire companies that attempted to put out the blaze.

In San Francisco, William Howard had arranged for his fellow merchants to pay cash tributes to his favorite firehouse, but some volunteers went further. For a small consideration a storeowner could be certain of his store's *not* burning to the ground. Compared to the endless ranks of truly crooked men, a slightly dishonest man like Broderick, who was honest in his personal dealings, might be the most honest man in town. "Broderick was no hypocrite in this," one volunteer said, "but actually quite outspoken. He would have preferred to have the support of the honest element in town, but respectable citizens held back from voting out of fear." Broderick fought fire with fire. Because honest citizens would *not* stand up to the criminal element's shoulder strikers, he sent his own bullies against them in their stead. "I say this with pain," Broderick admitted. "I have not had the admiration from men of the class from which I sprang that might be expected. They submit too lamely to oppression and are too prone to neglect their rights and duties as citizens." Thus, he worked with men who would obediently carry out his orders and countenanced the most flagrant licentiousness among them, though he personally was devoid of greed and lived a highly moral personal life.

As Cushing watched the jabbing, punching boxer continue up Montgomery Street, he felt he was watching a brilliant actor. Yankee Sullivan drank from seventy to eighty shots of whiskey a day and gathered information as Broderick's secret agent. Shadowboxing from one dive to another, he ended up at one in Sydney Town. Slumping over the counter, he drank and cocked one cauliflower ear, trying to discover if the incendiary was one of a fierce band of hundreds of Australian ex-convicts. The times—hard, ugly, unwashed, and vulgar—were lawless, and the most lawless lived in at the base of Loma Alta and along upper Pacific Street. It was a sordid region of waterfront saloons and boardinghouses filled with gamblers and thieves. Veined with innumerable paths, such as Moketown and Dead Man's Alley, it loomed in the center of the rectangle created by Broadway, Washington, Montgomery, and Stockton streets. Because Kearny Street and Dupont Avenue led into this "carnival of crime," a local travel guide mapped the precise locality so that their readers might keep away: "Give it a *wide berth* as you value your life!" Within a decade it would be known better as the Barbary Coast.

"All petty corruption in San Francisco pales before the society-cankering rapacity of the Sydney," the *Alta* said. The Ducks' own country, a land colonized initially by expelled British convicts, had deported them. These former prisoners and ticket-of-leave men of New South Wales and Van Diemen's Land penal colonies had been released on one condition: They must never again set foot in a British dominion. They entered their kingdom at the foot of the northeast corner of Davis and Pacific, the first street cut through the sand hills behind the cove. They moored their skiffs, unloaded, and reached the Pacific Street landing by climbing a set of slimy stone steps fronting a rude bulkhead. They armed themselves with pistols, stilettos, and bowie knives and robbed everyone who dared pass through their kingdom. Secure in their numbers, the Ducks committed their most revolting crimes in bright daylight under the eyes of the authorities. At night these sneak thieves, footpads, arsonists, and swindlers plundered houses, met the slightest resistance with murder, and used flames to hide their crimes. The Board of Selectmen regularly looted the treasury to pay them protection money.

Broderick, who was not above recruiting men from Sydney Town to accomplish his aims, suspected a Duck had set the two city-destroying fires. Suspiciously, the two blazes had broken out when the Lightkeeper's Wind was blowing *away* from Sydney Town. "Whoever this firebug is," he said, "he is extraordinarily well versed in the operations of the fire departments outside Sydney Town." The Ducks frequented the Tam O'Shanter, the Magpie, the Noggin of Ale, the Hilo Johnny, the Jolly Waterman, the Bird in Hand, and "Hell" Haggerty's Goat and Compass groggery at the base of Telegraph Hill. At one of these bars, Yankee Sullivan heard some riveting intelligence. The Lightkeeper had already planned the next big fire.

On May 30, 1850, the Council voted to pay the mayor and city recorder salaries of $10,000 each and increase the pay of its aldermen to $6,000, but it had no money for a paid fire department. Livid, Edward Gilbert, editor of the *Alta* newspaper, rallied the populace to protest this inequity. That night citizens held gatherings and speeches in the square and decided in a week or two to form a huge parade and march upon the council to expel them physically if something wasn't done before then. No one knew, of course, that before the parade could start the Lightkeeper would strike again with a third and greater city-decimating conflagration.

CHAPTER FIVE

Rainbow Rivers of Gold and Silver

By 8:00 A.M. on mail day, June 14, 1850, the one-year anniversary of the *Philadelphia* dockside arson, San Francisco was already doomed. Under unusually strong trade winds, the *California* steamed through the Golden Gate carrying 114 bags of mail. Even though Captain George Coffin, a Sacramento and San Joaquin rivers trader, got to the post office at the corner of Washington and Stockton streets by seven-thirty, a half hour early, two long lines were already stretched around the building. Just before the clerk slid back the post office window to begin the day, he glanced downhill and observed smoke behind the Merchant's Hotel at Clay and Kearny, the outer edge of Syndey Town. In the Square smoke was boiling out the doors of the Sacramento House's bakery. Like so many great disasters the worst blaze so far began with a tiny malfunction. Someone had stuffed a rag inside the flue of the bakery's chimney. Coffin heard the alarm bell of the Montgomery Engine House up the hill ring out its "frightful ding-dong-clang." In the Square, the new Monumental bell clanged, a noisy, insistent toll. Other bells pealed, other gongs rang. The alarm drew hundreds, then thousands. The Square became a dense mass of human beings who, in spite of new laws, had come only to watch.

On Telegraph Hill, Richard Lunt Hale, a young, dark-bearded New England prospector, was standing outside his shanty when he saw a puff of smoke between the hill and shore from the direction of the bay.

"I did not pay much attention to it at first," he said, "but even as I looked the smoke grew in volume, but without warning, tongues of flame shot out in several directions." A raging, rolling whirlwind of fire was tearing through the tent city, gathering impetus from the strong wind. As the bells rang, men rushed down the hillside to join the excited crowd. Captain Palmer B. Hewlett, known as Don Pedro, lived in a house higher up toward the telegraph station. He saw a high cloud of smoke near Kearny Street beyond the Square, returned to the breakfast table, and cautioned his visitors. "You'd better start looking after your baggage if it's in the city."

"Oh, Don Pedro, it cannot reach the place where our trunks are—Riddle's store on Sacramento Street," his visitors said placidly.

"If you don't hurry, the fire will be there before you are," Don Pedro said.

To please their host, all three guests walked down to the edge of a little ravine. Just then someone crying "Fire!" raced down the steep hill. The trio quickened their pace. Before they passed Pacific Street, flames were rushing everywhere. They sprinted the rest of the way to Riddle and Eaton's and, climbing to the second floor, got their trunks. Before they reached the ground floor again, Riddle's roof was afire.

"Everybody out! Fire!" cried Joseph C. Palmer, a close but corrupt political ally of Broderick. He was a banker and a foreman of the stylish St. Francis Hook and Ladder, a mostly German company. "Start her lively, boys," Palmer cried and lifted his trumpet. His blaring notes rose above the crowd, but the fire spoke louder. The firemen with their enormous "teapots" were better prepared, but this time the roads failed. The St. Francis Hook and Ladder's engine, with just a short distance to travel from their three-story brick building on the west side of Dupont Street near Sacramento Street, thundered downhill to the Square, but before reaching Commercial Alley it became ensnared in mud. The volunteers pulled on their tow ropes but could not budge it. Dutch Charley Duane, their newly elected assistant foreman, could not free the engine either, in spite of his prodigious strength. The black creep of flame, unhampered, consumed whatever it desired between Clay, California, and Kearny streets. Finally, Broderick One stayed it from crossing Kearny and going uptown by exploding an immense old adobe on the corner of Clay and Kearny. An artesian well on the corner of Clay and Montgomery streets furnished enough water to save the valuable block near it and part of other blocks. The well's cost was a mere $140. The new

Council, in power for more than six weeks, had provided for only one of the promised wells, though their increased salary was already in effect.

"The flames were utterly beyond control," said Hale, who had come down to help fight the fire. "The dry cloth of the tents, the flimsy wooden shacks caught and burned like tinder, while the strong wind lashed the flames before it until there was nothing more for it to gorge its all consuming appetite upon." South of the city, miners and farmers in the hills observed an odd light tinting the underbelly of clouds over San Francisco—the reflection of the fire moving toward the prized new piers. As the flames pushed toward them, they touched the foot of Commercial Street where the considerable premises of the three most important mercantile houses in San Francisco—Simmons, Hutchinson & Company, S. H. Williams & Company, and Macondray & Company—sat east of Clay Street fronting the bay. Their stored merchandise was immensely valuable. The volunteers raced to save them. Three giant pyramids of lumber, a million board feet of planks piled up in their yards, dwarfed the firefighters battling in the baking mud. "The scene was sublime when these pyramids, like those in Egypt, got well on fire," Captain Coffin recorded in his journal. The lumber ignited explosively. Boards sizzled and smoked. Slivers sang and snapped. Knotholes filled with moisture cracked like all the firecrackers in China exploding at once. The pyramids of lumber stacked at the foot of Commercial Street burned brighter.

Retorts of powder exploding in other blocks followed every minute like gunshots, but no amount of black powder could save the wood warehouses between Montgomery Street and the water. Over at City Hall, a company of marines forced spectators back as soldiers marched chests of gold dust to a secure area. As they rolled closer to the docks, a team of Ducks blocked their way. The men of a U.S. warship whipped a path for the soldiers with the broad side of their swords and enabled them to reach the shoreline. As if magnetically drawn, the blaze leaped for the new waterfront and anchored ships. How many besotted sailors would go up in flames on their straw-filled, gin-soaked mattresses? At the mudflat, the soldiers dropped the chests into the muck and jumped on top to force them under. Bluejackets shoveled mud over them, then ran from the advancing flames. An advancing wall of flames herded five hundred pitiful citizens out onto Long Wharf. Sobbing, they watched flames crawl relentlessly toward them. The refugees, Coffin among them, were driven into the heart of the Ghost Fleet. The cool metropolis of deserted ships offered temporary refuge, but now the castaways were cut off from all communication with the city. With a sudden shift in the wind, the dancing cinders and black smoke suddenly doubled back shoreward to where the fire had begun, the Merchant's Hotel. The door of the furnace had reopened. Unbelievably, the blaze began to reignite the already burned areas. As the fire burned up the available oxygen, its color altered from yellow to red. Momentarily spared, the castaways on Long Wharf listened to screams from the burning shore. The fire on shore persisted most of the day.

Night fell. Flames colored the sky with a copper glow. Outlanders saw a shroud of ashes forming over the docks. Small craft caught fire. Larger vessels began to smolder. As if from a pepper mill the cloud of gray ash settled out over the Ghost Fleet. Black unburned smoke boiled upward until it reached fresh oxygen, then exploded in flames on top of the dense shroud of smoke and lit the sky again. Now one end of San Francisco rose from fire, the other from water. DeWitt & Harrison's storehouse, midblock on the north side of Pacific Street, was threatened. Kohler recalled that about a dozen years earlier, when the Bowery Theater caught fire, Old Matt Carey of Engine Company Twenty-six had protected the adjacent buildings by hanging wet carpets, mats, and blankets over them. In San Francisco, storefronts along Washington Street had been hung with blankets during the Christmas Eve fire but had not been dampened enough, and those buildings were lost. Kohler had DeWitt & Harrison's commodities warehouse roof covered with soaked blankets and had wet the walls of buildings in advance of the fire. To attack directly with water would create scalding steam. In the midst of all this fire it was odd to see torch boys, leading volunteers to the fire by torch through the darkened bogs. The Ducks were there ahead of them, hindering rescues so they could loot.

Sawyer, hair singed, arms blistered, and eyes watering, saw two Ducks who had plundered some buildings race to pile their swag in a vacant lot and return again. A stranger stood at the forefront of a crowd, pinhole eyes alight with flame. Sawyer found his eyes focused on him. In spite of the heat, the man was leaning into the blaze smiling and extending his palms as if warming himself. The mob swept by him and he vanished as if he had never existed.

Throughout Friday night, the five hundred refugees on Long Wharf huddled at its far end and gauged the blaze's progress through the fog. At dawn Saturday, the fire made the water ruddy and tinted the morning fog a salmon color, then red. Finally the red curtain dimmed and sank to a smoldering orange. As the fire subsided and heavy smoke rolled over the refugees, the town on shore and shipping in the cove became indistinguishable from each other. They felt a "fatal euphoria" come over them. The fog burned away late in the morning and the first rays of dull, gray sunlight penetrated the canopy of ashes shrouding the city. The volunteers had saved some of the waterfront, though the low tide had rendered many of their water wagons useless. Abandoned, these pumpers lay as charred rubble on the pier. Dozens of ships crowded at their moorings were damaged, but Captain Coffin's sloop, *Sophronia*, was not among them—the first good fortune he had had since a recent unproductive trading expedition to Marysville. Solemnly he and the others left the long pier to inspect the charred sites of former homes and businesses.

At the quartermaster's, gun barrels had twisted like snakes. Coffin reached the burning pyramids of lumber. "When everything else was swept away, they stood like fiery giants . . . the genii of the catastrophe," he recalled, "with innumerable arms and tongues of flame, constantly spitting out flashes and cinders. Everything else was swept away." A gravelike pall lay over the former downtown. Not a breath of air stirred. Block upon block of glowing embers emitted a suffocating vapor. The city was like a lava flow. Jagged trenches of deep red, bright orange, and yellow glowed under the blackened crust, eerily lighting the landscape. The burned-out business district was low, dark, and red. Coffin weaved among the ruins. Buildings crumbled to dust at the first freshening of the prevailing sea wind. Precious metals accented the blackened landscape. At Coffin's feet gold and silver had melted into the ground and pooled in glittering rivers. Rainbow lakes of glass, once the windows of happy homes, reflected his face in brilliant colors. As the sun ascended, these mirrors became blinding. Spoons, crockery, forks, and knives had melted together in heaps. Tons of fused black nails littered the dunes in the shape of the kegs that had contained them. Iron warehouses had shrunken into unrecognizable cages. A fireproof safe had burst open and was empty.

Coffin met an acquaintance who had been burned out three times in six months. "Come," Coffin said, patting him on the back, "no dumps, up and at it again." "No, I am done for now," he said. "Between the first two fires I had time to recover myself, but from the third of May to the thirteenth of June is not long enough. Only let me have six months' interval and I shall be prepared, but forty days is not enough. No, no, the risk is too great! I shall sell my lot and try my fortune in some other place." To his left, survivors were lunching on roast ham, baked chicken, hot preserves, vegetables, and sardines—all cooked by the fire and blackly burning in drifts.

New England gold hunter Richard Hale surveyed the damage. "In a very short time," he said, "only smoking heaps of ashes and charred debris told where San Francisco had stood, for the town had burned to the very sand." He returned to his home on the hill to find his shack had survived. "The heights had not been swept," he said as he entered and sat down. His single door and window let in a view of the town and the corner of the bay beyond. "Below us lay a smoking, ashy waste, flat to the sand." The city lost its expensive new wood-plank roads. An examination showed that cheap pine had been substituted for the pricey redwood planks. More graft in the city of graft. Still deeply in debt for the road's construction, the Council would have to issue bonds and impose stiff taxes to regain its credit balance so they could replank the streets with more cheap wood. The conflagration had hit the residential section as never before—four hundred major buildings, a four-block-square area, had been consumed at a cost of almost $3 million. The fire was again attributed to incendiarism. "Some of the largest losers by the recent fire," reported the *Alta*, will in the end be the greatest gainers. Editor Gilbert estimated that the opening of Commercial Street would enhance the value of the land abutting it, greatly exceeding the value of the buildings destroyed. Much of the property was in the hands of commission merchants and the biggest losses would fall upon New England and New York shippers. The San Francisco merchants had in truth benefited.

Two days after the fire, the Square resounded with the rap of busy hammers. Men raced from every direction clutching hammers and saws and tripping over smoking timbers. With manic enthusiasm, almost hysteria, these undaunted citizens flew to instantly rebuild as they had done two times before and would do again. "One would suppose our people would become discouraged by such rueful reversals," John Mc-Crackan said, "but instead of that they seem rather to gain new impulses and energy." Swarming to work, they duplicated past mistakes. Singing, they attacked the rubble again, nailing smoking boards onto the shells of still-smoldering houses with still-hot hammers. "Onward!" They were working on San Francisco time. The owner of a melted warehouse was already bossing a master carpenter and putting up a new store. The floor of the new El Dorado was laid before dark. At daylight the next morning a frame was raised. In a single week a new establishment of rococo elegance with lascivious paintings on the walls would be up and running. In three days three stores would be occupied and operating.

Coffin headed back to the waterfront. "The three huge pyramids stood there for three days and nights," he recalled, "gloating over the general destruction till at last the same devouring element having eaten them off their balance, they toppled and fell in a crash of fire and smoke, the grand finale to a stupendous pyrotechnic exhibition." Street preachers shuffled through the smoking embers bellowing that God was leveling San Francisco for its debauchery, sharpsters, and thieves. They were probably right, but the noise of busy hammers drowned them out, leaving their dour sermons to hang over the city like another shroud of ashes. Barrels of gunpowder stored in basements over many blocks remained a constant threat, as did the desiccated redwood structures, ignitable ship hulks, discarded goods, dry-as-bone timbers, and oil-drenched buildings. As Coffin tried to sleep on the *Talma*, he could practically hear the flutter of kerosene, whale oil, and camphene lamps, of fat wax candles and the hiss of open stoves. Another strong wind swept in from the ocean. Howling, it blew away the cinders and dried the living firetrap, making it ready for the next big burning. People were already taking bets on when. In two weeks all would be as it had been except for the Montgomery Street banks, impervious as eggshells, that had burned. Since the fine for refusal to aid firefighters had been ineffective, the Council raised the penalty to $500. No one would pay that either.

All the volunteers had torn ligaments, scalds, injuries caused by falls, and considerable smoke in their lungs. Sawyer had injured his hand. He and new volunteer Mike Gully argued over the best balms for burns. Kohler commonly used a mixture of nitrate of silver, sulfate of iron, bicarbonate of soda, white paint, and sulfate of zinc to heal burns, but Gully suggested Sawyer hold his burn *patiently* in cold water so no blisters would form. Good advice.

Widespread discussion over who had been setting the blazes raged. The leading theory was that the Ducks were igniting San Francisco as part of their protection racket. Some thought the Hounds were using the ensuing confusion to loot stores and rob citizens. "No matter what the answer is," the mayor said, "we've got to improve buildings." First, he banned the use of highly combustible building materials. Citizens raided the San Mateo hills for thousands of feet of new redwood, filled in ditches that had impeded the volunteers, and dug some artesian wells. There was talk of using corrugated metal and granite blocks for the new buildings, but by now the same old firetraps as before had been erected. Citizens met at the St. Francis Hotel to further organize the unpaid fire department. Local government had little control over the volunteers. They could construct their engine houses wherever they wanted but tended to overprotect some neighborhoods and underprotect others. In July the mayor signed an ordinance to propose the establishment of a charter. Within a week Broderick, who was emerging as political boss of the city, twisted arms and got the charter approved. Another two fire companies were created, not regional but nationalistic departments, which only made friction between the cantankerous volunteers worse. As Sawyer had seen in New York City as the number of companies grew, they became more competitive. In the East, firefighting had become less community service than armed combat. Around Pell Street and in the Bowery residents still spoke of the 1836 battle between Lady Washington Company and the Peterson Engine Company when hundreds of volunteers and bystanders were caught up in a knock-down, drag-out, and bloody slugfest. New York Engine Company Number Two, notorious for its bitter rivalries with companies Nineteen and Twenty-six, was disbanded for brawling, as was the Hudson Company.

The next new San Francisco company was California Engine Company Number Four. It displayed none of the lavish gold braid of Social Three. Their uniforms were plain as boiled potatoes, though they had them shipped all the way to New York to be cleaned at a cost of $1,300. Their modest dress caused them to be called the Simple Fire Company, or Simple Four. Cook Brothers & Company lent them their first water engine. It was simple, too, but would soon be replaced by a Hunneman pumper. William Hunneman, an apprentice of Paul Revere and Ephraim Thayer, built and designed more than seven hundred manual engines. Simple Four's procedures for responding to fires, though, were complicated and required two sets of men—one for a cart and one for the engine, which made their response time to a fire slow. Their engine house, a lean three-story building with a white flagpole and Moorish grillwork, stood on Sacramento Street as far east as the edge of Happy Valley. A year earlier squatters had pitched their tents on the eastern portion of the cove and named the sandy level Happy Valley. It was neither happy nor a valley, only an unhappy region of plague. Most of Simple Four's members lived and toiled there in its planning mills or in the Peter Donahue foundry. One of its rugged laborers, William S. O'Brien, Number Four's foreman, became one of the Big Four millionaires who controlled interests in the Comstock Bonanza, the richest strike ever. Sam Brannan, who suppressed the squatter movement, had so far been unable to oust the settlers and before long would advocate that the city take violent action. An inordinate number of future detectives and police chiefs sprang from Four's ranks. Isaiah Wrigley Lees, a machinist in a foundry, became San Francisco's chief of police and widely known as the greatest detective in the nation.

Hearing the alarm by day, volunteers all over the city threw aside their cashbooks and ledgers, kicked off their shoes, jumped into their boots, and hit the ground running. Hearing the alarm in the evening, they leaped from their theater seats. Hearing the alarm at midnight, they started from sleep, pulled up their trousers in one motion, and got to the engine house half dressed to wheel their pitiful engines out and pull and push for the fire. The first heavy strokes of the alarm bell had barely ceased when the brighter peals of engine bells supplanted them. A few minutes' delay and all San Francisco might be ablaze, and who could stop it this time if not them?

Knickerbocker Five joined Broderick One and Manhattan Two as a volunteer band composed exclusively of New Yorkers, though mostly of German ancestry. Their first firehouse on Merchant Street had been destroyed by fire. Their new $10,000 three-story brick-and-stone-cut house was on the north side of Sacramento Street between Sansome and Leidesdorff streets. Five's mahogany Van Ness piano box–type pumper was a small wheezy engine named Two and a Half. When they were not dragging Two and a Half around, they pulled a three-thousand-pound New York piano box type called Yankee Doodle. The local practice of firemen's singing chanties at the blaze began with Number Five. Their most spirited, deep-voiced songster was John "Curly Jack" Carroll, a man of imposing height. When refugees from the Sacramento deluge were evacuated by riverboat to the steamship company in San Francisco, they were put up at the Sarsfield Hotel next door. Twenty-four hours later, a rainy Sunday at 10:00 A.M., Curly Jack Carroll, dressed in his splendid wedding threads—polished silk top hat and tails—dropped by rival Big Six, so called because the Baltimoreans pulled the biggest

engine of all, to discuss the wedding ceremony with his best man, Foreman J. H. Cutter. Two hours before his wedding the fire bell rang for Big
Six's district. A fire in a clutter of wooden tenement houses had leaped
to the Sarsfield Hotel and trapped the Sacramento refugees inside.

Curly Jack threw off his top hat, pulled on his helmet, and in his
hundred-dollar tux raced to the scene with Big Six. As a torrential
downpour beat at them, Six pushed and pulled their Philadelphia-style,
4,200-pound double-decker up slick, steep hills and still beat the other
fire units to the hotel. The trapped refugees had panicked, the wooden
window casements had caught fire, and many were leaping from the
balcony into the front street. A woman was ready to toss her infant to
the crowd below when Curly Jack threw back his head and spontaneously burst into song. "Oh, we'll hunt the buffalo," he sang, a song he
had carried with him from New York. His deep bass voice rose melodi-
cally above the cries of the trapped and calmed them. This respite gave
Manhattan Two time to arrive. As the volunteers beat at the flames
and set up ladders, all the men began singing. Their song gave rhythm
and order to their methodical pumping. Curly Jack only stopped singing when he spied a trapped woman on the top floor and plunged into
the smoking building after her. He fought fire for five hours and then
stumbled home late Sunday afternoon, fortified himself with a tumbler
or two of whiskey, and collapsed on his bed. As he slept, his prospec-
tive father-in-law showed up at Sarsfield Hall brandishing a six-shooter
and looking for him. On Monday, sixteen hours later, Curly Jack awoke,
realized he had slept through his wedding, and rushed to his bride. No
one knows what she said to her soot-covered groom, but when he did
marry, it was ten years later and not to her.

In San Francisco, fire and music went together perfectly, like fire
and arson. Five sang their way through supper and sang while they
fought blazes. They sang their way to fires and sang their way back. As
they cleared rubble with their fire hooks, they sang—"Oh, we won't be
home until morning." Soon these lusty, boisterous, musical volunteers
made Five the singing fire company. While Social Three had the best
singers, Five sneered at them as sentimental fellows who relaxed between pumpings to sing "Suwannee River." All his life Big Six's assistant
foreman, Steve Bunner, found intense delight in singing "Hunt the Buffalo," which became the anthem at the volunteers' funerals. When Five's
volunteer Cherry was dying, he asked his fellows to give him a grand
funeral because he had no money. At his funeral all the firehouses flew

their flags at half-staff and filled the sky with rockets. Residual sparks from the pyrotechnics set a building afire.

The volunteers went on sweating, singing, and straining over steep hills and rough terrain, the only light provided by boys and teens with torches. Broderick One, Manhattan Two, Social Three, California Four, and then Knickerbocker Five and Big Six became unrestrained in their desire to be first at the scene. The honor of putting out a blaze first became the ultimate mark of pride and a goal worthy of any transgression—including bloodshed and, potentially, murder. This new discord disrupted what little harmony had been achieved recently between the volunteers. Big Six's Charley "the Bone-breaker" McMahon punched a rival fireman so hard he broke a bone in his own hand. Three's obsessive drinking made them belligerent and it would grow worse over the years until one morning every member woke up with a hangover and decided never to suffer through another such New Year's Day, swore total abstinence on the spot, and dashed their liquor bottles into the street below. Their foreman, Franklin Whitney, organized the Dashaway Club, the first temperance league in San Francisco. Whitney was unhappy that they were forced to use Free's toy mining pump as an engine, so he had Volunteer Tom Battelle speak to Bill Howard, who brought a beautifully painted $4,000 pumper in from Boston on his ship, *Windsor Fay.*

Sawyer knew with dread certainty that the Lightkeeper would strike. The question was when. He would not stop of his own accord. He would have to be stopped, but how could they when getting to the fire was just as dangerous as fighting it? He worried that during the next blaze the planked streets themselves might catch fire, and then what would they do? With no gutters, the gold-hungry townsfolk assigned the plentiful winter rains the task of carrying filth down the east and west streets into the cove. In summer the garbage remained where it had been dumped, drying hard in the sun and forming a crusty, sticky patina that, to Sawyer's surprise, assisted horses to gain their footing. Tons of unclaimed cargo were stacked on shore. No one was interested enough to buy or steal it and highly paid ferrymen had no time to track down the rightful owners. When formerly valuable items became a glut, auctioneers chucked perfectly good merchandise into the pits along Clay and Jackson streets. When the cost of storing merchandise was greater than its value, merchants used the items as landfill. Downtown street foundations were composed of barrels of flour and sugar, cement, spoiled beef in barrels, tins of lard, tin cheese boxes, chests of coffee, rolls of sheet lead, crinolines, revolvers, bales of hay, and crates of patented gold-washing machines designed by men who never saw a placer mine. The sidewalk running along Leidesdorff Street from Montgomery to the Pacific Mail Office was made of one-hundred-pound boxes of first-class Virginia tobacco. The day the price of four thousand pounds of chewing tobacco dropped to three cents per pound, the owners buried fifty large casks. The next week tobacco was valuable again. One landfill consisted of two shiploads of Spanish brandy dumped over two acres of waterfront ground.

South of Market, bounded by Folsom and Mission and Fourth and Tenth streets, was a quicksand bog that sucked anyone crossing out of sight. Each spring the city did maintenance on the single road to the cemetery that cost $15 per square inch. Because the city was flat busted, all the roads remained quagmires and a hazard for the volunteers and their torch boys. Here and there nestled a small refuge, but immense dunes still covered much of San Francisco. The town's hills had always presented a predicament. No level ground existed beyond the narrow crescent rim forming the beach. The shore itself was a coastal desert of windblown sand, bare tawny hills, and formidable granite mountains. At times Sawyer thought Broderick One's job was impossible. Their ancient engine, the Mankiller, was barely functioning. Because there were still no new fires, the movement toward fire safety declined and the pursuit of business again took precedence, and as time went on, harmony among increasingly competitive volunteer units grew discordant and then vanished altogether.

As for who the arsonist was, Broderick believed the long-sought fire fiend was a member of the gang clustered around Telegraph Hill. With his ties in Sydney Town and a secret undercover informant, he continued to narrow the field. Riding the swells alongside the deserted hulks, Captain Coffin eyed the cove. The tough river trader kept track of the comings and goings in the city of deserted ships around Long Wharf, and it was here that the answer to Broderick's riddle lay. The fog was working its way across the bay's nearly four-hundred-square-mile surface and enveloping the ship buildings that entrepreneurs had connected to city streets by narrow docks, fragile catwalks, and massive wharves. Coffin watched a man float his skiff beneath a portion of Long Wharf and remain there. There was the flicker of a lantern, the glint of a knife. Thieves sometimes tunneled into storehouses on the wharf above by sawing away the floor planks beneath safes and letting the gold drop into their boats. The shadowy figure had come from the direction of Sydney Town and might be planning the next city-leveling fire. Coffin lost the man in the fog but was certain he had gone away with three men. He thought he recognized the first man as English Jim Stuart, the leader of the most vicious gang of thieves, grafters, and murderers in town.

Meanwhile, the Council had decided to plank east-to-west streets, such as California and Sacramento, from the waterfront to Stockton Street. Only Nob Hill's steepness halted planking in that direction. As the city grew, workers built new roads but did not bother leveling lots down to street level. The hills above Stockton Street had been too steep for wagons to climb without ending up in a tangle at the bottom, so the city planners decreed Stockton be laid out as much as fifty feet lower than the existing topography. This made for some decidedly odd homes. Houses constructed before the grade of the street was fixed suddenly found themselves perched high above Stockton Street, which now cut through the hillside. The torch boys had to run through narrow ravines with high cliffs on either side with rooftop lots that might be on fire. The potential to be crushed by an avalanche of fire was a real issue. Sawyer, running in the wide trench of Stockton Street, dodged pebbles and avoided fine sand showering on both sides. Earth sometimes gave way beneath a stranded house and sent it tumbling down into the road. He studied houses above on both sides. Cliff-dweller families climbed ladders to their front doors—now twenty-five to forty feet above street level—drew up all their food, wood, and water by rope, or climbed rickety wooden stairs. By night they crouched in front of their camphor lamps and pondered why they had so few callers.

While these houses tottered above the rim of a gulch, necessity had made an important thoroughfare; dwellings in lower-lying areas had the opposite problem. The regraded roads formed a high embankment, nearly burying the block of houses at its foot. Residents became archaeologists, excavating the falling earth each evening to tunnel to their buried front doors. No flat land existed between Nob Hill and the water's edge along Montgomery Street. Wide California Street had to be planked by the following year. Between California and Broadway was the densest area of business. Small portions of Montgomery and Washington streets had been cobblestoned, but the numbering of houses on Washington would not begin until the following May. Then San Francis-

cans could ride or walk from one end of the town to the other over rea-
sonably dry ground. By year's end, seventeen streets would be planked
for almost ten blocks. It was one step ahead, two steps backward as
repeated battering by iron-rimmed wagon wheels and sharp horseshoes
ruined the new planking. "Planking has served well in the infancy of
the city," the press commented, "but it is probable that so perishable a
material will soon give place to cobblestones or Macadamized paving,
or even square-dressed blocks of granite or whinstone." An enterprising
local, Charles Polhemus, built a forty-foot-wide plank road from Third
to Sixteenth Street, the edge of the Mission District. He charged a toll:
twenty-five cents per horseman, seventy-five cents for a wagon with two
horses, and a buck for a four-horse team.

Alta editor Edward Gilbert stormed from his office. Though he
owned the most important paper in town, he was perpetually discon-
tented. He hated what he saw in the city and wished he could do away
with the whole thing. Along the waterfront a man was found with a cord
around his neck, another with a crushed skull, and another with knife
wounds in his back. In an argument over a cigar, teenager Domingo
Basquez stabbed a man to death. Gilbert passed warehouses where
miners inside wagered on dogfights. Over on Kearny and Commercial
and Clay streets, rat races and rat circuses flourished. Plays presented
at theaters like the Lyceum and Bella Union appealed to the basest emo-
tions. As for the arsons, he did not think the Ducks were behind them.
No, he had another theory: A merchant had instigated the fires. Some
merchants had been outbid, out-ordered, and beaten to San Francisco
by their rivals. Before the Christmas Eve fire, their warehouses had
been swollen with unsold goods with more shipments of the same arriving with every steamer. Afterward the fire prices rose 20 percent and
merchants cleared their inventories.

Seeing corruption all around him, Gilbert walked to the bright
lights of the Square, the center of all debauchery. All-night gambling
dens such as the Parker House were raking in gold dust. "The city
shouldn't be this way," he thought. "Somebody should do something to
clean this wickedness up." Why, there were more saloons than boardinghouses in town; more gambling dens than hotels. He stalked across
to Delmonico's for a steak and sliced tomatoes. As he ate, he jotted down
ideas for an editorial: "Systematic pillaging by organized gangs during
the confusion of each fire suggests the presence of profit-motivated arsonists such as merchants." "Yes," he vowed, "someone should do some-

thing." He heard the crackle of flames in the distance—"My God!" he thought. "The Ducks are quacking!" In the heat and tumult, the cry "*Quack! Quack! Quack!*" went up everywhere.

It was not a complete city-destroying conflagration this time, but the volunteers, Sawyer, and the torch boys ran as if it were. Sweat dampened Sawyer's new red shirt. As they guided the fire engines, blue wharf rats and brown Australian kangaroo rats scurried from the torchlight. The Sydney Town Ducks were deadly, but ducks lay eggs and those eggs eventually hatch into ducklings potentially more lethal. Since these children had grown up in the atmosphere of their parents' depravity, they began to rob and pillage on their own as soon as they left the nest. Known as the Tarflat Hoodlums, they roved south of Market and over most of unhappy Happy Valley, waylaying, beating, and robbing anyone they met. In their black coats, blue spring-bottom trousers, and buff-colored felt hats, they treated mothers and their little girls no better than men and boys. When an officer intervened, the Tarflatters beat him nearly to death. The call of gold had drawn the most reckless young men to San Francisco: the best artists, intellectuals, farmers, merchants, and clerks. It also attracted the worst: cutthroats, ex-convicts, profiteers, pirates, traders, deserters, renegades, crooked politicians, and the Lightkeeper. Gold made it the most diverse city on the globe. Every nationality—British, Norwegian, Italian, French, Spanish, German, and Dutch immigrants—filled its streets. Baptist ministers and cheapjacks mingled with Philadelphia Quakers and mountain men. South Sea Islanders and Chinese in blue jackets trudged alongside California Spaniards. Thus the volunteer companies were composed of whichever ethnic group was most representative in the particular neighborhood where the firehouse stood. New companies were all French, all Irish (the Hibernia), and all German (the St. Francis Hook and Ladder), who wore handlebar mustaches, brown linen pantaloons, Hessian boots, and loose brown coats. The Germans played their violins during the fires to cheer on the volunteers. Each morning on Stockton Street between Pacific and Broadway streets, the all-French Lafayette Company Number Two drilled, gave standing and passing salutes until their arms were sore, rolled drums, and flourished fifes. In their plumed helmets they wheeled back and forth in divisions at double time beneath the flag of France. Lafayette Two's vexing habit was the wild aggrandizement of anything that could be connected, even remotely, to their beautiful France. They organized their hook and ladder brigade exactly as the

Paris Fire Department did, wore uniforms granted by Napoléon, and marched to blazes wearing lace brocade, silks, and dainty fragrances. The local French community of fifty thousand numbered the same as the German community, but they were so ever present in daily life that San Franciscans never thought to consider them foreigners. They congregated in cabarets on Jackson Street, where there were shops with signs in French; two French-language newspapers; a French gambling house, the Polka; and the popular Adelphi Theatre. In some districts, streets looked more like France in architecture than Paris did. Like the Swiss and German communities, they had their own hospital. Instead of the Teutonic Russ Gardens, Lafayette Two gathered farther down the road at the Willows, a Gallic amusement park with a zoo, bear pit, and sea lions. The men of Lafayette Two adored sauces, wine, cheeses, and sourdough bread. Their robust chief stoked his belly with onions, spices, and andouillette of tripe, smoked his pipe, drank his wine, and shared croissants with his friends. Two's fine artists decorated their engines with beautiful end and side panels of views of their beloved Paris.

As the ethnic and regional firehouses trumpeted their superiority over one another and the French over everyone, it was only a matter of time before a real battle broke out. The French might be great shakes on land, but they were laughingstocks at sea. Dutch Charley joked that French whalers, known as Crappoes (toads), set sail from French ports with tallow candles onboard. "They foresee they will not catch enough whales to obtain oil for light," he said. Lafayette Two retained their fine manners and courtly ways, if not their tempers, as they made sweeping bows of plumed helmets, but when the inevitable donnybrook broke out, the white gloves came off. In the midst of this escalating tension between volunteer companies, the Lightkeeper would strike again. At times like this Sawyer feared the arsonist might be one of the firefighters from Social Three, Big Six, Lafayette Two, or even Broderick One. The fire companies had become so competitive that setting a fire might enable one company to reach the scene before the others. A man thought a hero to the public might want to appear even more heroic by setting a fire so he could put it out to the applause of the city.

Gilbert adjusted his gold-rimmed glasses and gave his long, narrow galleys a final glance. Tomorrow's *Alta* would recommend that the police force be increased again to catch the arsonist. The May fire had also reawakened interest in establishing an actual fire department. The gaps between the blazes coincided with the temporary storage of great deposits of gold awaiting shipment back east. In each of the fires, stores of gold were looted during the confusion. Still thinking, Gilbert walked to the two-thousand-pound main press—a Washington hand printer, a rugged version of the classic flatbed mainstay of frontier editors, the R. Hoe Imperial. The printer inserted lead slugs for spacing, tightened the metal frame, and applied ink from a leather roller.

"A possibility," Gilbert thought, "a number of merchants have ordered tons of expensive merchandise. It takes a considerable number of months to sail here. In that time items formally in demand become too plentiful. Vessels arrive daily with goods fit only for the Montgomery Street bogs." Small fires had broken out all over town, posing the danger of a general conflagration just as several ships all bearing the same cargo anchored. "Such surpluses to the merchants meant a fortune lost overnight. Our arsonist might be a prosperous merchant with a fat overstock and the fires his way of clearing his books and collecting the insurance." George Wilkes, Broderick's earliest tutor and adviser in New York, would have agreed. "The warehouses of San Francisco were glutted to the roofs," Wilkes wrote in a letter to Broderick, "but the precious commission merchants of San Francisco could not make returns to their Atlantic shippers. And then came the terrible conflagrations which gave them a clear balance sheet." "Thieves, thieves, incendiaries!" shouted Gilbert suddenly. "Hang them! Hang them." The printer wiped his inky fingers on his leather apron, inserted a sheet of Chinese paper onto the hinged wooden tympan, folded it over the inked type, slid the bed carrying the form to a position beneath the cloth-covered platen, and pulled back on a leather-covered bar to force the platen downward against the bed of metal type and produce an impression. Gilbert paused as he took the first copy. "What if the Lightkeeper had an even darker motive. What if he was one of the volunteer firemen?"

<hr/>

The dust of April and the showers of May turned all of San Francisco into a slough of liquid mud that ruled their lives. Sawyer rolled up his trousers and plunged on. Mud oozed through his worn boots. A two-wheeled covered wagon, deep in the mud, had been backed to the verge of a hill. Its owner had constructed a table from a couple of boxes with boards laid across. On top of a chest were a few loaves, pies, bread and butter, buns and cakes. A teakettle was bubbling over an iron furnace. Sawyer selected a sweet bun and had lunch. Still eating, he walked to the eighty-foot-high sand mountain on Market Street and Third Street and another sixty-foot-high sand hill on Second Street. He trudged on, longing to be at sea as a fire engineer, kindling fires instead of putting them out. But he could not go yet. What was it they said about New York firemen? "Faithful and fearless," he recalled. He was both. Sawyer, still hungry, accepted a fatty chunk of white sausage, a concoction of fresh veal and pork called bockwurst from a vendor, and plowed on.

By June the mud pits on Market Street, the broadest part of the dismal bog, had covered over with a thin, hard crust spiderwebbed with cracks burned there by the heat. In July, with the end of "June Gloom," the sun baked the whitewashed board shanties and oilpaper walls and made them matchboxes. The people inside hid behind their muslin and Osnaburg partitions or rocked all night in tumbledown chairs. In the heat, wharf rats snoozing beneath the raised plank sidewalks had become indolent, but the sand fleas had grown bolder. Restlessly the fleas flitted about in sultry winds that daily increased in ferocity. Violent, hot gusts off the bay shook block upon block of warehouses. The hillsides became brown.

To defeat the sandy and boggy roads that made daily commerce and firefighting so difficult, the city fathers had decided to cover over the main streets with planking. But lumber in this wood-scarce city was again costly thanks to the last fire. At over $400 per one thousand board feet, lumber had to be freighted down from Oregon. To fetch local brush from the surrounding hills cost far more in wagon fees and overpriced manpower. Finally, the Council scheduled serious planking to begin and decided to worry about paying later. It would be the least of their worries.

PART II

THE

LIGHTKEEPER

September 17, 1850–June 22, 1851

The faults of [Broderick's] career were seen to be the results of his origin, his early orphanage and his youthful associations, but the man himself stood revealed as one whom God had endowed with personal incorruptibility, a grave, earnest, honest, brave man, who in the midst of unparalleled corruption in his own party kept his own hands clean and his record straight.

—*The Works of Hubert Howe Bancroft: History of California*

One of Sam Clemens's diversions in the city, whenever it rained so heavily that it would have been unwise to trudge about on mere routine calls at the wharf or the courts, was to play penny ante at the Turkish bath downstairs with the proprietor and a friend of them both, a fireman. The company was amusing and it is probable that Sam found the talk of this fireman more to his liking. Tom Sawyer (such indeed was his name) had been a Brooklyn gamin who took to the sea, had worked on vessels in the Mexican trade, and had served with great heroism in a shipwreck, rescuing many lives: a great exploit no doubt, for he had to swim about in a water boiling with sharks. It was a fortunate acquaintance for the ex-fireman. When the book *Tom Sawyer* came out, he had embarked in business as a tavern keeper. . . . Thenceforth he basked in renown, thriving mightily.

—Idwal Jones, *Ark of Empire, San Francisco's Montgomery Block*

Eliza "Lillie" Hitchcock

CHAPTER SIX

Tug-of-War

There was a terrible night fire in Nevada City on September 17, 1850, but from natural causes, not arson. Gongs sounded as a blazing feedback loop consumed the tinderlike pine houses in the town. The red glare fell far back into a pine forest of dry bark, needled tufts, and dead spines smelling of pitch and turpentine. In San Francisco all was well for a change. A fresh harvest moon dominated the sky. A warm wind swept in from the bay—the so-called Lightkeeper's Wind as Sawyer had named it and which could be considered a trade wind, if the trade was arson. In San Jose, Broderick slept contentedly. Almost everyone in San Francisco was asleep, too—except the gamblers, johns, and the incendiary who had pulled on his hooded greatcoat and set off into the fog. Whoever he was, in whatever disguise he wore in daily life, he was practicing his true occupation at 4:00 A.M. A trail of sweat coursed down his cheek as he labored through the mud to reach his target. His eyes glittered. Prometheus was bringing the gift of fire to the city; Vulcan, the fire god, was forging it.

All the inmates of the Philadelphia House Saloon on the northern side of Jackson between Dupont and Kearny streets were slumbering before their open fires when the gongs sounded. They woke to terror in their rooms of white muslin walls and oilcloth floors. Hearts beating fast, they pulled on their clothes and staggered toward the nearby Washington Market. They fled, leaving their windows and doors open

to provide oxygen for the fire. Swiftly the fire created its own winds
through the updraft, and the stairway became a chimney flue to upper
rooms. "Not again, not again!" they murmured. "No! For the love of God,
No!" Many were awakened a few blocks away on Battery Street by the
cry of "*Fuego, fuego!*" In the tumult the cry, "*Quack! Quack! Quack!*"
went up in the muddy pond. The Sydney Ducks were robbing and mur-
dering and cackling as they did. At his firehouse, Sawyer cried, "Drop
everything. Hit the ground running. Jump into your boots, pull up your
trousers, and get to the engine." By 4:10 A.M. volunteers were heaving
at the pump handles and hurling themselves at the blaze. The roar of
flames drowned out cries for help, but the victims were lucky. The fire

moved torpidly because it was night. Night winds go downhill because of the cooler temperatures and move slower than during the day because of higher humidity. Day gusts usually fly uphill because the sun heats the ground and convection carries the fire upward. Burning buildings throw off their own heat, and as the hot gases rise, the vacuum pulls in more oxygen to ignite the unburned carbon in the smoke. That heat creates a convection current and upward tornado that carries the embers for miles to start more fires.

During this fourth great fire the flames ravaged the greater part of the blocks between Dupont Avenue and Montgomery Street embraced by Washington and Pacific streets. The devastation reached half a million dollars, though officials estimated twice that amount. At least during the fire all personal feuds between ethnic and regional firehouses were temporarily forgotten as the volunteers worked together to one purpose. The arson cleared a hundred one-story wooden shanties. Sawyer went inside the few that had survived. As he had suspected, their interiors were lined with flammable paper and baize (coarse woolen cloth with a nap on one side). The destruction of so many firetraps opened up a large centrally located area where larger, fire-retardant buildings could be constructed. Because the June fire had been so recent, most of the larger buildings had not been rebuilt and thus could not be lost again.

The cost of replacing buildings was becoming cheaper as each year the cost of labor dropped and wood from Oregon became more easily obtainable. Dr. Merritt, a physician who had a sideline of importing knockdown houses from back east, made certain his customers were satisfied. The day before the fire, one of his clients discovered a door missing from his order and had gone to Dr. Merritt to demand it. He promised to deliver it in the morning, so he got up early, carried the door to his customer's house, and found only a mound of ashes in the spot.

In San Jose, Senator Broderick was busy lobbying for more durable structures for San Francisco. The city erected some iron prefab buildings with heavy iron shutters and masonry and put up a few three- and four-story brick warehouses, painted a depressingly ugly red, on Montgomery Street. Finally they began a two-and-a-quarter-mile plank road between Portsmouth Square and Mission Dolores. The city also repaired Long Wharf, seriously damaged in the third big fire, at a cost of $180,000 and sent it stretching two thousand feet into the cove so eastern merchants' speedy clipper ships could tie up in deepwater. Captains increased wages to hold trustworthy crews, but the days of seamen's deserting in the cove were ending as the gold mines played out.

The city's first modern fire engine, en route from New York, was slated to arrive on the first anniversary of the Christmas Eve fire. Sam Brannan, hide merchant Bill Howard, and Talbot Green, all major financial supporters of Company Three, had each pledged $600 to the city's firefighting effort. Green had had a street named after him before it was revealed he was really Paul Geddes of Lewisburg, Pennsylvania, who had a second wife and had absconded with $8,000 from a Pennsylvania bank. Green went east to clear his name and never returned. Brannan had to settle his $600, but nothing could dampen his enthusiasm for that splendid Hunneman engine he had ordered with $20,000 of his own money to ride during the upcoming Fireman's Day Parade. On September 20, Kohler's term as chief engineer ended and the volunteer companies voted on his replacement. Andrew McCarty was elected, but three days later the Council realized that though the Protection Company had cast 104 votes, they had only fifty members. The results were thrown out and Kohler was formally reelected on October 19 to another eight-month term.

A day earlier Dr. Jacob Stillman, who had observed many of the tragedies in the city, had finally been on his way out of San Francisco. "Good riddance," he said. He had kept a careful journal of his tribulations over the last fourteen months. "It is man here that passes into sere and yellow leaf and not trees," he said. Just then the *California*'s sister mail ship, the *Oregon*, steamed through the Gate and anchored halfway between the city and Alcatraz Island. Flags were fluttering from her rigging. Stillman observed a large banner in the bunting he could not read. The *Oregon*'s crew began firing cannons from her deck and sailors on other ships began discharging their artillery. Next, big guns roared from the fort. Thousands were converging on the waterfront, some firing revolvers. Shouts filled the streets. On Long Wharf, Sawyer, Kohler, and Senator Broderick tried to read the *Oregon*'s banner. The eighteen-year-old's eyes were sharpest. "Just you read it! We're the thirty-first state!" Sawyer yelled. "Now we're at home again. We are *in* the States!"

"Far better than being a state," added Senator Broderick, who was the symbol of every Californian against slavery, half the population, "we are a *free* state!" And that, thought Sawyer, in spite of Broderick's skating on the edge of the law, in spite of his rough friends and rougher tactics to make the changes he wanted, was why he idealized the man.

Every great man was just about a hundred years ahead of his fellows. To him the senator stood for all that was noble in the city. He was, after all, only slightly dishonest in a thoroughly dishonest city. Until now the common answer to the question of a person's nationality had been, "I am a San Franciscan." Now everyone answered, "I am an American!"

The Council appropriated $5,000 for a celebration the next day, but the impatient citizens arranged the grand affair that night at $20 a head. They held the American Ball at the California Exchange on the corner of Clay and Kearny streets. Because supper was served at the Union Hotel at Merchant and Kearny, the owners built a carpeted bridge from their modest building to the Exchange so women would not have to go out on the boggy streets and tread over sacks of beans in their fine gowns to reach the ball. The sheriff, appointed chief of twenty-eight marshals, kept the event secure and the American Ball was a glittering success—and none of the women even got their shoes muddy. With Kohler's reelection as chief engineer of Broderick One, Sawyer saw his chances for any future advancement diminished. He got along poorly with Kohler, who could be ostentatious and once paid $1,500 for a single seat at Irish-born opera diva Catherine Hayes's concert, even had his men shower the stage with gold nuggets, jewels, and fifty-dollar pieces in heaps at her feet.

Sawyer walked to the corner of Gold and Sansome where Sansome Hook and Ladder Number Three kept their small firehouse and aggressively added his two cents' worth to the latest volunteer group to form. He suggested a division of labor—hose men would fight the fire and ladder men would rescue victims and use their hooks to pull down walls. Sansome Three was in charge of blasting caps and black powder for all the other companies. Blowing up buildings in the path of an uncontrollable fire had proved to be the one foolproof means of containing a blaze. Until now Three had stored the explosives in the biggest cart in the new state, one large enough to hold fifty-foot ladders but maneuverable enough to be kept out of a fire's path. A bigger, more substantial fireproof engine house, though, was really the answer. Sansome Three was sustained by rich businessmen, among them their foreman, A. DeWitt, co-owner of DeWitt & Harrison's warehouse, who paid for a new $44,000 headquarters on Montgomery Street. The furniture alone cost $5,000. "Ah," Sawyer thought, "if only the rest of San Francisco was built so well."

Bill Daingerfield, an eastern lawyer who dreamed of making big money by buying real estate and selling political secrets, joined

Broderick One as a volunteer. When Daingerfield's new properties in Shasta burned down, he wrote his family back east: "I will make a fortune and a large one, in the next few years, I will have information that I can sell to speculators at a high price, as I will have full knowledge of the character of all the lands put into market." He predicted a profit of $9,000 in his first year, and that then the governor would make him a judge. As a judge he would have even greater secrets to sell. Until then he would fight fire and sell a new kind of property he had discovered. He had decided to invest in city water lots, plots of water in the cove that when filled in could be built upon. Senator Broderick had invented the water lot by introducing a bill in a sleight of hand in the Senate that transferred title to the waterfront from the state of California to San Francisco. After the bill passed, the city turned over the water lots to a ring of predatory politicians who were managing municipal affairs. The city marked streets and offered rows of building lots that still were submerged a quarter of a mile offshore. When the plots were auctioned off, Broderick and Brannan had first bid on the most valuable. Though Daingerfield never became rich, in three years the governor would make him a judge. Never more than moderately successful, he would die while hearing a case. His days with Broderick One, though, were his happiest because then his dreams were boundless and possible of fulfillment, and hope still existed.

Between fires, Sawyer did a little river work on the San Joaquin and Sacramento river steamers, in shallow San Pablo and Suisun bays, and traded periodically in Sacramento and Marysville. On October 31, another arson gave the volunteers a scare. The blaze, kindled by an unknown hand, set afire the City Hospital. Dutch Charley and Archie Watson of Protection Two arrived first, got 150 patients out, and then discovered the fire had communicated to a one-and-a-half-story garret. Dutch Charley and Archie found no one inside, but they were cut off by flames. Dutch axed a hole in the roof to escape and sent Archie out first. "After shouting through my trumpet to the St. Francis Hook and Ladder Company for a ladder to be placed against the house," Dutch Charley recalled, "I followed Archie. We slid to the edge of the roof where the ladder was hoisted and then went down through the flames which burst out from the windows on both sides and singed our hair as we passed." On the lawn outside, Mayor Geary, a normally unassuming man, was issuing orders directly in conflict with those of Chief Kohler. Finally Kohler had had enough. "Keep your mouth shut or leave the ground instantly," he snapped. When the mayor refused, Kohler ordered Dutch Charley to place Geary under arrest. Only after he had escorted him some yards toward jail did the mayor agree to "clear out of here."

On December 14 a second intentional blaze ignited inside Cooke Brothers and Co.'s iron building at the foot of Sacramento Street below Montgomery. Another million dollars in merchandise and several iron buildings went up in smoke, but its breadth did not gain the status of a city-destroying fire. Now the city treasury was as empty as the reservoirs. So far two big fires had been kept from spreading. The volunteers had to celebrate that fact. The city still stood, but the people thought every cry was a signal of impending destruction. At any moment the Lightkeeper might murder again with the striking of a single spark.

As Sawyer returned home, he thought of the seven volunteer companies formed after Broderick One, Social Three, Big Six, and the rest. Volunteer Seven had not a shred of personality. Vigilant Nine had even less. Admittedly, Pacific Eight, popularly called Sailor Eight, had a striking persona. Because their firehouse was by the water—near Pacific Wharf on the west side of Front Street between the Jackson and Broadway Street wharves—they fought fire as if they were at sea. Their members wore white cotton duck, swaggered like sailors, and operated the pumps of their New York–style engine as if pumping bilge water. They hauled at hoses and ropes as if raising sails and sang rousing sea chanteys as they battled flames.

Crescent Ten showed a strong Cajun identity. Most of its members were from New Orleans. Because Ten marched looking straight ahead, people began calling them *Proud* Ten. Proud Ten, the most athletic in town, except for the acrobatic all-German St. Francis Company, rejoiced in their supremacy of strength, quickness of perception, and fleetness of foot. When the Council set the date of the next Firemen's Parade as May 4, the anniversary of the second great fire, the swiftest was selected to hold the tongue and roll their New York side-lever engine downhill in the trial run the day before. Because Proud Ten's engine house on the north side of Pacific Street between Kearny and Montgomery streets was close to many of the big fires, they usually got to the blaze first. One day Ten arrived so prematurely, they had extinguished the flames and were returning home before any other company got under way. As each passed, Ten razzed the latecomers. "Clean sweep, fellows!" they whooped. "We've made a clean sweep!" Ten's foreman mounted a broom on top of their engine to stand for a clean sweep and carried it to every call to taunt the others, but eventually it proved cumbersome. "Let's replace the broom with a foxtail," Ten's steward, "Cockeyed Frank," suggested, "and put the foxtail up as a trophy. Any volunteer company that beats all the others to a fire can fly it on their engine." Soon a tug-of-war began among the volunteers for the foxtail, a highly sought prize. The most intense competition was between Proud Ten and Manhattan Two. Winning the foxtail encouraged dishonest practices among the smoke eaters, who laid elaborate plots and counterplots, sent men ahead to guard any available hydrants against rival brigades until their own engine arrived, or overtook an engine and ran it into a wall. There were three bell ringers at City Hall, each elected for one year by a board of delegates. Two and Ten tried to engineer their own man's appointment to tilt the odds in their favor.

A contradiction in a fireman's life was the frequent use of fire to fight fire—backfires, torches to light their way, and burning lanterns in their windows to inform comrades they were on the way to the blaze or to signal all was well. They staged their fake fires, usually empty shacks set aflame, when their firehouse was filled with men and their engine ready to roll. Most fake fires were staged in the Seventh District in the direction of Bush or Rincon Hill and beyond because it would promise a downhill trip. In staging a fire they needed a bright blaze; otherwise the bell ringer might be "called up" and "broke." Ten staged several fires to draw Two into a losing race. In response, Two planted fresh relief runners along a predetermined route to take over for exhausted firemen pulling their engine. They slowed just enough for the fresh runner to jump under the rope, take hold, and be off without missing a beat.

As Two made a good run to the Seventh District ahead of everyone, a fireman cried, "Up Jackson to Kearny. I don't care where the fire is. Up Jackson Street!" The regular run was down Montgomery. At Kearny, Two met Ten coming down Kearny straight for them. Both engines halted—side by side—and refused to budge while the building burned down. Another day an alarm sounded—a minor warehouse fire in Happy Valley. "Everybody out! Fire. Start her lively, boys," called the Engine Four chief to his hose boys. Strapping long trumpets over their shoulders, they dashed to Battery and Sacramento streets. Simultaneously Four's engines turned into a narrow alley and ran alongside a rival, rubbing hubs while the men hurled curses and traded blows. Then one engine hit a bump and crashed into the other; thus began a three-hour battle with ax handles and spanners. Four Company, suspended for actions against another company, was ordered to "turn tongue in," forbidden to answer alarms until the suspension was removed.

New volunteer companies followed: Empire Company Number Eleven housed their Van Ness piano box engine with patented running gear in their firehouse on the north side of Bush Street. Pennsylvania Twelve was called the High-toned Twelve because the men wore expensive frock coats, plug hats, and flashy jewelry on their red shirts. Despite muddy roads, they wore patent leather boots and approached any blaze as if sneaking up on it. Afraid to wet their boots, they dropped their rope at the sight of any puddle. Two, Three, and Ten companies held Company Twelve in contempt, calling them the Featherbed Firemen and Patent Leather Firemen. The well-dressed Philadelphians battled flames in spotless brocades yet barely raised a sweat. They threw fancy dress balls and soirees at every opportunity. On the day of a ball, the dandies drove the town barbers mad with their demands for the closest shaves, precise haircuts, and perfect curls. Their guests got high-toned, too, buying expensive outfits and filling the bathhouses and steam rooms on the day of the ball. Who looked classier: the swaggering Twelve in white gloves and claw-hammer evening suits or their fashionable supporters? Twelve decorated their engine house with flowers and moved their engines into the street so their guests could dance. As the night wore on, everyone was dancing in the streets.

When Twelve lost $500 in an engine-pull race with Big Six, they refused to accept their award of second place and ordered the fanciest engine available. Their huge advance payment more than paid for it, but they sent extra money to speed things along. The Philadelphia manufacturer was baffled. "What is this for," he wrote back. "How shall we apply this generous second payment to the construction of your new engine?" Back flashed an answer from the fashion plate firemen, "Spend the excess on abundant silver and gold ornamentation. Lay it on lavishly as possible. Our mighty engine must be as elegant and stylish as ourselves. We understand that may not be possible, but do your best." Twelve's engine order distracted all volunteers from the rugged occupation of fighting fire. "Sam Brannan wants paintings on his silver machine," Sawyer said. "Now Twelve wants silver and gold ornaments. Doesn't any firehouse just want an efficient firefighting machine?"

On January 6, 1851, the volunteers met to take stock of their first year fighting fire. After extinguishing a blaze, several foremen had coffee and muffins at the Clipper Restaurant, their customary meeting place.

The low-ceilinged eatery above the Custom House and post office was built entirely of ship's timbers. Waiters carried out coffee in two huge tin pots with wooden handles and poured from both spouts simultaneously. A toy railway running the length of the restaurant delivered the food. The miniature flatcars, operated by a handle like the crank of a hand organ, rattled down tracks from the kitchen carrying muffins to the firefighters. It circled back to the kitchen and returned, whistling, with hot dishes at three for a quarter. It took dexterity to grab tureens of soup and plates of fish, game, and beef cuts as they rolled past. The supervisors, still wearing their helmets, tied napkins around their necks and began to eat.

Outside the window in front of Flood & O'Brien's Saloon, people plunged through the thick mud along Washington Street. Ashes and debris from the fires had produced more mud than ever before. From the Point to the sandy, eastern suburbs stretched a vast mud sea filled with potato parings, onion tops, eggshells, cabbage leaves, and fish bones. From the cove's edge to the Square, the city literally floated on a bog. Man and horse floundered, splashed, and struggled for dry land. "Mud is the element in which we are now compelled to exist," the papers reported. "It is in every street, and a man is crossed by it at every crossing." San Francisco was not a town, but a "quagmire" and "chaos!" a visiting Frenchman complained. "When one finally chances it, one either walks somewhat in advance or else copies those who have preceded you or follows the pedestrians who know the way, putting one's foot where they put theirs." "It was proposed to cross the street on a hewn timber," wrote a local woman about a bridge built over mud for pedestrians, "which was nearly one hundred feet and at a height of twelve feet, I should think, from the green slimy mud. I succeeded pretty well until about halfway over when, finding myself dizzy, I was obliged to stop and get down on my knees, and hold on to the timber. . . . I was afraid to proceed lest I should fall into the mud and water below, and, for the same reason unable to retrace my steps. . . . That was my introduction to the town of San Francisco in 1851."

Outside, Sawyer trudged through the bog, studying each alley. He was always hearing of a bold robbery or attempted murder by the organized bands of criminals, but could walk every night and at all hours from the Square to the head of Clay Street and never see a policeman or watchman. A policeman was scarcely found even by day. With so few cops, the Hounds and Ducks always knew their whereabouts and pursued their crimes without fear of exposure. Thus the Lightkeeper was able to move about unimpeded. Where he would strike next obsessed everyone, especially Sawyer. All through February, San Franciscans listened with dread for the first sharp tap of the Monumental fire bell and howl of the rising wind. The next time it rang its long, steady strokes would certainly play a funeral dirge. During the first half of the month, small fires caused havoc. Not a single night passed that the warning bell did not peal of a small suburban fire. Questioning, alarmed, feeling their way in the unlit streets, citizens wondered if San Francisco could survive the next big fire and were so nervous that the striking note of any bell cleared a theater in an instant. On March 2, the *Alta* judged the volunteers' occupation a good and grand one and lauded their "skill and courage under circumstances involving great personal danger, and often much inconvenience and pecuniary loss to individuals, who, at the call of duty, cheerfully forsook their own private business to save the community from a terrible calamity." Fine words, but while everyone counted on the volunteers, they still needed more fire-resistant dwellings. A New England prefab wooden house was raised at the north end of Taylor Street, its precut sections assembled in such a confused manner, the second story didn't fit over the first.

On March 4, 1851, at 4:00 A.M., a cry of fire went up. Two steamboats at Central Wharf between Clay Street Wharf and Howison's Wharf burst into flame and threatened other vessels at anchor. That evening someone set a fire in a store. A strong wind scattered the cinders and burned down ten other buildings. Other near misses led the volunteers to believe they had the situation under control. Near the end of April, someone set fire to dry grass at the rear of a building. Every day police heard rumors of a plot to burn down the city. On April 23 a false alarm sounded in the dead of night. In the confusion eight prisoners escaped the city prison. During visits, their spouses had smuggled in augers and other tools used to dig a passage through the thin brick wall that formed the foundation of City Hall. "We live in such a cauldron of excitement in this town," a citizen said, "that it is impossible to collect our ideas to write a letter: thefts, robberies, murders, and fires follow each other in such rapid succession that we hardly recover from the effects of one horrible tragedy before another piece of unmitigated villainy demands our attention."

That the May 1851 fire fell exactly on the anniversary of the May 1850 blaze shattered any doubts the earlier fires had been anything but arson and that the Lightkeeper still walked among them.

DIAGRAM OF THE BURNT DISTRICT, MAY 4, 1851

CHAPTER SEVEN

The Melting House

An unrelenting northwest wind whispered between Telegraph and Russian hills, an invisible river, sweeping the city clean of moisture and throwing up clouds of choking dust. The howling failed to keep many awake. Most were already up and pacing, dreading what they knew would come. To reduce their chances of total ruin, vigilant storekeepers cached their merchandise at the edge of town or rented storage by the artesian wells east of Montgomery Street. Citizens kept their valuables neatly piled on their bedside tables for immediate escape. A lawyer left his law books packed in boxes beneath their empty shelves. On the wharves, entrepreneurs moored their boats beneath the piers so that in case of a fire they could sail away at a moment's notice. A merchant tethered a scow under his waterfront store and had only to drop through a trapdoor and row to safety. Others planned escape into the mysterious Ghost Fleet that had so far remained as impervious as Sydney Town to flame and might even be home to the Lightkeeper.

From the Ghost Fleet the flickering torches of Sydney Town were plainly visible to the north. The "Coveys" were gathering from Murderer's Corner at Jackson and Kearny to Clarke's Point on the outskirts and at the main dives—the Thunderbolt, Cock o' the Walk, the Coliseum, and the Billy Goat, the most dangerous place in Sydney Town. The Billy Goat's proprietor and chief bartender, a middle-aged Irishman,

James "Yankee" Sullivan

kept order with a hickory wagon spoke and a derringer. His customers were certain the arsonist would strike again on the anniversary of the second great fire on May 4. "This fire will be a diversion," they said, "for the greatest plundering any city ever experienced."

Meanwhile, San Franciscans were doing all they could to protect themselves. They prayed the prefabricated twelve-by-fifteen-foot metal houses they had bought through the mail would protect them. The iron sheets, grooved so the roof and sides slid into place, were shipped in boxes nine feet long, one foot deep, and two feet wide. "Attractive" one- and two-room metal houses from Boston were sold for $100 and up, touted as cheaper than wood, rustproof, and fireproof. They had their defects. When it showered, raindrops on the roof sounded like a bar- rage of musket balls. Under the blazing California sun, the highly con- ductive walls became blazing and the outer unpainted surface blinded neighbors with its reflected light. Sheet metal house builders offered a powerful anticorrosive paint to cover the galvanized iron, but under the sun it emitted a sickening odor. Then one company provided ventilating equipment to lessen the paint odor; but this failed as miserably as the fireproof paint. The brown-painted iron buildings were "the most un- sightly things possible." When night fell, the interiors dropped to arctic temperatures that froze the occupants. A wooden interior insulation was available. All one had to do was build an entire wooden house in- side the metal one.

In spite of all this, several hundred of these sheet metal homes had been erected in 1850. San Franciscans also bought huge metal warehouses from Germany, France, Belgium, Australia, and Britain. For $2,000, John Walker of London and E. T. Bellhouse of Manchester offered preassembled corrugated metal buildings of the finest British sheet metal. Walker shipped a seventy-five-foot-long, forty-foot-wide, two-story counting house with its own front porch and odd convex iron roof. One, of zinc and corrugated iron, served as George Dornin's res- taurant on Montgomery between Jackson and Pacific streets. Another became the Graham House at Portsmouth Square. A sheet iron building became little Trinity Church on Pine Street above Montgomery. Curi- ous iron houses with rounded roofs took up a half block at the corner of Jackson and Battery streets. Some ended up on the hills above the shore, but because they were constructed of one-inch-thick plates, their castings were incredibly heavy. Inevitably, the ground gradually gave way beneath them and they plunged over the cliffs or sank slowly into the ground.

The first two days of May were cool. People peered nervously over their shoulders as they fried their salt pork and potatoes on portable miners' stoves and drank thin coffee. The anniversary of the May fire was almost here. Dutch Charley raged, paced, and consulted his calen- dar. Almost a year earlier the great inferno had occurred at the worst possible time: while everyone slept. Dutch Charley's hunch was that the next blaze would be kindled on May 4, absolute proof that the fires could not be accidental. He almost found himself hoping it would happen. He listened for the Lightkeeper's Wind to rise and watched for the signalers on Telegraph Hill to light their fires against the wall of fog rolling through the Golden Gate.

May 3 was pleasant. That night sleepless San Franciscans began to measure the hours until 4:00 A.M., the exact anniversary of the previous year's fire. Early risers, breakfasting on fried fish and chocolate, waited breathlessly for the well-known clang of the huge signal bell. Its tone differentiated it from all the other bells in the city. The restless multitude ticked off the minutes, then seconds. They need not have bothered—the blaze had already been kindled. The fifth fire exploded at the very edge of midnight, and so Sawyer always thought of it as the Great Fire of May 3 *and* May 4, 1851. It was ignited in a Clay Street upholstery shop on the southwest side of the Square. Shortly before the blaze was noticed (it had been slyly licking at the dried-out shingles of the hotel roof), a ragged man recognized as a "habitue of Sydney Town" was seen running from the paint shop. He had barely vanished down the road when the whole upper story filled with flame. The paint shop on the west side of Portsmouth Square, an irresistible morsel, provided a plentiful supply of inflammable paints and oil for a midnight snack. In less than five minutes it collapsed into itself, an implosion that sent flames on droplets of burning oil splashing over two adjacent houses. The wind, which had lulled away at sunset, had returned an hour before the fire broke out. It was high and from the northwest, blowing *away* from Sydney Town—the Lightkeeper's Wind. Reenergized by the heat of the conflagration, the gale fanned the flames and gave them life.

As the cry of "Fire!" echoed across the square, unsleeping citizens boiled out of their rooms. Because an arsonist had already burned the highly combustible town to the ground four times, a fifth time would be unthinkable and so they were stunned. Again the bell of the Monumental Fire Company at Brenham Place clanged. At the fire's epicenter all three buildings were fully engulfed before Big Six could drag its pumpers the short distance across the Square. Their engines, the Mechanical, the Union, and the Franklin, lacked enough hose and water to do the job properly. Sawyer's hook and ladder company had the same problem. They rushed to refill their water wagons by attaching a suction pipe to the house and lowering it into one of the cisterns. Down went the pipe and up it came dry. The volunteers raced to the next well, but it was dry, too. Most of the clay cisterns mandated by the Council were dry, too, as the firefighters discovered over the next minutes.

In the cove a ship's captain retired early, but as worried as the rest of the citizens, he could not sleep. As he lay listening, he heard the first twang of what he called "that infernal bell." He reached topside and saw the whole northeast side of the Square in flames. The heat had reawakened a furious nor'wester. The Lightkeeper's Wind rushed down the gully between Signal Hill and the Heights, driving the fire mass directly over the section that had burned last June. He could not leave the vessel but had to stay and stamp out the burning coals raining from the sky. "Those man toys they call fire engines were rattling away to the scene," he wrote, "with the shouts of the companies and the tinkling of their polished bells, but they are of no more use than a syringe from the medicine chest. . . . All the fire engines in America cannot stop a San Francisco conflagration." He watched the engines struggling. "Before them raced the most important members of the company," one official observed, "the torch boys holding their torches high as they ran, so that the way could be seen through the unlighted streets." As the fire progressed, a man sprinted ahead of them all and started smaller fires.

The Lightkeeper was sweating now and taking a chance on being caught. The mostly wooden buildings around the Square were extremely combustible. J. Helm and Company, Gildermeister & De Frenery, and the new El Dorado on Kearny Street were all brick. This blaze would test their invincibility against fire, but how would the new metal fireproof houses fare? Near the Square some townsfolk were jeering the firefighters and declining to help in spite of the stiff new fines the Council had imposed. "Twenty! Forty! Fifty dollars a load—only help me remove my goods!" begged a merchant, down on his knees in the mud. The watchers only folded their arms. "Among the spectators there was generally a great want of concentrated effort," Harvard philosopher Josiah Royce noted in his California state history. "In short, as one sees, the whole affair was a perfect expression of the civilization of the moment."

Horses pulling loaded drays pulled wagons of fire. As a Good Samaritan helped some French lithographers save their parcels, a man carried off their carpet bag. As he sprinted to recover it, a flaming wagon ran over him. This blaze, the swiftest of the five that had already engulfed the city, came at the worst possible time. The city was between city councils—the old board had adjourned and the new one had not yet been sworn. Nobody was empowered to order buildings blown up to check the path of the flames. Broderick, who had been elected president pro tempore of the State Senate a month earlier, was in Sacramento with Kohler and most of the volunteers who were attending a firemen's conference. It fell to Sawyer, California Four, the torch boys, a few other companies, and Broderick's shoulder strikers who had remained behind to save the city.

The fierce gale spread a broad flame over the city, a flickering roof growing to a half mile in length. Updrafts carried embers for miles. The stiff wind whipped the fire furiously, sending up one block in the flicker of an eye. Riding on the wind's back, the flames jumped Kearny Street. The wind slackened, gathered its strength, and replenished, then returned as a stiff gale that violently blew flames southeast, north, and then east again. The volunteers retreated to regroup and plan.

The Lightkeeper's Wind drove a howling ball of cinders and superheated smoke into Montgomery, Sacramento, and Commercial streets. Albert Bernard de Russailh was halfway to his office on Commercial Street when he saw the fire wheel around his way. He set off running. Breathless, he reached his office and dashed inside. The rear of his building was already on fire. When the ceiling collapsed, he staggered, bleeding from cuts on his forehead and nose, and crawled a few feet before dropping to the floor unconscious. As the fire outside rolled and dived, it simultaneously destroyed houses on both sides of Commercial Street. One house began burning at the top, down slowly, story by story, to the basement. Over the crash of falling timbers the volunteers heard the terrified screams of people inside the structures. The cries were faint. The blaze's hoarse voice rumbled like a locomotive and drowned out everything. Mike Gully of Broderick One and Barney Cosgrove of California Four had to shout just to be heard. They were the speediest firefighters of the day and toiled to save the old Custom House on Dupont Street. This last relic of Old San Francisco on the northwest corner of the Square held books, ships' papers, and gold in its vault. Gully and Cosgrove fought with hooks, sacks, axes, and even their scorched hands to rescue the leaky one-story landmark. Their skin was blistered and clothing smoking when the wind momentarily turned southeast and gave them some hope the old adobe structure would be spared. If they were lucky, the fire would now be confined to the hills to the north. But the wind thrashed north, then east, and in a rush of black fire returned with a vengeance to burn the adobe building to its foundation.

As the volunteers were driven back, they wondered, "Could anything of value be salvaged from these ruins?"

Captain Hante of the Revenue Cutter Service, on the cutter *Polk*, had another way of battling fire. He stationed thirty guards around the *new* brick Custom House on the northwest corner of Montgomery and California. Working feverishly, his men saved a million dollars of specie by tossing it down a well, and preserved practically all the vault gold, $3 million worth, and naval department papers. Any record more than two years old was at the old Custom House. Nearly two thousand tons of merchandise inside the U.S. bonded warehouse were rescued. A brick and iron building north of the Custom House, on Montgomery Street, was aflame. On Sacramento a brick bank crumbled in an explosion of fire. The new raised planked sidewalks, dry and flammable as tinder, rested above hollows that acted as funnels to channel superheated air along the length of the street and from thoroughfare to thoroughfare. People leaped for their lives as sudden blasts of flame erupted through cracks in the sidewalk. In some places the raised planking broke through and plunged them into the fire. Agonized, a man rolled in the mire to extinguish his flaming clothes and died.

In the choking smoke Sawyer's breath came hard. As young and fleet as he was, he had to fight to stay on his feet. Across the street flames curled seductively along the walls lining the burning sidewalks. The planked wooden road itself was burning, its surface crackling and flickering as one immense fiery field. The flaming street shriveled all the new frame houses on both sides of Clay Street. Every structure between Clay and California streets ignited. On the floor of his office, Albert de Russailh slowly regained consciousness. Smoke and flames were swirling around him. He felt the earth shake. Firemen were blasting firebreaks to take away the fire's fuel. Then he heard sharp, well-defined retorts in the distance as firefighters pulled down timbers and walls. In a minute he heard another rumble: the muffled roar of more buildings exploding. Merchants were voluntarily blowing up their businesses. Unforced destruction, the unchallenged dynamiting of a building, remained the volunteer fire companies' most effective means of halting a fire's march. Not much had changed since the Christmas Eve fire. Stored barrels of gunpowder were exploding, quaking the ground and hurling houses into the red sky. As the thunder of explosions marched closer, Russailh rose, escaped down the stairs, and ran along the planked road for a block until he realized the street was on fire and so were his boots. Covered in sweat, he turned and, exhausted, collapsed on the floor of the Hotel de l'Alliance where he slept unaware of flames licking within inches of him and choking smoke drifting over his head.

All around the sleeping man people became insane through panic, heat, greed, despair. One man shot and killed a Mexican woman. A man on Washington Street lost his house, and then blew out his brains with a revolver. A merchant, burned out five times since he had been in San Francisco, slaughtered his family in madness, then shot himself, too. A former millionaire, his high silk hat and clothes ablaze, revolved in the gutter while laughing insanely and beating his lion-headed cane against blackened bricks. Carriages and wagons jammed together in a tangle of reins and locked wheels. Horses broke loose and charged along the flaming roads.

A powerful wind whipped around to blow a blanket of black smoke out over the bay. Washington, Sansome, and Bush streets flared into roaring furnaces. Frame houses vanished like frost on a windowpane. Flames spread rapidly north of Portsmouth Square, consuming buildings in no particular order, randomly knocking at every other back door. Timbers crashed in showers of burning splinters. Forced back by the flames, the crowd trampled everything before it. Severely burned men clawed their way to safety. Terrified horses bolted from blazing liveries. Wagons carrying the injured to makeshift hospitals overturned in the deep mud of the unburned area. The copious provisions of whiskey the thirsty town so prized propelled curtains of blue fire skyward. The glare was blinding. California Four and Broderick One and a few citizens fought on, rudderless without the chiefs and engineers.

As it had on the previous June 14, the firestorm churned hungrily toward the wharves, chasing citizens in bedclothes east along Commercial Street and far out onto the end of Long Wharf. The Great Boston Fire of 1760 had halted at the water's edge. Most fires usually did. This blaze was different. Long Wharf caught and went, then the Montgomery Street Wharf, and then the next landing. Insatiable, the fire leaped from the piers out onto two hundred abandoned ships mired in the mudflats along the piers. The trapped armada had already suffered casualties. Volunteers cried, "Knock it down." Working with irons, hooks, axes, and crowbars, they disconnected the remaining wooden wharves from land, saving some of the waterfront and dozens of ships crowded at their moorings. A few seaworthy ships forced their way through the tangled chains holding them in the morass and sailed toward the Golden Gate and safety.

Unbelievably, the fire urged its way *against* the wind to Stockton Street and fought its way from there a block over to Powell Street. The gale ran along Powell in a southeasterly direction, crossed Sacramento and California streets, and howled toward Market Street. Stuart and Raines on Jackson Street was lost. The conflagration leaped Jackson and Pacific streets to Broadway, where it licked over the arid high ground and ate its way past Sansome, Battery, and Front streets to Clarke's Point. Now a gigantic flickering noose of flame encircled the entire town and inexorably began to tighten.

Flames had surrounded banker James Naglee's warehouse, an important repository, by the time the St. Francis Hook and Ladder Company reached it. The engine had so little water pressure, its two narrow streams of water vaporized on contact with the hot bricks. Scald cascaded over the men like needle pricks. Soon all were swimming in an ocean of steam. "More men," bellowed a temporary foreman through his silver trumpet. "For the love of God, more men over here!" In the distance Sawyer heard the clank of fire brakes, another engine coming, and the screams of the burned and dying. Heavy black smoke under great pressure was issuing from the upper-story windows of a hotel across from Taaffe & McCahill's huge mail-order warehouse at Sacramento and Montgomery streets. From the color and pattern, he knew there was tremendous heat in that smoke. Deep orange meant the temperature exceeded 2000 degrees and white signaled a blaze of 2370 degrees. Dazzling white meant the temperature was climbing beyond the limits of the iron boiler and had to be damped down. The underventilated fire had created a thick mix of accumulated fire gases.

Dense mushrooms of smoke boiled from the burning hotel at high velocity. There was partial autoignition on the hotel's exterior as fire gases exited and mixed with the air, but this superheated cloud of fuel was too rich to ignite. Inside, reradiation from ceilings, walls, and objects fed one another. As a backdraft entered the hotel along a thermal runway, there was a total autoignition of superheated fire gases where incoming air met the smoke. A fireball erupted. Energy released from the fire burned uncontrollably and became hotter. A man trying to escape from a neighboring building ran into thick black smoke issuing from the hotel and became enveloped in fire. He ran a few steps, fell, and was consumed before Sawyer's eyes.

Inside Naglee's warehouse, a quartet of nine-to-twelve traders had shut themselves up behind barrels of water they believed would enable them to ride out the inferno. The thin brick walls they confidently relied upon had already begun to crumble. Spirits and chemicals within the warehouse ignited. The lurid colors blinded the traders inside. They still might live if they could endure the next hours of incredible heat. They huddled together behind the cooling water barrels.

Outside, three firefighters were cut off. Running for their lives, they reached the safety of an alley, only to be crushed by bricks falling directly on them. A whirlwind of sparks spun over the mountain of bricks as if to mark their grave. California Four feared that DeWitt & Harrison's commodities storehouse in midblock on the north side of Pacific Street might automatically ignite next. The warehouse's owners had no water, but they did have kegs of vinegar. By the time the volunteers reached the storehouse, Harrison had gotten to the roof and drenched the building with eighty-three thousand gallons of stored vinegar, and DeWitt's men were beating out the rest of the flames with vinegar-soaked blankets. Ahead, Taaffe & McCahill's three-story metal store was anchored imposingly on the corner of Sacramento and Montgomery streets, south of the City Hotel and close to the quartermaster's house. Inside Taaffe's crouched six stubborn traders as loath to leave their merchandise and gold and silver in the advance of the flames as the four traders huddled inside Naglee's.

"We'll sit the fire out," said one. "Of course," agreed another. "Our new building is corrugated iron and fireproof." The men slammed the massive iron doors, one-inch-thick metal plates and castings of insurmountable weight, and bolted the thick shutters. Secure, they crouched behind double sheets of iron. They listened to the dull thud of falling debris against their metal fortress and tensed as the inferno rumbled up to the doors and covered the metal warehouse like a fiery blanket. Sawyer and other volunteers arrived out front but were driven back. Shielding his face, he could only watch as the fire began to curl the iron. The cheap metal began glowing. Conduction directly transferred heat through the wall and made the inhabitants of the warehouse sweat. By now they doubted their decision to ride out the firestorm. If things got bad, they knew they could always fling open the strong metal shutters or slide back the thick iron doors and escape.

A fringe of thin smoke quivered along the window casements, gave a puff, and in an instant the windows became perfect rectangles of woollike smoke. Heavy black smoke issued from the upper story under great pressure. It was perfect for black fire: boiling smoke, underventilated fire, and a heavy rich mix of fire gases accumulating within. The fog frames blackened as the six traders watched. They heard the volunteers outside crying for them to escape. Long tongues of bright yellow flames belched from small rents in the metal coffin. Outside, the volunteers screamed louder for the men to evacuate. By then it was too late. While white signaled a blaze of 2370 degrees, dazzling white meant the temperature was climbing beyond the limits of the cheap iron. The exterior of the metal building and the ore inside was melting and flowing into white-hot puddles at the firefighters' feet. As the smoke around the window frames darkened, the six men inside ran to the shutters to open them. They would not budge.

"What's wrong?" one asked. "Pull harder."

The twin sheets of bolted metal trembled and grew cherry red—too hot to touch. The great double-layered iron shutters, as advertised, did not melt. Instead, they expanded in the heat and sealed the windows permanently. Next the men raced to the huge iron doors, but the fire had welded these to the building. The double sheets of bolted iron began to tremble. The traders, who were suffocating, pounded miserably on the door, burning their fists, and then ran back to the shutters. The color of the flames altered to orange. Flashovers of superheated gases radiated across the ceiling and downward, setting crates of merchandise afire. Radiation raised the temperature of objects to their ignition point. Their ledger books were already burning. Glass became molten. The traders' lungs filled with fluid; their throats closed in spasm. They were being roasted alive in a huge furnace. The moisture was sucked from their lungs and their skin began to bubble. Fiery explosions of smoke began consuming the available oxygen. Smoke turns to carbon when it reaches a temperature of 1000 degrees. The traders' lungs were black by now. Carbon monoxide killed the merchants mercifully quick at this point.

Outside, the volunteers observed the heaving red and white sea brooding at the iron windows and smelled sulfur and charred meat. More of the impervious "fireproof" iron structure collapsed into heaps and puddled into glowing slag. Twisting, groaning, and glowing, Taaffe & McCahill's warehouse grew suddenly white hot—so incandescent it blinded their eyes. The volunteers said nothing. The iron warehouse inflated to unimaginable size. The strain was unbearable. It had to blow at any moment.

"Get back, boys," Sawyer called. Retreating as far as they could, they took refuge in a burned-out lot. The iron building expanded to its limit, shook violently, once, twice, and exploded its fastenings. Red-hot bolts scattered like bullets, puncturing men and structures alike. Shutters burst out. Long-tongued flames twisted the iron into monstrous shapes. Gold and silver inside melted, flowed among the twisted black iron, and created one grotesque piece of metal. The doors coalesced into a caricature of their former shape. The bulging storehouse, having lost its integrity, shriveled. It collapsed before their eyes to become a dripping, molten metal coffin. Chastened, the volunteers left the warehouse and mechanically went on pulling down houses in the path of the fire. Whirlwinds of flames and smoke columns walked alongside them, running clockwise and counterclockwise and creating additional whirlwinds that carried sparks miles away. Sawyer now knew smoke could roar. He held his ears as timbers dropped in his path. Escape seemed impossible. In the choking smoke the volunteers' breathing came in gasps as they rushed blindly looking for safety. All were exhausted. The blaze rumbled westward and northeastward at the same time. Fresh air was blown in as the wind changed and filled the fire with oxygen. Other torch boys led firemen through shortcuts and down seldom-used alleyways until they reached salvation.

The blaze swept past them—a momentary darkening, then a gush of sparks followed by superheated air, gases, and a broad column of red shrouding everything with glare and the sound of a locomotive rumbling over broken tracks. An umbrella of dark smoke projected a reflection of the blaze on the underside of clouds. On the outskirts of town, people saw the ghastly light above San Francisco. As far as Monterey the fire cast an unearthly light below. The vast sheet of flame was so bright it attracted flocks of birds from surrounding marshes. Against the black smoke the birds were specks of burnished gold. Drawn to the flames, they flew into them and vanished one after another in tiny puffs of steam.

Former convicts robbed and assaulted citizens fleeing the city. Gangs of Ducks, principally members of Jack Edwards's gang, began robbing and assaulting people on the outskirts of town. As looting began in the suburbs, thieves in the city bided their time. The Coveys could not loot properly until the fire burned out. A few, eager to begin pillaging, pulled wet bedsheets over their heads and dashed headlong into burning stores. Few came out again. The ones who did dragged steaming valuables to the road, pulled them to a secure spot, and rushed back for more. While they were gone, their fellow Coveys robbed them. Empty strongboxes littered the smoldering ground like mortar shells. Any fireproof safe that had burst open was now empty. Merchants kept moving their valuables ahead of the fire, but it was a losing battle.

A half block away, men cried out in agony, but the inferno's train-like bellow drowned them out. In a deserted hollow on the northwestern corner of Jackson and Montgomery was a shallow basin of weeds that was a pool in summer. The depression was stacked with rescued merchandise: a jeweler's plate-glass showcase, velvet lined and overflowing with sparkling rings, stickpins, bracelets, and brooches belonging to Hayes & Lyndall's Clay Street store. It lay unprotected while its owner had gone back to salvage more goods. A band of drunken Ducks trotted down the slope of Montgomery Street and sprang upon the case.

Heinrich Schliemann, the future discoverer of the lost city of Troy and archaeological excavator of Mycenae, was in San Francisco that night. "The roaring of the storm, the crackling of the gunpowder," he wrote, "the cracking of the fallen store walls, the cries of the people and the wonderful spectacle of an immense city burning up in a dark night all joined to make this catastrophe awful in the extreme." "Not all great fires are started by Greeks hiding in Trojan horses or mad Roman emperors with fiddles," a survivor complained. "Some are Ducks with tapers."

The city burned all night. At dawn the boom of the firefighters' explosives rumbled like the dirge of funeral drums. The Ghost Fleet lost the *Callao, Byron, Galen, Roma, Autumn,* the *General Harrison,* a store ship, and two other converted vessels. Flames damaged the seemingly impervious *Niantic* and *Euphemia.* The *Apollo* and the *Georgian* ship warehouses shimmered with fire as did the catwalks and wharves connecting them to the city. Many more iron buildings failed—the City Hotel, Captain Folsom's building, and an adjoining brick building were gone. So were the U.S. Assay Office, Dodge's Express, the California Exchange, the Union Hotel, Gregory's Express, Delmonico's, two adjoining buildings—the Starr and Minturn—the *Courier* and *Balance* offices, and Moffat's Lab, which was brick. Sawyer knew that on the east side of Montgomery, between Washington and Jackson, stood three stories of a supposedly fireproof building. "The fire will halt its march here," he predicted. "It can never get through these thick walls and iron-bolted shutters." No sooner had he said this than the fire reached the buildings and he was proved right. Meanwhile, crowds forced north by the fantastic heat had halted at the corner of Jackson Street and saw other walls melting like snowdrifts. A change came over the crowd for the first time. They had been afraid before; now they were angry.

The people had lost their last bit of faith in a fireproof house or that anyone could stop the Lightkeeper, who set his blazes with impunity, greater frequency, and obvious relish. It was no coincidence that the fifth all-encompassing fire had broken out on May 4, 1851, the anniversary of the second city-destroying fire and the same day as the Firemen's Parade. Systematic pillaging by organized gangs of army deserters and ex-convicts during the confusion and in every one of the devastating fires so far suggested the presence of a profit-motivated Lightkeeper. The gangs had been waiting. "The conflagration had to be the work of an incendiary," citizens said. There is no doubt now. Their fury mounted against the arsonist's "brazen chaos." An investigation pinpointed the genesis of the blaze to the Clay Street upholstery shop. The space above Bryant's Hotel was occupied by Baker & Meserve's shop and should have been fireproof. According to the owners, residents had taken the lanterns out of their rooms at 10:00 P.M., no fires had been used about the house "for any purpose whatever," and the fireplace had not yet been damped down to ash and coals to restart for the morning fire.

❧

Yes, the blaze had been a diversion to allow strong-arm toughs to loot the great stores of gold dust that miners had in safekeeping awaiting transportation back east. Prospectors keenly missed the presence of any secure banks in the mining regions. While they panned and shored up tunnels, they had to leave their ore unguarded and stood pickaxes in their holes so no one would meddle with their claims. Astonishingly, the markings were commonly honored. An El Dorado gambler lost $45,000 at the turn of a card but said only, "I left my tools in the hole and I'll get plenty more gold when I get back and the water falls." Ethics in these uncommonly dishonest times were confusing.

Just before dawn, Mayor Geary announced that $200,000 worth of gold was missing. Later he would leave the city with an unexplained $200,000 fortune he had somehow accumulated on the job during his three years in office. Yet his wealth had not been derived from trade—he had none—or from illegally buying city lots or any of the other doubtful city transactions in which both Brannan and Broderick indulged.

Red Davis and Curly Bill sailed from Rincon Point at the height of the conflagration to bury looted gold. Lit by the burning city, the two Sydney Town Ducks felt the Lightkeeper's Wind at their backs and heard the California Engine Company bell ringing on Market Street and the odd cadence of the Monumental firehouse bell in the Square. As they progressed on their two-mile journey, a low white fog crept across the bay and covered over the red waters surrounding the burning city. Sheriff John "Coffee Jack" Hays, a tough customer, might be hot on their watery trail. He once led his volunteers against fifteen-to-one odds to smash a Comanche war party. The former Texas Ranger, greatest of them all, could outride and outshoot almost anybody except Billy Mulligan, who scared even the Ducks. Between the Ducks' present position and Sand Island was Goat Island, to the south. Abruptly the 140-acre island rose steeply from the water silhouetted against a bank of white fog. Using Goat Island as a seamark, they lined up its north end with a grove of redwoods on the East Bay hills, which guided them safely past the sunken ledge of Blossom Rock, a secret and deadly obstacle to ships northwest of Goat Island. They saw a fifty-foot-high cliff and summit of trees and pulled hard for a curving white beach on the eastern side. Cautiously they circled to the island's tiny cove. Along the coastline was a peaceful stretch of beach and beyond that tangled thickets. Smugglers often buried opium and contraband there until their confederates could row out to the island to retrieve it. They heard a flutter of wings and raucous cries as a pelican flock flew up the island slope. They beached their boat, hauled out bags, and went to bury their stolen gold. Goat Island, a perfect temporary bank for miners, Spanish pirates, wise chiefs, and medicine men (there was a sweat lodge there), offered the additional interest of more gold to discover. If only some of the wealth reported buried on Goat Island was intact, it deserved the name Treasure Island. The Ducks saw a bark moored off Goat Island, one of the rival Hounds' ships, and went ashore to hide their treasure. Meanwhile, a government vessel parted the fog and pursued the bark, which outran the federal ship. Later authorities found some of the stolen loot in Sydney Town.

In San Francisco the dawn gave the shell-shocked survivors their first good look at the devastation caused by the deadliest arson in San Francisco's history. "So many whirlwinds of destruction had swept over the devoted city at short intervals, and with such fearful strides," survivor Ralph Andrews wrote, "that the whole community was as excitable as if they had stood on the brink of a crater." Captain George B. Coffin rushed to Stuart and Raines's lot to see if his nautical equipment had survived the fire. "Not a piece is left large enough to make a clothespin," Stuart told him, then turned away, already contracting with a builder for a new store. "I need it to be ready for occupancy in one week," he ordered. Disheartened, Coffin went to see the rest of his beloved city. "A space of a hundred acres which at sunset stood thickly studded with buildings," he wrote in his log, "was cleared away at 4:00 A.M." The metal homes and warehouses the Gold Rush Society had placed such faith in had failed miserably. They had been nothing more than tinderboxes. Thirty-six to sixty-eight of the so-called fire-resistant buildings had melted. Only seventeen of the structures could be salvaged. "They are little more than a woodpile enclosed in noncombustible walls," a survivor said.

When one newspaper editor tried to transport his press to a safer location to print a fire edition, fire destroyed his press. All the newspaper offices had burned except the badly damaged *Alta*. At 5:00 A.M., Edward Gilbert, its contentious but cowardly editor, sat down to write: "San Francisco is once again in ashes. The smoke and flames are ascending from several squares of our city, as if the God of Destruction had seated himself in our midst. Here and there a brick building stood like a tomb among a nation of groves, yet even they, in most cases, have nothing but their walls standing." He considered early estimates of $7 million in property loss too low. The fire was still burning in places. He calculated the loss at $10 to $12 million. Others estimated the loss as high as $17 million, with the possible loss of a hundred lives. Gilbert wrote: "The municipality of this mushroom place was at the moment in debt, for the expenses of the city government, over one million dollars; and this calamity of the great fire was surely a fitting work for such a municipal organization to accomplish over night." He believed the fires had cleansed the city of evil. "We can and will begin again, fresh and reborn without sin."

At 7:00 A.M. the final remnants of the fire reached a sparsely built section of town, ran up against an unfinished brick structure, and died. Hard brick withstands ignition temperatures up to 1000 degrees. When the fog burned away, the city's tallest structures were a few chimneys shaking against the slate sky. Devastation stretched three quarters of a mile long and a quarter mile wide. Every house on Leidesdorff was gone. Eerily, among acres of devastation, an isolated house or two stood untouched. Coffin stumbled to Sacramento and Montgomery streets to learn the fate of the traders who locked themselves inside Taaffe & McCahill's iron warehouse. "Their burnt and mangled bodies were found among the ruins near the door," he wrote. "It is supposed that, finding the building no longer tenable, they had endeavored to escape, but the intense heat had so warped the iron doors and windows that they could not be opened. Their bones were burned to a cinder." The victims had rushed to the same spot and perished together, their bones indistinguishable from one another. Mr. Wells, the Boston banker, had remained in his fireproof building too long, but he did escape. Wells, dreadfully burned, would carry the marks to his grave. Coffin wondered why the apparently fireproof Wells & Company building had been destroyed and descended into its cellar to find out. When the cellar workers fled, they left a door open and one of the little windows at the rear that provided light, the only window not shuttered by iron. The draft had brought "a perfect hurricane" of flames into a basement filled with liquors. On the first floor contractors were already laying plans to replace the building within weeks.

At the Naglee warehouse, of the four men shut up in their vault for four hours, James, Noyes, Forst, and Mudge, only Mudge was seriously burned, but Edward Cahill, last seen inside his flaming store, was presumed lost. On the corner of Montgomery and Sacramento streets lay the charred remains of Leon Greenebaum, Reuben Backer, M. Nassbaum, and O. Rossenthall. They would be buried at 2:00 P.M. at the Israelite burying ground. At California and Montgomery streets, by Naylor's brick building, Heath Davis had lost his four-story brick building, the city's first, that he had leased as the new Custom House.

All the warehouses in town but three had been destroyed. Gildermeister & De Frenery's brick building on Montgomery between Sacramento and Commercial streets was saved by its thick rear walls. Jesse and Joe Seligman's single-story shop at California and Sansome survived because of its twenty-two-inch-thick brick walls and heavy iron shutters. Immediately the Seligmans, as owners of one of the few business district buildings still standing, gave up being mining supply salesmen and became bankers. When they opened Burgoyne's safe, they found $1.5 million and all the papers and deposits inside not even singed. Meanwhile, a citizen named Mr. Argenti formed a patrol of guards at his own expense to protect the ruins of his neighbors.

Five large store ships full of merchandise were still burning. One, the *Niantic*, so miraculously saved in the previous June's fire, had been enclosed in a wall of sheet iron for protection and might still be salvaged, at least below water. At the foot of the Jackson Street Wharf neighbors saved a big warehouse but nearly lost their lives. All around it, the tops of ten thousand piles in the mud had burned down to the water's edge. At 8:00 A.M., an hour after the fire burned out, Sawyer, half drowned and half toasted, and smelling of plaster and wood, shambled back to his engine house to sleep. His hair was singed, his eyes red, his lungs sooty, and every muscle in his body was screaming. While he slept, weary survivors wandered glassy-eyed though smoldering streets. A lucky few had salvaged their goods and stored them onboard the British vessel *R. K. Hurtley* of Liverpool. The unlucky many carried furniture with no place to put it. Shelter on the outskirts of town was costly: $150 for the use of a tent for ten days. One family set up housekeeping in the street, arranging their family portraits around a post. A man ran back into his office, which had suddenly burst into flame again. He perished from smoke inhalation. Monumental Six volunteer James Welch burned to death.

Over at the St. Francis Hotel, two burned-out men ascended the outside stair to the second floor. Inside, a tall, powerfully built man, dreadfully burned, was standing behind the door, eyes closed, head drooped upon his chest, and wrists crossed as if he were shackled. His beard and all the hair below his hat had been burned off, as if shaven. When he spoke, it was through scorched, mangled lips. His voice was muffled, yet oddly familiar. "Excuse me, but I do not know where I am," the stranger whispered, "or how I came to be here. Don't you know me? I am your counselor, Elbridge Gerry Austin."

At Kearny and Washington streets, unlucky Tom Maguire stood over more ruins. The previous April, the stocky impresario had added an auditorium on the second floor of his Parker House in recognition of the "Swedish Nightingale," Jenny Lind, who had won the hearts of the New York volunteers by donating her concert proceeds to them. When she left Manhattan, the firefighters presented her with an elaborately engraved box of pure California gold. The wooden three-story Jenny Lind Theatre, where James Stark directed productions of *Hamlet, Mac-*

beth, and *King Lear,* cost Maguire and his partner, J. B. Hart, $40,000. Maguire had been counting on income from the theater to pay off their debts within four months. But he was a determined man whose success was amazing, considering he was totally illiterate. He planned to erect a second Jenny Lind Theatre on the same site. The Empire and American theaters and the Adelphi were destroyed; Dutch Charley and his partner, George Baker, lost their new saloon in the Crockett Building; and the five-story Union Hotel pitched into the street, though Williard the bookkeeper, thought to have been burned to death inside, was found alive.

Sawyer slept until 7:00 P.M. After a light supper, he slept again. When he awoke, refreshed but aching, he returned to the Square, where three thousand people had stacked their belongings and slept all night in the open, lit by flickering light. Others dug through ashes with bare, scalded hands, scrabbling for melted gold and silver. Some were crazed by the tragedy, but most met the fire with the same heroic humor as before. They were always at their finest when it was too late to do anything. "As a whole," Editor Gilbert wrote, "the community was soon as cheery as ever, and at least a trifle wiser than before, not so much in its immediate following conduct as in its plans for the future." "Everybody seems in good-humor," agreed young Frank Marryat, a visiting British adventurer and artist, "and there is no reason why the stranger, who has lost nothing by the calamity, should allow himself to be plunged into melancholy reflections! Planks and lumber are already being carted in all directions, and so soon as the embers cool, the work of rebuilding will commence. . . . The highest praise that I can accord to the San Francisco volunteer firemen is to . . . say that they are zealous and intrepid and that their services are gratuitous." One merchant asked another, "Burnt out?" "Yes," he replied, "and burst up." "Flat?" "Flat as a damned pancake!" "Anyway, it's a great country." "Nothing shorter." San Franciscans were proud of their fires—grand fires, heroic fires, the finest ever seen. They had fire in their veins and each blaze brought a new and finer city.

Among the toppled iron posts and tottering chimneys, street preachers bellowed, but their sermons, in spite of being weighty with doom, were carried away like feathers in the updraft. People moved from the center of town to the north end. Their new neighbors were the gangs of Sydney Town, who had been burned out when the wind suddenly turned. While San Francisco mourned and nailed hot boards together, refugees in the north end had to go about armed, sleep with pistols under their pillows, and wake to the constant sound of gunfire. The inferno had been "set by an incarnate fiend for the purpose of robbery." The *Herald* wrote: "It appears now beyond doubt that the recent confla- gration . . . was the work of an incendiary." There was no shortage of suspects. Senator Broderick believed a gang of ex-convicts had ignited the devastating series of conflagrations to provide diversions allowing toughs to loot the ample stores of gold. Careful merchants, aware that looting was the aftermath of every fire, had locked up their merchandise onboard vessels in the harbor. When folks heard Ducks might have bur- ied the looted $200,000 on Goat Island, hundreds set sail to dig it up. One enterprising volunteer *did* make a fortune. He galloped to the next town before news of the blaze reached there and cornered the building supply market before prices went up. He had been canny—within ten days the indefatigable San Franciscans would have rebuilt three hun- dred structures. The blaze had consumed between 2,000 and 2,500 homes this time. Complete ruin and partial ruin spread for twenty-two city blocks westward and northeastward. Sixteen blocks had burned in the first two hours. Between seventeen and eighteen square blocks had been completely vaporized and six other blocks had been dam- aged. Three-quarters of the business district between Pine and Pacific, from Kearny to Battery on the water, disappeared. Except for two forlorn buildings at the corner of Vallejo Street, the fire devoured everything east of Sansome Street. Colonel Poore's new building built out over the bay marked the northernmost limit of the conflagration. From Clarke's Point, the cessation of fire in that direction, to Happy Valley, nothing re- mained except foundations standing over water. Half the new wharves had been incinerated, a loss accounting for half the cost of the fire. Of the five great blazes, the anniversary fire was more costly than all the previous fires combined: $12 million. The mayor estimated the cost higher: $20 million. The total number of structures destroyed by the arsonist over the last year now stood near 4,000, the most disastrous series of fires ever inflicted on a major American city. How many lives were lost will never be known. Estimates ranged from three hundred to a thousand. Trampled corpses lay deep under the muddy ooze and no one was doing any digging, only building over them.

On May 5, J. Goldsborough Bruff, a local artist, topographer, and historian, took a walk through the smoking streets. Temporary structures were rising like weeds among the charred rubble. "Forty-eight hours since, what a difference!" he wrote.

> *Compact streets, of neat, and very lofty and elegant houses; stores of every description, well filled with goods and thronged with the gay and busy bustle of pleasure and business! Now black and shattered walls, and heaps of smoking and burning ruins; confused piles of goods and chattels, and multitudes of houseless people! My bedding was burnt—Mr. Thomas McCalla of Washington City died.*

Next day he noted that many enterprises had resumed operations on a reduced scale. At the Washington and Kearny corner, the Council had set up a tent by the Verandah Saloon to aid survivors and worked under the din of the Verandah's slightly mad one-man band. He had a drum strapped to his back and fastened to his elbows, pipes tied to his chin, and cymbals attached to his wrists. His iron-soled boots kept time. Holding their ears, the Council members drew up plans to erect $2.5 million worth of the same "inflammable" businesses and homes at the base of Telegraph Hill as before. Had they learned nothing? Not quite. The Council had a clue. One out of five *brick* structures on Market Street had not burned. Workmen were contracted to rebuild the Union Hotel as a $250,000 *brick* building, refit the Adelphi Theater now at Dupont Street, and build a new fireproof Parker House. The Council located several privately owned fire engines to facilitate the establishment of Clarke's Point's own efficient fire station because much of the city's private wealth was stored in highly flammable houses there.

Friday, May 9, dawned bleak. High winds blew suffocating ashes throughout San Francisco. At the northwestern corner of the Square workmen cleared the ruined walls of the old adobe Custom House to dig down to the melted gold in its vault. Editor Gilbert was gratified by the demolition of this "last sad relic." "Possession was held by Palmer, Cook & Company under a lease for three years from Colonel Collier," he wrote. "The lot forms part and parcel of the Square, and no individual should be permitted to occupy so formidable a notch." On May 15, someone tried to burn down the Verandah Saloon on the corner of Washington and Kearny streets. The brick house had been closed for several hours when the arsonist set his fire. It burned through the upper part of a door to a small storeroom that he had soaked with oil and filled the passage and upper-story rooms with flames. An alert watchman saw the smoke at 1:00 A.M. and exhausted himself putting it out by carrying buckets back and forth. A minute more and casks of brandy in the basement would have ignited, trapping those sleeping upstairs. That the arsonist had brought oil to the fire scene was a clue to his identity, but no one saw it yet. The next day someone attempted to torch the City Hospital. When a firebug set another fire on Pike Street, the *Alta* suggested more alarms of fire could be expected anytime because "we have a band of desperadoes in our midst who have long gone unwhipped by Justice." A shipload of Australian ex-convicts had arrived in May. Seven hundred more were due in weeks.

At heart the public appreciated each volunteer for his self-sacrifice. Enthusiastic fans trailed behind their neighborhood or ethnic favorites, cheering them on as if they were a sports team. As they clapped, chanted, and sang, everyone was thinking the same thing: "Why can't someone catch the arsonist?"

All roads led to the waterfront but did not stop there. Piers extended from the tips of all principal roads—Market, California, Sacramento, Clay, Washington, Jackson, Pacific, and Broadway streets—and as new wharves walked on stilts out over distant tidal flats, the existing streets rode their backs. On Sunday afternoon a lone, skeletal figure strode on long legs southeast along the mudflat waterfront. The bedraggled scarecrow with black tousled hair, pockmarked face, and soot-blackened hands reached a run-down waterfront flophouse on Long Wharf, Stuart and George Simmonds' Collier House, and climbed the outside stairs to his second-floor room. He paused at the door and looked around. His neighbors were always watching. He had the rough appearance of a Hound, but his Australian accent and his companions, all ticket-of-leave men from Van Diemen's Land, betrayed him as a "Sydney Duck of notoriously bad character." Born in London, in his youth he had been transported on charges of arson and robbery to the New South Wales penal colony for life. Possibly his mother had been an ex-convict, too, but he never knew for sure. Deported like other Australian convicts, he arrived in San Francisco in November 1849, about the same time as notorious gang leader English Jim Stuart, and gravitated toward the waterfront and the base of Telegraph Hill.

He was frequently seen around town: Sam Brannan had seen him come up in court a dozen times and get off as often, and had glimpsed him around the wharves, where he was a sometime lighterman on the

Whitehall Bay taxies. When the Lightkeeper's partner, a member of English Jim Stuart's gang like himself, provided Stuart with a tip about the gold shipments of a wealthy waterfront merchant, the Lightkeeper and the rest of the gang met at Mrs. Mary Ann Hogan's rooming house to plan the robbery. It was their common meeting place, though Stuart sometimes roomed at Mrs. Hogan's hotel, which was used by criminals who needed a place to hide.

People stopping at the Collier House noticed something odd about the lodger: He frequently smelled of oil. Edward Johns and his roommate, Henry Tufts, lived in number two on the second floor directly over the butcher's shop and next door to the Lightkeeper, who lived in number three. William Hellman occupied the room on the other side, number four, and of all the neighbors, he was most curious about him. The lodger sometimes left in the middle of the night and often returned lathered with sweat. His midnight forays suspiciously coincided with three or four failed attempts to burn down San Francisco again.

The lodger spent the afternoon in bed surveying his meager belongings—a bowie knife, two wooden boxes of matches, some boys' clothing, jars of oil, lumps of coal, and some wooden shavings—which fit comfortably into a battered trunk. The miserable bed with two mattresses, a cook stove, a pine table, an oil lamp, and some flowered curtains belonged to the Collier House. The lodger yawned. He was content. He had work to do. A summer fire perhaps.

◆◆◆◆◆◆

On May 20, Eliza "Lillie" Wychie Hitchcock asked, "Where are the buildings?" The little girl had just arrived in San Francisco aboard the *Tennessee*, a wooden side-wheel steamer. The slender seven-year-old with large brown eyes and chestnut hair had made the difficult journey with her parents down the Atlantic Coast, over the Isthmus from the Chagres River to Panama, and along the Pacific coast with a capacity for 150 cabin passengers, 50 children, and 350 in steerage. She surveyed the cove—jammed with decaying ships and fringed by drab slopes of low brush and scrub. On the summit a gray windmill turned slowly. "Then that is not the army fort?" asked Lillie's mother, Martha, gesturing toward the tent city on the high slopes. "No," said Mr. Taaffe, who had lost his metal warehouse, "most of the burned-out families are living in tents and everyone is short of supplies." That night the refugees on Telegraph Hill ate boiled beans for supper, but the Hitchcocks were luckier. Captain Joseph Folsom and homely Henry Halleck drove them in a hired rig to Bill Howard's old estate at Stockton and Washington. Gilbert, the feisty duel-challenging editor, boarded there, too. Over dinner he discussed the arsonist. A blaze had broken out on the deck of the *Tennessee* on their way up the California coast and had terrified Lillie. That night she awoke screaming of fire. As San Francisco rebuilt, the little girl rode horseback along the muddied streets, went "fishing for rats" under the raised sidewalks, trotted her donkey cart around Mac-Condray's grounds, or watched the many daylight fires that volunteers promptly extinguished. One day a bullet whizzed by her head while she was walking in the dunes south of Market. Instead of turning and running, she rushed up the hill to locate the origin of the shot.

The Hitchcocks swiftly adopted the role of well-to-do aristocrats and Martha became her old grand-mannered self. The arsonist was rarely spoken of, though she wondered whether his motives were anything like her own. "I was heartsick at being forced to burn the house down," Martha explained, fluttering her eyelashes, "but I had to as the only way to drive the wretched homeless out." Two years earlier decay had ruined her family estate, the Hunter Plantation in Huntington, North Carolina. Weeds filled the garden; one corner of the mansion was sagging. When the court auctioned off the property, Martha raised money to reclaim it. Taxes ultimately dragged the once grand plantation under. Squatters overran the sweet potato fields, set up shanties under the weeping willows, and swarmed along the creeks. It inflamed Martha that two particularly disreputable vagrants had set up housekeeping in the main house. Rather than endure strangers camping in the rooms she had played in as a child, Martha got out the coal oil. Just after dawn one morning, she torched her family plantation. As "the most Southern woman" in San Francisco, she enticed into her home any local members of Southern aristocracy, though an occasional non-Southern celebrity crept into her parlor. She was not fond of Broderick. "We do not allow among us common people who climb a golden ladder above the herd to which they belong," she said in her fluttery way. "I include their wives, if they have any." Broderick had no wife. He was "Nature's perfect bachelor," according to historian Kevin Mullen.

Lillie's life changed the day Pat Fitzmaurice drove her to a tea party and took a detour to check on the progress of his new hotel, Fitzmaurice House. While he went over the blueprints with his contractor, Lillie and two of the five Fitzmaurice children, Patrick, twelve, and Joanna, nine, crept into the half-constructed building to explore the second floor. Without warning smoke began boiling up the staircase. Patrick and Joanna tore away from Lillie and were halfway down when a falling beam pinned them to the burning stairs. Lillie heard them moaning in the rubble but could not see them through the smoke. Then she heard nothing more. Trapped on the upper floor, she cried for help. Flames rose higher and smoke funneled out the front door, alerting Fitzmaurice. Screaming, he rushed upstairs, but the remaining planks gave way. His men dragged him to safety but could not breach the sheet of flame to reach Lillie. Outside the uncompleted hotel, John Boynton, a tall, handsome, mustached part-time smoke eater for Knickerbocker Five, was passing and heard Lillie's screams. Flinging his pack containing a fire ax and coil of rope over his shoulder, he scaled the side of the hotel to the unfinished roof. Smoke was billowing from a hole that he chopped wider through which to lower himself. Superheated gases radiating downward from the first-floor ceiling had set fire to stores of lumber. Boynton blindly felt around until he found Lillie and revived her. "It's too late for your friends," he said, sweeping her up, "come with me." Lillie wrapped her arm tightly around Boynton's neck and he climbed, hand over hand, up his rope. Workers, who had reached the roof by now, hauled them up to safety. The city mourned the loss of the Fitzmaurice children as Boynton, trumpeter Bill Fairman, singing Curly Jack Carroll, and the rest of Five's volunteers raced to a nighttime fire. Mother Mulcahy's hog ranch on the Mission Road was ablaze. Lillie was on the piazza holding her mother's hand when she felt the ground rumble and heard the pad of bare feet and thunder of boots. Martha saw a crowd of whooping and hollering torch boys running before the engines, dogs darting between their legs. Torches lifted, the runners' eyes darted everywhere at once. Martha shook her head in disgust.

"As we dashed past the Oriental," Boynton wrote, "I saw the bright-eyed, piquant little girl I'd rescued. . . . As we swept closely by on the narrow, she cried to us, 'Hurrah for my dear Number Five.'" Five cheered back. "Let me go, Mama," said Lillie, "and stand while the jackey holds the butt." Martha was stunned Lillie would want to run with these raga-muffins to a fire. Behind the engines ran other boys who were not above pilfering things at the fires. Lillie rushed to her father, who was more appreciative. When Five, with Lillie running alongside, reached the hog ranch, they learned Mother Mulchay had already died in the fire. By the time Five returned to their fire hall that night, Lillie's father had a barrel of brandy for Boyton and his men and a thousand dollars toward a new pumper to replace their old piano box engine. "But it was Lillie Hitchcock's heart which throbbed with eternal love for the members of Number Five," Boynton recalled. "From then on she belonged to us as much as we belonged to her." Lillie would stand in the window at night, surrounded by children who lived in the Oriental Hotel—Will and Eugene Dewey, Harry Pierson, Desiree Morse, and Cordelia Dessare—and wave at Five's volunteers as they returned. Boynton even allowed them to pull Five's bell cord.

Later, Lillie, Eugene, Will, and Harry were returning from school one day when they saw Five's engine pass. As they ran after the volunteers, Desiree and Cordelia joined them. Five, short of hands that day, was gamely struggling to beat Manhattan Two and Howard Three to the summit of steep Telegraph Hill. At the top a small shack was burning near the signal announcing arriving ships. Soon Five fell behind, unable to move the horseless piano box engine another foot with their tow ropes. When Lillie saw them losing the honor of being first, she threw down her books, raced up to the engine, and looked for a vacant place on the rope. "Come on, you men!" she shouted to bystanders along the road. "Everybody pull and we can beat 'em!" "It's not my funeral," yawned one man. In reply, Lillie seized the tow rope in both hands and began to drag it as if she could move the heavy water wagon by herself. Eugene joined her, then Harry, and finally a half-dozen shamed men who leaped from the crowd and began to pull with her. Lillie's encouragement gave Five renewed strength. They went up the slope "like a red streak" and got water on the fire first. From that day on, whenever Lillie saw Five's men rumbling to a fire, she sprinted alongside them.

Dr. Hitchcock finally grew frustrated with her trailing the engines. "Lillie," he argued, "you must stop this foolishness or I will put a stop to your pursuing fires." After a visit to her father's inherited plantation on the Georgia coast, Lillie returned to San Francisco, her passion for chasing fire strong as ever. Eventually her parents shipped her to a San Jose convent school where for the first two weeks she lost sleep and stopped eating. The third week a classmate swinging her pencil on a string accidentally stabbed her eye and fluid leaked out. Lillie took a hack home. Badly injured, her sight began to fail. She spent months in her darkened hotel suite as doctors monitored her health. Each day she grew thinner, more ashen. Boynton and her firefighting friends missed

Lillie. "When she doesn't turn up," said one, "it's because of that mother of hers—she's a snob." Lillie rallied only when she heard Five's raised voices singing their way to a blaze. Bouquets of flowers addressed to "our mascot" and "our sweetheart" filled her room. To aid her recovery, Five rose each dawn to spread tan bark on the street in front of her hotel to deaden the sound of passing wagons. Nearby, the Risdon Iron Works would set up a deafening racket, so Five, unionists themselves, talked the ironworks into ceasing their boiler making until Lillie got better. When the bandages were removed, her eyesight returned. Her parents, gratified by Five's attentions, relented and allowed Lillie to go to them. She slipped into her black skirt and red woolen blouse as her father said, "Give my regards to your gentlemen. They are fine men. There is no way I can deny that." He watched her splendid little figure running alongside the heavy engine. Fighting fire had healed her.

The men presented her with a shiny black helmet bearing the word *Five,* which she wore every time they answered the tap of an alarm. When garland-bedecked Five's engine was lifted up on the Platt's Hall stage, they sat Lillie in the driver's seat and presented her with a tiny fireman's cap embedded with a diamond and a gold pin with the numeral 5. She would neither enter a party without her pin nor chase after the engines without sending back home for it. She was overjoyed when Five made her their official mascot. Thanks to the Hitchcocks' wealth, they soon had a luxurious new three-story fireproof brick station with iron gates and leaded-glass windows. Exquisite wrought-iron work on the second floor framed a golden number 5.

Lillie always kept a light burning in her window until Five had hauled their engine home and was soon treating the tired, dirty men to an after-fire supper. She dropped everything when she heard the fire bell ring and rushed to beat out sparks with her apron and fill leather buckets as fast as any volunteer. One time a fireman yelled, "Get that girl out of here. This is a man's job." In answer Lillie ran to the engine, seized the hose, and directed a stream of water on the fire. "Start her lively, boys!" she cried. "Everybody out! Fire!" She became a familiar sight racing alongside Five's engine in her blue silk dress, chestnut curls flying behind. Once, Lillie missed a fire because her family was visiting in another part of town. Concerned, Five sent a delegation to see if she was well. When Lillie did not sight Five, she counted the strokes of the fire bell to identify the ward and once beat them to a fire by riding in the hack her father had engaged to take her to a party. Enraptured, she often sat in the Oriental Hotel's lobby enthralling her audience with stories about the brave firefighters and blazes she had seen. At night Five's sweetheart cast her eyes toward the dark streets outside the hotel and wondered if somewhere an arsonist was prowling again ready to destroy the city and kill her friends.

One afternoon Lillie was returning from a wedding rehearsal at Grace Church in her white tulle, star-spangled dress when she heard the fire alarm ring and saw an engine turn onto Market Street. She had the coachman stop her carriage, hailed the fireman father of her classmate, and demanded to be taken along. At the Market Street blaze she saw a sea of red-shirted men up on ladders playing their hoses on the flames and began cheering Five on. The pipeman of Big Six, Five's rival, up on an adjacent ladder, took one look at Lillie's Paris dress and taunted, "See, I told you she was only a featherbedder. Look at the sissy member of Number Five." In response, Five's pipeman turned the full force of his hose on the beautifully dressed girl, who, shocked at first, saw that a friend had dunked her and only laughed and waved. "Told you she was no featherbedder," said the Five pipeman. "She's one of the boys." After that even rival fire companies included her in their parades.

CHAPTER EIGHT

The Lodger

All day Sunday the lodger lay on his back, arms clasped behind his neck. He fell asleep smiling over the regulations posted on the wall that warned about smoking in bed. He awoke thirsty, hefted the big china waterward, and lifted a cover that was only a piece of redwood with a nail in the center for a handle. He took a sip with the coconut-shell dipper, then brewed tea to shake off the chill. "What is it that makes cold in this city so much more freezing than anywhere else?" he thought. Once a century it snowed in San Francisco, he knew. Perhaps it was time again. He heard tapping outside, pushed back his chair, and drew back the curtain. A man was nailing a circular to a storefront. At sunset the lodger crept out to read it. The reward for the arsonist's capture was $5,000. He shivered. It was colder than ever and he would like a big roaring fire about now. He rubbed his callused hands together to warm himself. His hands smelled faintly of oil. The sinking sun lit up his smile with red—like fire.

On May 28, T. Butler King, failed banker and collector of customs, assembled his employees, armed them with cutlasses and pistols, and marched them across the rain-soaked Square. "King made an ass of himself generally," the townsfolk agreed. Holding a bludgeon in one hand and a huge Colt in the other, he marched briskly over puddles from the previous week's rain. Crowds around the Custom House on Montgomery and California streets watched as the melted vault containing

$3 million of gold was lifted to the surface. Hauling a carload of gold and surviving city treasures, King and his rugged guards began the first of several trips to the new vault at the northwest corner of Washington and Kearny streets. Sadly, this suggested that San Francisco was so lawless that it needed an army to move treasure in bright daylight along the city's most populous streets. En route some jokers bribed the waiters of a public eating house to charge the convoy with butter knives. All the guards ran away except King, who, ass or not, held his ground and raised his cutlass to defend the gold.

On May 30, a nighttime arson attempt was made on Pike Street. Robberies resumed and the dull thudding of slungshots echoed through the city. "Can we not catch these rascals," lamented the *Alta.* "There is a flagstaff in the Square with a block for a rope to run through," Gilbert wrote of a 110-foot fir flagpole, a gift to the city from Portland, at the gable end of the old adobe City Hotel. "To what better use could it be put than to run up to its very truck, some of those who infest the city, setting fire to the buildings."

"San Francisco has continued to grow broader and deeper and more substantial," Captain George Coffin observed. When he sailed there in July 1849, the city limits extended to the west only a mile and a half beyond the Square and to the south only two miles as a city of tents. Now the Montgomery Block, the first buildings impervious to fire, was being constructed and Montgomery Street rebuilt with fireproof buildings with brick walls two to three feet thick and no exposed woodwork. The doors and windows had iron shutters. The roofs were slated with partition walls rising six feet above them. John Parrott, former U.S. consul at Mazatlan and the top banker in town, ordered a Georgian-style three-story structure built with granite from China, San Francisco's most accessible quarry. His Parrott Block would serve as a bank on the northwest corner of Montgomery and California. The granite was imported, but the foundation was local—Yerba Buena Island blue rubblestone. As they laid the last tier in June, the granite blocks arrived, each "trimmed to the T-square," cut to intersect and marked with a chiseled Chinese character to designate its place. When Bernard Peyton, the contractor, opened the instruction booklet, he was stumped. The directions were in Chinese. Unable to assemble the bank, he sent to China for Cantonese stonemasons to solve the puzzle. When the bark *Dragon* arrived, the Chinese foreman unrolled a key sheet from a length of bamboo and put his men to work. As coolies in their native garb with bare feet silently matched the blocks, the building lifted prettily. With only an hour's break, the Chinese labored from dawn to dusk for a half pound of rice, half a fish, and a dollar. Having contracted for ninety days, the coolies finished on time and sailed for home on the next tide.

"It makes no sense," Broderick complained. "We send for bricks from the Atlantic states and Australia instead of making our own." The discovery of large clay deposits where Mission Creek empties into the bay would permit the opening of several local brickworks to manufacture sixty thousand bricks a day. With plentiful bricks, merchants began to construct two-to-three-foot-thick brick warehouses using lava from Hawaii as foundations. Builders cemented on slate roofs and screwed double sets of iron shutters over the doors and windows of the best fireproof, burglarproof buildings yet seen. During the day they folded the shutters back and at night closed them. Intense radiant heat from a fire, conducted inside by the iron shutters, still might ruin inventories, so one owner erected water tanks on his roof to flood the interior if an alarm rang out. Around the outside of the central district genteel wooden cottages with iron fences enclosing front gardens flourished. Buildings demonstrated a magnificent improvement in strength and grandeur with their Gothic spires, mansard roofs, octagonal structures, and cast-iron grillwork. It took droves of northeastern architects to fireproof the city's construction—new brick buildings with double iron shutters and large tanks of water on the roofs. The first granite-faced building of the Parrott Block, a cluster of handsome fireproof structures of brick, granite, and iron, would be completed by late December. Henry Halleck, the prominent lawyer, drafted plans for a completely fireproof building on the southeast corner of the intersection of Montgomery and Washington streets. He got his $3 million worth—a Florentine facade closed at the back, framed stone columns and artesian wells, deep groundwork, and metal bulkhead doors packed with asbestos. Deep-set windows of French and Belgian glass covered with heavy double iron shutters locked out any fire. Two-foot-thick walls made up of two million bricks rested on a raft of ship planking. It stood on redwood piles dovetailed into tiers bolted, anchored, and tied with earthquake-resistant cables in a deeply excavated basement. The whole shebang floated on water. Halleck did not get his open courtyard in the center. It would create a vacuum to draw in flames if a fire should sweep in from hillside or waterside. He settled for a light well. Behind its heavy firewalls, the building would survive every big quake for the next hundred years, and only then be replaced by a modern pyramidal skyscraper. In 1853, the Montgomery Block would provide quarters for Colonel Joe Lawrence's *Golden Era;* Ed Stahle's steam baths, where Sawyer would meet Twain; and rooms for dozens of professional men, scientists, lawyers, and artists. Gold from the diggings arriving on carts clattered up from the docks under a dozen musket guards. A Chinese bookkeeper called the count as gold in nugget and cornmeal form was unloaded and trundled to Adams and Company's offices on the Merchant Street side. Their foot-thick outer iron doors kept out fire but also kept it in. Inside, gold was melted, refined, and cast into ingots in their red-hot furnace in a brick-lined cellar. The bars were lowered into the coolness of a deep, iron-shafted vault.

Political patronage to the volunteers dwindled as the city began to contribute its part to the construction of firehouses and oversee a revamping of the fourteen engine companies and three hook and ladder units. Five's firehouse had been demolished. Their new building on Sacramento Street between Sansome and Leidesdorff streets was a huge improvement. On March 25, the California State Legislature enacted a bill that exempted all volunteers from both jury duty and military service. Years later, when Sawyer and a group of firemen formed the Exempt Fire Company, the grateful state voted them an engine house and their own fire equipment.

On May 1, the Rassette House, a wooden five-story firetrap on Bush Street, caught fire and Dutch Charley distinguished himself by saving four hundred citizens trapped inside. The *Pacific News* wrote, "Charley Duane comes forth from the blazing rafters of the Rassette and the old St. Francis, half-drowned and half-roasted, a redeemed man and useful citizen." The first day of June 1851 came. San Francisco's gravity-flow reservoir stood at empty after such a dry winter. Only a bare film of moisture coated the tar-sealed bases of the cisterns. Several small fires were set in the outskirts of town and the fire bell tolled at least once each night. "This rascal, this arsonist—I am beside myself with worry," wailed the mayor on the drizzly morning of June 2. "Will we ever have a clue to who he is?" He was about to get his answer.

At 9:00 A.M., over on Long Wharf, angry words were being exchanged at the Collier House between the lodger and Henry Stowell, the lower-floor proprietor and bartender. Finally Stowell ordered the lodger to leave his hotel by evening. "And take along those two other parties who had also engaged your room," he snapped. The lodger shot the landlord a menacing look, surprised that Stowell had known about his companions. How much had he heard of their plans? "I'll have my trunk out by 5:00 P.M.," he said.

At 2:00 P.M. June 2, Lewis Hellman, in room number four, exchanged a few words with the lodger, who had been boarding there longer than he had. According to another second-floor neighbor, Edward Johns, the lodger had moved into the Collier House on May 5, the day after the May anniversary fire, the most costly and deadly of the five fires so far. The lodger told Hellman he was going to the mines. At 3:00 P.M., in front of the house, he spoke to another second-floor neighbor, Joshua Nickerson, who lived above the Contra Costa Market. They had spoken earlier that morning, too. "He had taken a part of his things out, but did not give up the key," Nickerson said. Earlier he had noticed a burned spot in the lodger's room. "The place burnt was not quite so large as my hand," he said. Hellman saw him take his blanket and go off. He was back by 4:00 P.M. and hailed Hellman on Long Wharf. "I don't believe I'll go to the mines today," he told him. "I'll go tomorrow." Two hours later he returned and asked Hellman peevishly, "Why won't the landlord give me a room to live in? He gave you one. He said he did not wish to rent the room, and wanted it himself. Why can I not have it again?" Hellman smiled. "This is probably true," he said. "The agents did not care about letting it again." Around 8:00 P.M., George Simmonds visited the Collier House bar to collect rents and saw lamp oil dripping down through the cloth ceiling. He pointed this out to Stowell. "You better go upstairs and see what they are doing," Simmonds said. Stowell went up and found the door locked. In coming down the bartender met the lodger on the stairs. "What do you want?" he snapped. "I came to see where oil dripping below is coming from. Come down and I will get a light and go upstairs and we will find it."

The lodger followed him into the bar, where Stowell pointed to the oil spot. "Does that not come from your room?" "It does not," he replied. "Well I think it does." They went upstairs to see if there was any oil in the entry. There was none. "Do you pretend to say that the oil does not come from your room?" Stowell said. "It does not," the lodger said. "There is no oil in my rooms." They came downstairs again and Stowell pointed to the oil spot a second time. "It must come from your room." "It does not." "Then I let the matter drop," Stowell said later. "I got a chair, stood on it and felt the spot and said, 'Yes, it's oil.'"

Around 10:30 P.M., Hellman was sitting in his room sewing when he became aware of the light step of a man ascending the stairway. He heard the door to the lodger's room open softly and someone come out soon after, lock the door, and go downstairs. Five or ten minutes afterward, he heard the same soft tread in the hall. Someone had tiptoed up the stairs. When Hellman opened his door a crack to peer into the corridor, he glimpsed the lodger standing with his back to his door. "He stayed in his room, number three, a few minutes," Hellman said. He "locked his door and went off again—just the same step not to make any noise between five and ten minutes after the same man came up again in the same way as not to make any noise—stepping slowly—I wanted to see what was going on—opened my door and saw the lodger standing before his door. Then I locked my door." Hellman returned to sewing and then to bed.

In the room on the other side of the lodger's, Johns and his roommate were trying to get some sleep. Johns heard someone stealthily ascend the stairs and then the thump and scrape of a trunk being moved. He got up and peeked out and saw the lodger in the passage with a large trunk. Hellman, from his bed, heard the lodger go downstairs. Johns, at his door, heard low whispering and the friction of many matches.

When the man came up again, Johns knew it was the same man by the cracking of his boots. He went down again and then was the friction of many matches in the room again. What took so many matches to light? Three visits within an hour. On the man's last visit someone was with him, whispering. Johns listened but could not make out any words. The lodger closed his door again, locked it, and started back downstairs. Right away Johns smelled smoke.

Stephen Keith, one of the roomers, knocked on Hellman's door. "There must be some fire somewhere in the house," he said. "Is there fire in your room?" "No, there's no fire in my room," Hellman said. Keith met the lodger in the hall and asked the same question. "There is no fire in there," he said. The two went downstairs together to the butcher's shop and found no fire there. "It must be upstairs and you must go with me to help me find it." Keith hunted around and left the lodger at the top of the stairs. "Don't leave," Keith ordered him. Another boarder coming up met the lodger on the stairs. "Where is the fire?" he asked. "I don't know," the lodger said, "but I suppose it is downstairs." A minute or so later, another boarder ran upstairs and rapped on Hellman's door. "Is there a fire in your room?" he asked. Hellman shook his head and they looked around upstairs but found nothing. Returning along the hall, they smelled smoke issuing from the lodger's locked room and began yelling for help.

Around 10:45 P.M., Police Officer Bryan Donally was walking his beat on Long Wharf when he heard George Simmonds cry, "Police! Come up!" Donally asked what the matter was. "There's a fire upstairs in the Collier House on Long Wharf and there are some suspicious characters you should look out for." Donally learned there were three or four persons present when the alarm was given and some sleeping in the rooms upstairs, about ten persons. Donally started up the outer stairs and saw two men struggling at the top. One, Stephen Keith, was preventing a scarecrowlike man in black from coming down with his trunk because there was doubt over who owned it. Donally had reached the fourth step when he spoke to the lodger. "He did not answer me for some time," he said. "He averted his eyes. There was a light in the sign outside and considerable light in the entry. I noted he was pockmarked and had his boots outside his pantaloons." He got a good look at the suspect, who was trying to conceal his face. Another man was behind them, also hiding his face.

"Keep an eye on him," he ordered Keith. "There's something wrong here." He went upstairs to look after the fire. "There was considerable smoke in the entry. I opened the doors of several rooms but could not find the source. Mr. Tufts and Mr. Johns came out of their rooms and wanted to find out where the fire was." Donally went downstairs, returned upstairs, and found the lodger's room. He could not see a handle or a lock on the door, but it was barred. He put his arm against the door, forced it open, and entered a room boiling with smoke. He looked to his left. There were two mattresses on the floor behind the door. Clothes, wood shavings, a boy's waistcoat, two empty wooden matchboxes, and a bowie knife were strewn about. The clothes smelled oily, but there was no pot or jug of oil in the room. Donally stooped, saw there was a hole in the ticking of the top mattress where a round object had been inserted. He kicked at the mattresses. There was a pool of oil around them and a larger pool of oil on top. "Here's the fire," he cried. When he lifted the top mattress, the lower mattress burst into flame. The catalyst was a smoldering coal. "It began to blaze between the two mattresses. I cried for water and another officer." He threw the top mattress down the outside stairs just as a roomer brought water in leather buckets from the downstairs bar. Together they extinguished the fire in the calico mattress on the bottom. Donally came downstairs, asked who occupied the room, and was told it was the man he had detained on the stairs. "He went away," Hellman said. "It was dark, but I saw him run off." The lodger had escaped and his mysterious companion had vanished.

Outside in the darkness Simple Four was just responding from Happy Valley with their red and gold pumper. Donally was joined by three other officers. Collier House residents had earlier reported the taciturn lodger as suspicious and had mentioned his late-night trips. In half an hour Donally tracked the lodger to a four-story brick building with an iron balcony, the gilded El Dorado. Donally entered into the upper stories where miners, gamblers, and women of the halls held court. He looked around. Standing at a monte table to the right of the dealer was the lodger with both hands in his pockets. When he saw Donally, he rested his foot on a bench and put his right hand to his face.

Donally, not certain this was the man from the Collier House, did not want to identify himself as a policeman in such a crowded room. He took his badge off his coat and slipped it in his pocket. He moved closer and asked the man to walk down on Long Wharf with him for company. They walked in the cool night listening to the rushing water. "I was down on Long Wharf at the time of the cry of fire," the lodger said. "Are you not the man who stopped me on the stair?" Donally said nothing. "I was going up to bed and smelled the smoke and came away. At the alarm of fire I went downstairs and took a drink." The lodger pretended to be drunk as they walked, but at times, forgetting his role, he walked perfectly straight. "I asked the proprietor and he said there must be some fire in the house. He knocked at my door, said there was fire in my room."

"Why did you leave the scene?" Donally asked. "I was burnt out at the last fire and I did not want to be burnt out again," the lodger said. "If you roomed in the house when the fire was discovered, why did you not stay there?" Donally asked. "I did not wish to get burnt," the lodger replied. "I have no doubt now you are the man I first arrested," Donally said and frog-marched his prisoner back to Stowell, who also identi- fied him as the man. "What you spill some oil up in your room for?" Stowell said, looking above where it had come through and stained the cloth ceiling. The lodger looked up at the stain but said nothing. Stowell continued, "As for the other man, I know him as a boatman and that he came from Australia. Although they were on good terms they often fought." From there Donally directed his prisoner toward the station house.

Ned Wakeman left shipping magnate Charles Minturn's office at the foot of Geary Street and began walking in the dark along Powell Street. A month earlier he had raced his stolen steamboat *New World* down from Sacramento in five and a half hours dock to dock and set what seemed an unbreakable record. On his way he met bluff Sam Brannan, an old friend. Before they could speak, they saw torch boys leading Simple Four's engine. It was jolting up the rutted street towed by exhausted firefighters headed back to their barn. A squad of frock- coated city policemen were running closely behind them jostling and shoving a tall, thin man in black with tousled hair. A trail of blood ran down his soot-blackened face. His eyes were wide and curiously pale. As the police squad advanced down Geary Street, Wakeman saw a dour-faced Scotsman, Captain Frederick W. Macondray, leading the volunteer police. Macondray, a mercantile, a Mexican War veteran, and an alderman who had been burned out in the last fire, had a stake in catching the arsonist. He looked plenty mad.

"It looks like they're going to have it out with those brass-buttoned pickpockets at last," Brannan cried with glee. Macondray's men marched the prisoner past them and in the torchlight Brannan got a good look at the lodger. "I recognize him; it's Ben Lewis! He's been questioned for half a dozen fires and turned loose every time." Brannan called to the police, "What do you plan on doing with him this time, Captain Ben Ray? Pin a medal on him? It's Ben Lewis!"

Historian H. H. Bancroft identified Ben Lewis as "a hardened ex-convict, a Sydney rascal" like English Jim Stuart, and number nine in the hierarchy of Stuart's twenty-member gang of murderers and robbers. That placed Lewis very high in the ranks of villainy. To paraphrase Bancroft, Ben Lewis was a villain—a great villain, an audacious villain, and every inch a villain. He achieved villainy, and if villainy was not thrust upon him, he had no hesitation in thrusting it upon others.

In the flickering light, Brannan turned back to Wakeman. "Thugs, thieves and shysters, and the law have joined forces and the time has come for honest men to take the law into their own hands! Arson. Some poor devil's store set on fire so the Ducks can move into the back door and move the loot while the owner's running out the front. Four times in the last year the town's been burned to the ground as a convenience to thieves and murderers. Not a single arsonist has been convicted."

The strange caravan crossed through the dirty Square to the City Hotel. Brannan, temper rising, caught up with them and forced his way to the hotel door, crying to Ned Wakeman, "It's time for action and I'm hoping we can count on you as one of us." "I'm with you," said Wakeman, a powerful, intimidating man who knew his Bible by heart and was ready to quote it. Twain characterized him as normally "hearty, jolly, boisterous, good-natured," but now he was itching to string up Lewis and recite a few passages over his corpse. Brannan and Wakeman saw Lewis slumped in an ornate chair close to the entrance. Brannan grabbed the prisoner's long hair, jerked his lean face into the light, and crowed, "Ben Lewis! I was right. He's done a half-dozen fires, Captain, just as I said." Brannan looked around angrily. "The police seem more concerned for Lewis's safety than the burning of innocent people."

Word of Lewis's arrest reached Mayor Calhoun Benham. To the handsome, black-haired Mexican War vet, the expertness of the water-front room fire suggested Lewis was an arsonist, possibly *the* arsonist they had sought. He studied the reports of the last city-destroying blaze, the anniversary fire, and found what he was looking for. A few minutes before eleven o'clock a man recognized as a habitué of Sydney Town had been seen running from the paint shop on the southern side of the Square. It troubled Benham that simultaneously other fires were kindled at various points downtown. This suggested that Lewis had an unnamed partner, possibly the stealthy man who had helped him move his trunk from his hotel room and then vanished. He read Donally's police report that night. According to the Collier House tenants, the two companions had openly boasted they would one day burn San Francisco to the ground. As in the earlier fires, the anniversary fire had been set on a night when the wind was blowing from the east and north—the so-called Lightkeeper's Wind that carried the flames away from Sydney Town, the only section not burned. The Duck's enclave suffered damage only when the wind unexpectedly changed direction.

That evening the Council convened to figure out how to approach Ben Lewis's arrest and agreed to meet the next day. A hearing was held in the Recorder's Court. At first there was little interest, but in late morning witnesses from the lodging house entered the court. Brushing rain from their drab pantaloons and dark green coats, they stomped mud from their short boots and were sworn in. Their testimony produced a strong implication of Lewis's guilt in setting fire to the house on Long Wharf. The case against Lewis, an ex-convict, was strong. More information was gathered. Lewis was now suspected of starting four of the major conflagrations that had razed the entire city. The hunt for the second and unseen man began quietly.

Colonel James was the defendant's counsel. "Who is present to prosecute?" Judge Waller asked. "No one is," said Colonel Stevenson, who owned the house on Long Wharf that Lewis had set fire to. The judge appointed the Honorable T. B. Van Buren of San Joaquin as prosecuting attorney. With few people in court, Van Buren summed up the case by noon. "A fire alarm was raised in the upper rooms of a lodging house on Long Wharf," he began. "This man, Lewis, was caught in the act of stealing a trunk from a room, and his room was found to be on fire." Lewis offered no evidence at all. News of the hearing circulated. By 1:00 P.M. Lewis had become the threatening symbol of lawlessness in San Francisco. In minutes a crowd gathered around the City Hall. At 2:00 P.M., while Lewis was still being arraigned, four thousand people rushed to Portsmouth Square. A cry swept the city: "Judge Lynch is holding court! They're going to hang a Sydney Covey!" Newsboys called on corners: "Come out and see the hanging."

Brannan recirculated an old handbill:

Are We to Be Robbed and
Assassinated in Our Domiciles?

If we are willing to let the felons burn us up, let us say so and the sooner it is done the better. Men that have no resentment ought to be abused and kicked by villains and cripples and everybody else.

As a protective measure, police surrounded City Hall. Now eight thousand angry citizens jammed the square. Brannan pulled up a crate and began to speak. "I'm very much surprised," he told the mob mockingly, "to hear people talk of grand juries, or recorders, or mayors. I'm tired of such claptrap myself. Fires, murders, beatings—Sydney Town is a growing hellhole. A decent woman won't live here—an honest man is doomed. These men are murderers, I say, as well as thieves. I know it, and I will die or see them hung by the neck. The laws and courts never yet hung a man in California and every morning we read fresh accounts of murder and robbery. *I want no technicalities!* Such things are devices to shield the guilty. Who will help return order?"

"We will," roared the mob.

"Who'll enlist?"

"We will!"

"Five hundred murders since gold was discovered and not one man punished yet." This was not true. "Not one man!" Brannan, having roused the rabble like a summer storm, jumped down and went up to Mayor Benham, whom he had seen monitoring the situation from his window. "There's a real crowd out there, three thousand and more and some with ropes," the mayor said, wiping his brow. "They want action, Mr. Mayor," Brannan said. "You better go out and tell them what you plan to do with Mr. Lewis before they decide for you. Lewis the arsonist should be turned over to the volunteer police, who would see to it that he is held in custody until he is made to answer for his crimes."

At 4:00 P.M., Lewis's defense attorney reviewed the evidence and declared it insufficient to justify a committal of the prisoner. "It is purely circumstantial," Colonel James said, "and does not in any manner charge the prisoner with anything that could not be accounted for as an accident."

Van Buren leaped to his feet to reply, but a scream of "Fire!" interrupted him. The spectators in the courtroom tried to rush out just as others rushed in, creating a gridlock at the entrance. As a fire engine noisily rattled past the court, Sheriff "Coffee Jack" Hays instantly concluded that Lewis's friends at Clarke's Point had set a fire as a diversion and intended to free Lewis in the confusion. He was right. The Ducks had torched a house on the corner of Front Street and Long Wharf. "Hold that man fast!" he said. "Quickly, men, see to the prisoner and look for his friends—they will attempt to rescue him, mark my words." Dozens of guards ringed the suspect. Though Lewis glared menacingly, his face was pallid with fear. When some of the crowd broke in and grabbed him, police sprang forward and took his arm in a brief tug-of-war. Lewis was thoroughly roughed up and half his clothes were torn off before the cops closed ranks around him. In the fierce struggle they hustled him into the clerk's room, an inner room. Sheriff Hays hustled Lewis to the station house and locked him up.

"On the evidence [of the rooming house arson]," Judge Waller said, "I feel I should feel bound to commit the prisoner." He was afraid that the mob might break in again and attack Lewis but felt it only proper that the defendant be brought back to hear his ruling. "I will commit him and will not admit him on bail." As the judge sent an officer to return Lewis to court, cries rose outside: "Hang him!" "Lynch the villain!" "Hang the fire-raising wretch!" "Bring him out—no mercy—no law delays!" Though the blaze had been swiftly extinguished, the alarm had drawn together an enormous crowd. The fierce tone of their chant broke up the court's deliberations. Waller paused, then reconsidered. "It will be best not to introduce the prisoner after all," he said as another rush was made on the courtroom. Had the impatient mob outside waited a few minutes more, Lewis would have been back in court and they easily could have laid their hands on him and gotten a rope around his neck.

From an adjacent building, Captain George Coffin observed Lewis and his police captors go up through a trapdoor onto the roof. He descended to the next floor and onto a balcony so he could watch the crowd encircling the courthouse. Below, a sea of excited faces cried, "Bring Lewis out! Bring Lewis out!" Speakers pro and con made appeals to the public. Colonel Jonathan Stevenson, the first speaker, urged prompt action and castigated the laxity of the law and the police.

"If the man is guilty, which I firmly believe, he should not be allowed to sleep but should be hung immediately." As owner of the lodging house that Lewis had torched, Colonel Stevenson had a vested interest. As he left his podium he was loudly applauded. Excited cries for Lewis's hanging rose louder than ever. Mayor Brenham appeared upon the upper platform to say he was astonished that any man could utter such sentiments. "The prisoner should have a fair trial," he began, "and if found guilty, punished but until then be safely guarded." The crowd's roar interrupted him. "I call upon the police and all good citizens to support the law at the peril of their lives." The mayor was drowned out again. Coffin observed a tall, pallid man at one end of the portico and a small red-faced man at the other end making speeches. Marshal Robert G. Crozier appeared upon the platform between the two. "The prisoner is no longer in the station house," he said. "He has been removed by police and is in safe custody. I do not know where he is now. Lewis was delivered into the sheriff's custody on Wednesday morning, June 4, and that is all I know."

"Justice will be done," said the lawyers as the case continued inside without the prisoner. The district attorney requested that Lewis be tried in twenty-four hours and summoned witnesses to appear before the grand jury, which the next day indicted the defendant. Judge Levi Parsons quashed the indictment against Lewis and informed the present grand jury that their term had expired. "You are no longer a legal body," Judge Parsons explained, "and no longer legally constituted. The grand jury is, in effect, abolished. Consequently, you cannot act in the matter of Ben Lewis." He reasoned that the grand jury had been called on May 26 by a substitute, Judge Robinson, during Parsons's temporary absence from the bench. Parsons discharged the jury no longer legally constituted to wait for the July term. The *Herald* had earlier criticized Parsons for practices they felt encouraged crime. Parsons had held its editors in contempt of court and when one editor refused to pay the levied fine, Parsons had had him jailed. Naturally, the *Herald* agreed with the mob:

Although strongly opposed, as must every lover of foul play, to the summary execution of even such a character as Lewis, without a patient and impartial trial—yet we must declare that we regard the demonstration of yesterday with the highest gratification that if the man be proved beyond a reasonable doubt to have committed this crime, the citizens will supply any deficiency that may exist in the law. We say this, fully alive to the expectation that we shall therefore be accused of advocating Lynch-law. If this man be guilty of setting fire to the house on Long wharf, and if the law does not adjudge him the penalty of death therefore, we do most unquestionably advocate Lynch-law.

"Judge Parsons, unless you assume the responsibility of acting in this case," the state's attorney warned, "the prisoner will probably walk free.

"No criminal cases can be tried until a new grand jury is in session," he said firmly, "and that will be no earlier than July first." As the recorder referred the case to the district court for another trial, a great cry erupted outside: "Bring him out!" Vigilante prosecutor and record keeper George E. Schenck's trial notes, pages four through fourteen of the committee papers, stated that Lewis's trial had led immediately to the organization of the vigilantes and took great pains to secure a complete transcript of the trial record in anticipation of the district court trial sometime in July. "On motion resolved that we recommend the General Committee proceed to the District Court House," Schenck wrote, "and remain there until the case of Lewis is disposed of—and if necessary to arrest and take Lewis and dispose of him as the People may direct." Brannan, no friend of the arrogant Judge Parsons, was livid. "This is an example of unpunished, triumphant crime," he roared. After demanding "no technicalities," he had gotten them anyway. The lodger's freedom on a technicality incited the bellowing crowd to fury.

The city was without a criminal court when all jails were crowded and escapes as common as down on a duck. At sunset one of the authorities tried to address the crowd and was hooted down. "Hear him! Hear him!" said some. "No, no!" others jeered. When he assured them Lewis would have a speedy trial and be promptly executed, the mob melted away, muttering that because the courts had failed to function, they might take matters into their own hands. Two hours later, the remaining protesters had cooled down and darkness claimed the Square. To be safe, the mayor readied the California and Washington Guards.

At 2:00 A.M., an on-duty volunteer cop and owner of a new building on Commercial Street saw four men in conversation near his house. As he approached, they moved away. Suspecting something, he went inside and discovered a pile of shavings just bursting into a full blaze under his stairwell. Had he not extinguished it, the city would have been burned again. This was the second attempt in a day to burn the city. "When different fires took place," wrote the *Annals*, "persons were repeatedly seen in the act of kindling loose inflammable material in outhouses and secret places. Many of these fires were believed to have been raised by incendiaries, solely for the opportunity which they afforded for plundering."

Coffee Jack placed Lewis in irons and rowed him out to a man-of-war in the cove. Because he had not actually been tried yet, Lewis was released on bail soon after to await a future trial. The arsonist was smug. He had little to fear if they found him guilty. The maximum penalty for arson was only two years in jail. The wind that had been brisk during the afternoon lulled at dusk for an hour, then freshened violently—perfect fire weather—the Lightkeeper's Wind revitalized. Hazy and cool weather with strong wind brought another fire alarm. Another house burned that evening. In the Square, light frame buildings trembled in the gale. As usual there was scarce water to fight fire. The people were more afraid than ever.

In this atmosphere, on Sunday, June 8, Chief Engineer Kohler presented an alarming review to the Council. Due to the May fire, he explained, many of the engine houses had been destroyed, their engines damaged and hose burned. "The apparatus of the Hook and Ladder Companies are likewise in a generally damaged, inadequate and unusable condition," he reported. "The cisterns are either empty or so out of repair as to render them useless. . . . Should a fire occur while the Department remains in its present crippled condition, nothing but the waters of the bay and the naked sand hills . . . could check its course." The city treasury was hopelessly empty with no prospect of immediate relief. "Our generous firemen have already expended their private means for the public good in organizing the Department, furnishing apparatus and keeping it in repair, to an extent that could not have been expected from them anywhere but in San Francisco. Not a dollar has ever been refunded to them—except in script—and to expect them to make still further sacrifices is unreasonable and unjust. What, then, shall be done? Must the Fire Department go to ruin, and the city to destruction, for the want of a few thousand dollars?" The frequent alarms spurred the *Alta* to ask, "Were a fire to break out there, what means could be used to extinguish it?" Because the reservoir in the Square had not been filled since the May fire and contained little or no water, the paper suggested a reservoir be built near the junction of Montgomery and Green streets capable of holding two million gallons of water. Pipes should be laid from the reservoir passing along all the streets exposed to fire, and hydrants installed at the corners of each square. Somehow the Council must make a provision for these expenses.

Before noon San Francisco had declared an open war of extermination on all arsonists. "Let us set about this work at once," the Council said. "Without this or some similar plan, the evil cannot be remedied, and if there is not spirit enough among us to do this, then in God's name, let the city be burned and our streets flow with the blood of murdered men." That afternoon, Robert Lammot visited Brannan in his office at Bush and Sansome to organize an efficient volunteer police patrol along the lines of the successful fire patrols on the city's outskirts. First they sent notes to one hundred men who could be trusted to keep their mouths shut. The next afternoon they convened at the California Engine Four engine house at Market and Bush to appoint a committee to draft a constitution for a crime-eradication group. That night one hundred men entered their names on the rolls of the newly named Committee of Vigilance. Volunteer William Coleman, a wealthy twenty-seven-year-old fresh from the goldfields, proposed that the vigilantes string up anyone even *suspected* of a crime. Captain Frederick Macondray was made captain of night patrols that would operate in shifts to guard the business district. Under Ned Wakeman the water police would safeguard the Embarcadero.

At midnight, Brannan, on his first informal patrol, kept a sharp eye out for arsonists. Cursing the unlit and cumbersome streets, he stopped to shake the mud from his boots and spied a shadowy figure. "Now what's he up to?" he thought. "Isn't that a pile of shavings at his feet?" He pounced on the figure, knocked the match from his hand, and dragged him struggling into the moonlight. "Haven't I seen you before?"

"Let me go," he said. "I'm a Mormon like yourself. I was only lighting my pipe."

"You lie. You're no Mormon. Mormons don't smoke! And where's your pipe?" The man felt about in his pockets. "I—I—I must have lost it." Brannan lit one of the man's matches. His white face shone in the flickering light. "No! You're one of Roberts' thievin' friends. You're a Hound. I remember you rightly enough, friend!" The man squirmed loose and sprinted into the darkness. Brannan tugged out his pistol as he ran, fired one shot but missed, and the suspect escaped. Was this one of Ben Lewis's friends trying to clear him with a decoy arson? Nonsense. Lewis was an Australian Duck from Sydney and this man was a New York Hound. The two gangs hated each other.

An enormous third eye surrounded by a sunburst and incised on a metal disk carried the words "Organized 9th June, 1851" and "12." "One of the new symbols to identify our group," Coleman said and recited the inscription *Fiat Justitia Ruat Coelum*: "'Let justice be done, though the heavens may fall.' It's an old motto with a new symbol—a giant open eye." The vigilantes had painted the symbol on one entire wall of their Committee of Vigilance headquarters. They had united into "an association for the maintenance of the peace and the preservation of the lives and property of the citizens of San Francisco." George Oakes, now a member of California Four, had helped form the unlawful committee with Brannan and James Neall and pledged to watch, pursue, and try "the outlaws infesting the city, through the regularly constituted courts, if possible. Through more summary process, if necessary." This meant lynching. The vigilantes agreed to meet upon the single strokes of the Monumental bell. The hanging men had only hours to wait before the death bell tolled for the first time.

A furious Senator Broderick, now president of the State Senate, immediately galloped to San Francisco. "I have always stood against any form of vigilantism," he said. "I do not think people should take the law into their own hands." He placed Vi Turner and several of his men inside the Vigilance Committee as spies to report back. With every increase in power he had become less corrupt—more a statesman, responsible leader, and lover of freedom. "He worships freedom above all things," said John W. Forney, Broderick's friend, "and I never saw him intolerant except when he doubted the integrity of those who refused to see the truth as he saw it, and he finally believed that all men must not be wicked themselves who could not or would not reject the wrong as he did."

In the late afternoon of Tuesday, June 10, a week after Ben Lewis's arrest, a huge, slightly deformed man with coarse red hair and beard emerged from the Ghost Fleet, furtively tied his boat beneath Long Wharf, and crept along the central wharf. Dressed in a full suit of black, Covey John Simpton was nearly invisible against the charred timbers. He reached a two-story shipping office at the end of Commercial Street on the Washington Block on Long Wharf and moved into the shadows to wait. For several days he had been casing George W. Virgin's shipping office. Simpton was so low, brutal, and foul that both the police and his Sydney Town cohorts knew him as "the Miscreant." Fourteen years earlier he had been transported for life for arson and attempted murder to New South Wales but had escaped and reached San Francisco in late 1849. The Miscreant, a confederate of the master criminal English Jim Stuart, had adopted his alias, John Jenkins, from a notorious Australian bushranger hanged in 1834. Simpton sold the Uncle Sam, his disreputable crib on Dupont Street, to Mr. Connally, who died a few days later. Immediately Simpton began consoling Connally's widow. At 8:00 P.M., sailing time, Simpton watched Shipping Agent Virgin leave his second-floor office and go downstairs with some money from his strongbox to deposit with the bartender. Simpton came up the outside stairs, barged into the unattended office, shoved a small safe containing $1,500 into a sack, and went out. As he was escaping, Virgin returned and raised an alarm. Several volunteers chased Simpton along Long Wharf and captured him after a watery chase.

As volunteer policeman David Arrowsmith escorted Simpton toward the station house, George Schenck, the Vigilante Committee secretary, intercepted them and talked openly of his suspicions that Simpton was involved in setting the anniversary fire. The Miscreant was unworried. A number of dishonest judges and lawyers and unscrupulous officials were in the Ducks' employ. Had they not just set Ben Lewis free? "You're a member of the Committee of Vigilance," Schenck told Arrowsmith, "why not take him to the committee rooms!" They dragged Simpton to a large storeroom in Brannan's building on Bush Street, near Market. Just before 10:00 P.M. Oakes rang the great bell with a billet of wood: two measured taps, a pause, two taps, another interval, and then silence, and again two notes. He tapped the bell some twenty times. The Monumental bell echoed the call, two strokes, then silence, two and two and two! Two centrally located firehouses a half mile apart, California Four and Big Six, repeated the message at intervals of one minute. A third company at the head of the square picked up the strokes. Their combined tolling summoned the vigilantes to hang whomever they thought guilty. The secret password, "Lewis," hissed among the vigilantes. "Lewis, Lewis, Lewis, Lewis." That hated name brought action from men who craved to shed the blood of the wicked. Coleman got to headquarters within half an hour. Most of the hanging men were already there. The Vigilance Committee's huge blue and white flag covered one brick wall. To one side Simpton stood defiantly inside a large holding cell. Above him were two stout beams to support hangman's ropes if needed. Bill Howard rushed in behind Coleman and placed his pistol on the long table. "As I understand it we are here to hang someone," he said, and because the defendant was an Australian, convened a kangaroo court. Simpton would be hanged at 2:00 A.M. in the Square. Throughout his "trial" Simpton had been so defiant and insulting it suggested that he expected momentarily to be rescued by his fellow Ducks. By torchlight a pack of heavily armed vigilantes escorted him a half mile to the west side of the Square. While still forty feet from the flagpole, the vigilantes gave the condemned man a glass of brandy and lit him a cigar that he smoked on the way to the southern end, where a jutting beam could serve as a gibbet. Simpton's arms were pinioned. Wakeman fitted the noose around the prisoner's neck. At the gable end of the City Hotel, Broderick, his Bully "B'hoys," and Officers Noyce and North and Captain Ben Ray appeared and charged the hanging men. Mayor Brenham, Sheriff "Coffee Jack" Hays, and Marshal Crozier were conspicuously absent. Broderick leaped atop a barrel and pleaded, "Come to your senses! Are you not Christians?" The scar on his cheek was livid. Now other rescuers, Sydney Ducks set on rescuing their confederate, began pulling on the prisoner's feet. The vigilantes won the tug-of-war, threw the rope over a joist projecting from the banking house of Palmer, Cook & Company. Brannan thundered, "Up. Up. Up! Let every citizen be a hangman at once." Twenty vigilantes gripped the slack end of the hemp, ran backward, and yanked the unrepentant robber off the ground. Oddly, his legs, scarred and callused from the long wear of shackles in the penal colony, never kicked. His face contorted no more than usual. Now Noyce knew why Simpton's cigar had gone out. He had been strangled during the tug-of-war. The vigilantes had hanged a dead man.

At 5:00 P.M., they laid Simpton's crumpled body on the floor of the Monumental Six Engine House. As darkness fell, the excited mob viewing the corpse moved to the courthouse and milled outside considering what to do about Ben Lewis. "Criminals had little to fear in merciful, gentle, careless California," Frank Soule lamented. "Jurors, eager to be at moneymaking again, are apt to take hasty charges from the bench." If caught, the Ducks shielded one another from arrest, conviction, and punishment. They controlled not only most of the vice, murder, crimping, extortion, and arson within San Francisco but also employed unscrupulous shysters and two-bit politicians to make payoffs for them. They intimidated incapable prosecutors, bribed police and juries, and elected criminals who controlled judges who were corrupt, ignorant of the law, or too timid to mete out just punishment.

Twice, Ben Lewis was brought before the district court for trial and twice his counsel unearthed judicial flaws in the indictment that quashed the proceedings. Each time, Lewis's lawyer used loopholes that allowed the ex-con to slip out of town. When the grand jury found the bill against Lewis for arson, the Executive Committee of the Vigilance Committee decided that after such a long postponement, the arsonist's time had come. They recommended that the General Committee take possession of Lewis and hang him where they had hung Simpton. The motion was tabled so a subcommittee of three could be appointed to superintend Lewis's trial in the legal courts, or if necessary, arrest and dispose of him. But Ben Lewis was nowhere to be found. With no arsonist in captivity to blame, much less his unknown partner at the Collier House, the papers excoriated the fire companies that had been arguing hotly against the lawlessness of the committee. The *Alta* alleged that volunteers served only to make money by threatening and extorting shopkeepers. On June 12, the vigilantes organized a rally in the Square. More than ten thousand bloodthirsty citizens gathered to authenticate the hanging men as essentially the new government of San Francisco. One lynching infallibly produces more lynchings. Mark Twain later suggested a brave man be stationed in each affected community to

> bring to light the deep disapproval of lynching hidden in the secret places of the heart. . . . Where shall these brave men be found? That is indeed a difficulty; they are not three hundred of them in the earth . . . martial personalities that can face mobs without flinching . . . such personalities are developed only by familiarity with danger and by the training and the seasoning which come of resisting it.

A day earlier, Clarke the attorney had spoken up against the lynchers and a jeering mob had roughed him up, threatened him with hanging, and chased him all the way home. An ineffectual puppet named Hoag took the slightly raised podium of the old government adobe standing above the Square and roused the crowd to give the vigilantes carte blanche to hang suspects without trial. Broderick entered the Square leading a phalanx of his big shoulder strikers: Dutch Charley, Moses Flanagan, Activity Burke, Bob Cushing, Terry Kelly, Woolly Kearney, and tiny Billy Mulligan, now the official county jailer. More followed until all his forty-niners, his forty-nine "B'hoys," carrying ax handles and pry bars—firefighters' tools, street fighters' tools—were cutting through

the mob in a V-shaped formation. A voice rang out: "Hang Broderick!"
Others took up the cry. Broderick's crash squad linked arms, lowered
their heads, and singled out the mob's most cowardly members first,
then cut out the brawniest, separated them, floored them, and turned
to do it again. Dutch Charley delivered head butts. Activity Burke gave
well-placed kicks. Billy Mulligan intimidated men with a simple look.
North, west, south—the crash squad struck, heads lowered like charg-
ing bulls. As men dropped like tenpins into the mud, calls for hanging
grew fainter, then ceased. The men cut a wide path to the raised platform where Broderick swung himself up over the rail with ease and
kicked Hoag halfway down the back stairs. He had studied law, history,
and literature but was so angry, his speech lacked its usual eloquence.
He was not a speaker but a common man. Not gifted with easy speech,
he was given to coarse invective when opposed. Now he lashed the thousands with all the force of his passionate nature. "Come up here, you
cravenly cowards!" he roared. "Scoundrels! You that are hallooing—
pull me off the stand yourselves. Isn't this a pretty scene there now—a
parcel of hirelings, menials, police officers and their companions—the
very stool pigeons I've been describing. Abject willing slaves! Slaves by
choice." He spoke firmly and coldly for twenty minutes. When a dozen
men tried to pull him over the thin rail into the mob, he kept his balance
and snatched up Hoag's list of resolutions. "These illegal pronounce-
ments supposedly cloaked in law," he bellowed, "they would make every man here a candidate for the noose or a murderer. This is what I
think of them! Evil words for the wind." He scattered the scraps like so
much confetti. One man who believed in justice by law had intimidated
the biggest gathering ever held in the city. Broderick drew himself up.
"This meeting is adjourned!" he roared, then vaulted the railing and led
his men from the Square. The next day cranky Mr. Gilbert condemned
Broderick, writing that the people were only "there enjoying their right
for peaceable assembled to consult and deliberate upon the best methods of maintaining order, protecting property and life and riding society
of the evils which have so long hung upon it like a blight and a curse."

Ben Lewis was still missing. Dutch Charley was certain he had
"shoved out," but the volunteers waited for the next arson anyway. The
last two volunteer fire companies formed—the Rough Diamond Company Thirteen and Tiger Engine Fourteen—were both a distance from
the heart of town where the larger fires took place. In fact, the Rough
Diamond, which had "grass growing under its wheels," rarely left its

Mission Dolores neighborhood. There was not a dandy, ex-boxer, or regional type among them, just commonplace men. Fourteen's members
sprang from Happy Valley's butchers and grocers on Second, near Howard Street. They eventually became known as the Millionaire Company
because an extraordinary number of them became millionaires. Claus
Spreckels, a neighborhood retail grocer, paid regular dues but did little
active firefighting and enlisted only because his neighborhood's social
events and politics congregated around Fourteen's firehouse. He went
from his fifty-foot-by-one-hundred-foot sugar refinery at Ninth and
Brannan to become the "King of Sugar." So far Fourteen had never experienced the intense rivalry that existed between Companies Five, Six,
Two, Four, and Ten, but their one donnybrook was a blowout.

When fire bells sounded for a blaze in Waverly Place, Fourteen's
engine was being repaired and they responded only with a hose cart.
Four, closer to the fire, pulled with two sets of men to handle a cart
and an engine. Fourteen overtook them on Clay Street and the two engines collided when the hubs of the wheels interlocked. Sam McDowell,
on the front of Fourteen's rope, wound the rope of his cart around a
basement railing at his side and held the rival engine fast. Four demanded they release its wheels; Fourteen demanded the right-of-way.
When Four refused, Tiger's foreman smashed his trumpet over a rival's
head. McDowell gave one man a bloody nose, the police arrested everyone, and the building burned to the ground. On the way to jail Scannell
halted the police and told them, "Release those boys. Boys, man your
ropes and return home." Of the fourteen companies, only two were hook
and ladder; the rest were underequipped. "The only difficulty is that the
City is so flat-broke that the companies cannot get good engines," Robert Lammot wrote, "or even have the old ones repaired."

As the anniversary of the June 14 fire approached, the fears of an
encore increased. Despite threats from the Ducks, the June anniversary came and went without a blaze. There were the nightly brush fires:
One hotel burned a little and provided an exhausting night's work for
the volunteers, but even these minor outbreaks became less frequent.
Still, the city crouched, poised for action. Had the cycle of costly arson
fires beginning with Christmas Eve, 1849, and continuing on May 3–4,
June 14, September 17, and May 4, 1851, ceased with the banishment
of Ben Lewis? Sawyer realized there was still danger. The identity and
whereabouts of Lewis's partner was unknown, as was the whereabouts
of Lewis himself.

Though no one enforced the existing ordinances mandating story pipe and chimney construction, the Council adopted new ordinances regulating construction materials. Washington Square was a waste and trash dump, but the highest danger lay in the thickly settled portions where overoccupied frame houses huddled close together and hand furnaces were commonly used. The town was still on edge. A man writing a letter flung down his pen and ran outside when he heard the Monumental fire bell. "People have learned by sad experience what a terrible thing fire is in San Francisco," he wrote, "and so, soon as one is known to exist, everything is dropped at once." Between 1845 and 1851, New Yorkers suffered $30 million in property losses, and fires were so commonplace that the volunteers were celebrated as tourist attractions. It was the same in San Francisco. As they battled flames, crowds bet on which team would extinguish the fire first. In the slums where Broderick had trained, volunteers in competing fire companies traded punches, bloodied knuckles, and fought pitched battles with the tools of their trade. In the end, there was often nothing left to applaud but ashes. One night an alarm sounded for a small fire at Sansome and Pine streets and a heated race between One, Three, Five, and Six took on unusual seriousness. Three was off the mark first. Five got rolling next as Foreman Frank Whitney slipped on his gold cape and with his golden trumpet called his Bostonians to their Hunneman engine. Curly Jack Carroll sang as they pulled old Two-and-a-Half along the dark streets. Big Six was off next and dispatched their Mechanical. "Big George" Hossefross, Dutch bearded and sweet faced, knew Six's Baltimoreans could pump water higher and faster than any other team. He later became the first man in California to apply hydraulic force to raising large buildings. Six's torch boys ran alongside the front wheels, and another two boys used their torches to lead forty pulling volunteers through the boggy streets.

Broderick One started last. Their boys snatched their torches from the wall rack as Kohler cried, "Start her lively, boys," to Daingerfield, Scannell, and Dutch Charley. "Onward! Pull her along and jump her, fellows." They rolled out their battered old engine. As torch boys ran alongside the Mankiller, torches cast the water engine's shadow against hastily raised three-stories along Montgomery. All the units reached the burning waterfront building on Pine Street at the same time; all turned the corner at once. Immediately there was a collision—metal bent, spokes broke, and men were jolted into the road. One's engine veered off into the mud and was least damaged. Three's water machine overturned. So did Six's. All the divisions rushed into an intersection scattered with fallen ladders and axes as the northwest wind sent a shower of sparks over them. A two-fisted free-for-all began. Three landed the first punches. A crowd gathered to applaud each of the various skirmishes. Five's pipemen abandoned the fight first, got up their ladder, and let their hose down into the bay. When Six righted their engine and rolled it closer to the fire, they began to battle again. Two of Five's men working the hand pump failed to notice the tide was out and their nozzle was pointed through the window of the Chinese laundry next door. They pumped a stream of mud onto baskets of freshly ironed shirts. The others brawled until the clatter of bricks and falling beams shocked them to their senses. The building had burned to ashes. It was an omen. It seemed that things could not get much worse, but they did.

A STREET SCENE ON A RAINY NIGHT

Davey Scannell

CHAPTER NINE

The Golden Ring

O n June 22, 1851, an arsonist struck again—the sixth great fire in eighteen months. Either he had been waiting until plenty of gold was on deposit or the need for a fire to warm his cold heart had seized him again. Wisely he had waited until the cisterns in the business part of the city were even lower than in the May fire. At 7:00 A.M. he stalked among the dwelling houses where, in spite of the Council's six-bucket rule, most homes had no water. On this Sabbath, the *Alta* announced that dancing by Senorita Abalos and a laughable farce, *The Widow's Victim,* were to be staged at a downtown theater. But hours before the show, that theater would be a heap of hot ashes, as would the *Alta* office. At 7:57 A.M. the air barely stirred. At 8:00 A.M. the wind began to rise. The gentle sea breeze that usually filled everyone's eyes with sand became a strong northwest gale that whipped through Spring Valley. When the wind was blowing like a hurricane, the arsonist set a fire inside a two-story wooden building on a hill.

Bennett and Kirby, the owners, occupied the kitchen with a friend, Lippincott, but let the bankers Delessert, Ligeron & Company use the front rooms. The fire, breaking out under the eaves, might have easily been extinguished if a supply of water had been at hand. None was nearer than the bay. At the rear of the building stood an empty house on the north side of Pacific. Next door, Morriss & Reynolds' carpenter shop was packed to the rafters with wood. Sparks from Bennett and Kirby's burning house set the woodshop afire. Conveniently for the arsonist, a well-stocked lumberyard was also just across the street. The flames stretched hungrily toward it. A few neighbors tried to check the fire by ripping down houses in its path, but no one can tear a house to pieces faster than a fire can burn it.

The lumberyard caught and drove off the neighbors as the fire spread along Pacific Street snapping up wooden homes until it reached Barroilhet's Gambling House. A huge warehouse of corrugated iron sheets nailed to a wooden frame caught fire. A considerable quantity of gunpowder was stored inside. The volunteers and torch boys scattered and were well back when the explosion leveled the ground over a vast area, but the force still knocked them off their feet. The four-story Graham House on the northwest corner of Pacific and Kearny streets was already ashes. At 10:30 A.M., just as church bells were tolling, the fire leaped Pacific Street. In minutes the block from Broadway to Stockton Street was aflame. Citizens ran to an alley near Stockton, ripped down a building in the flames' path, and slowed the blaze. The flames moved east from Stockton over onto Jackson Street. The powerful wind blew the fire to the intersection of Stockton and Jackson streets where Lieutenant McGowan and twenty-two other men were ripping down the corner houses. As it crossed the intersection, shouts of "Fire!" sent early risers racing back home to save what they could. Late sleepers scurried from their beds, pulled on clothes, and rushed outside where strong prevailing winds nourished the flames. The intense heat sucked the moisture from their lungs, singed their hair, and blistered their lips. The blaze then licked along Dupont Street, burning frame buildings at the rear of the ruined adobe. Up went the popular La Polka. The blaze made no distinction between gambling halls and churches, because it next targeted the Reverend Albert Williams's First Presbyterian Tabernacle on Stockton between Pacific and Broadway streets.

"At the first bell-ringing for the eleven o'clock service," the Reverend Mr. Williams recalled, "I was looking out my north study window from my residence [five blocks away] on California Street. I saw a dark cloud of smoke rising from the region of the church." The large New York Gothic edifice, an expensive prefab affair, had arrived in the fall and was ready for dedication. Freight, labor, and the funds to buy the lot had cost Williams's congregation $16,000. The worshippers had been on the way to the church services while the choir made special preparations for that day's choir music. "I reached the church in time to assist members of the congregation in saving the books, organ, and other moveable articles," Williams said. The fire had already burned the west pulpit end. "Last of all, I helped to detach the pulpit and bear it to a place of safety. The eastern Stockton Street front, supporting the belfry, last gave way, and the bell loosened from its loft height fell into the street and was broken . . . in so brief a time the church which we had waited so long, and in the use of which so much gratification had been derived, was entirely destroyed." Just below Pacific and Broadway, the blaze gobbled up the French Church on the west side of Stockton Street. The First Baptist Church should have been the next tasty morsel, but it was the only church out of five to survive.

The volunteers exploded buildings to halt the fire's progress. When they tried to blow up the Sacramento Hotel on Broadway, only one cask of powder ignited. A volunteer, cigar clenched in his jaw, strolled into the already flaming building with two more powder casks under his arms. The fire in the unvented room was rolling over the flax ceiling and starting down the linen wall behind him as he lit the fuses with his cigar. Calmly, he retreated, puffing as he went and adding to the smoke. In the doubled explosion behind him the hotel fell and a fiery belt arched over the street back to the engines. They had to be abandoned. This fire was especially cruel. From the Stockton Street area to Jackson Street lived a poorer class of French, Mexicans, washerwomen, laborers, and mechanics whose homes were the major sources of their income, and now those were gone. At Sacramento and Montgomery streets, Lillie Hitchcock and her parents were roused by the alarms. In the high wind, one house after another went up on the blocks surrounding them. Fire jumped Washington Street, made for Clay and Commercial streets, and then began licking at the Howard House, where the Hitchcocks were staying. Martha rushed to the attic, packed their clothes in a trunk, and with Lillie lugged the trunk downstairs and into a wagon. On the first floor, men tore down the rooms closest to the burning house next door. Dr. Hitchcock ripped up the Turkish carpets and then climbed to the roof and covered the tar with wet blankets. All their efforts proved ineffectual. As the Howard House burned, the Hitchcocks departed for Rincon Hill. From the back of the wagon, Martha studied the burning ships in the cove below with fascination. Images of the Huntington plantation's burning filled her mind.

Survivors were already sailing to the East Bay when a second blaze erupted on the outskirts of town. The incendiary had either galloped there on a fast horse or had a partner who had awaited his signal to act. The authorities agreed "that this fire is the work of not one, but two incendiaries." There had been warnings. The patrol of the Vigilance Committee had lately discovered more kindling fires than ever. As thick black clouds filled the streets, plunderers and looters marched lockstep across San Francisco, taking full advantage of the confusion to loot the gold stores. Because it was Sunday, Captain Coffin and Captain Haskel called onboard the *James Caskie* for Captain Jones and his wife to join them for church services. They were sitting in the Joneses' cabin when bells on shore began to peal. They supposed it was for the morning worship, until ships' bells of all tones, tin pans, and cow horns joined in. On deck they saw heavy smoke and flames rising far up the hill in the western section of the city. Coffin hurried to shore, ran west toward Powell Street, and saw his friend, Dr. Mitchell of the cutter *Ewing*, fighting fire.

A Frenchman, John Baptise Durand, aboard the *Monte Lambert* anchored far out, heard the alarms and rowed ashore to help a friend transport his goods. As he reached a flaming store on Pacific Street, the fire veered toward Ohio Street. He stooped to pick up a live coal to light his pipe. A crowd saw the gesture. Taking him for the arsonist, they beat and stomped him so severely he perished from his injuries later in the county jail. The coroner's verdict would be that he died from an inflammation of the brain caused by injuries received during the fire. A Mexican man, carrying a bale of goods from a burning building on Washington Street, was cornered by an enraged mob that demanded, "Put down the bundle." When he either refused or did not understand, he was kicked to death. Another man was luckier. When enraged citizens accused him of starting the fire, a police patrol intervened. "He's one of us," they vouched and were believed, though many of the cops were ex-Hounds and former Ducks in league with the thieves or even friends of Ben Lewis. Honest police apprehended some arson suspects, acquitted three on the spot, and held others in custody.

The Jackson Street fire had burned as far as Kearny Street when George Hubbard's friends saved him from his burning sick bed and carried him to the middle of the Square. He perished there in the heat in full sight on a heap of goods that caught fire several times during the day. Higher up on the hillside, tiny one- and two-story buildings "burned like shavings." When Captain Coffin reached the western side of Powell, three engines were squirting the blaze with leaking hoses. As he stood watching, he perceived something odd. The opposite side of the street, a continuous range of wooden buildings, changed from yellow to the color of burned coffee, then began to smoke. As glazing snapped and shattered, the vacuum sucked heat into the building interiors where cotton linings caught at once. An instant later the whole broadside of the street burst into flames. The volunteers abandoned two of their engines and saved a third at the risk of their lives. Several men were fatally burned. The flames raged farther down Jackson Street. Only half rebuilt, the business district was being destroyed again. The flimsiness of temporary buildings only fed the fire that attacked three storehouses and the new City Hall.

Coffin, shaken by the explosions, raced down to Stuart and Raines's Store, where he discovered the Newburyport delegation removing their stock. Captain Raines filled a trunk with treasure, piled it into a wheelbarrow, and charged Coffin to find a safe place to store it. He rolled the wheelbarrow to Front Street, but before he went far, the blaze had careened down between Broadway and Pacific streets. In danger of being trapped between two fires, he wheeled his barrow down to the lower end of Pacific Wharf, where for the next three hours he faithfully guarded Raines's gold.

Dutch Charley showed himself a hero again, saving blocks of houses from burning. Abruptly the blaze turned south toward Washington Street and the *Alta* office in the wooden buildings between Kearny and the Bella Union. The Howard Company tried in vain to save Gilbert's newspaper by blowing up the California Restaurant adjoining his office. Nor could a private fire engine and a tank of water salvage the building, presses, and the type. Printing on borrowed presses and using type set up in the offices of a competitor, Gilbert bitterly wrote a single line: "We are sick with what we have seen and felt and need not say any more."

Sawyer, feeling the wind whistle around him, feared that this time nothing might be left of San Francisco. The cloying smoke was like syrup. He began to cough. Firemen do not eat smoke. Smoke eats them. The fire assumed a celestial quality. Little whirlwinds of hot air spiraled around them and then united to create one huge vortex. The giant ring rose above the firefighters. When it was directly overhead, the invisible ring of superheated air slowly began to turn clockwise. Gradually it took on the hue of the fire and became a golden ring. It spun faster until it created an updraft rising miles into the stratosphere. The center of the ring, hotter still, ate up all the oxygen to create a counterclockwise downdraft of sparks and lethal gases that was forced on the firemen. As the inner ring rotated, it became a dark circle of smoke, wheels within wheels relentlessly turning like a mill.

Sawyer held a moistened finger aloft. "The wind is altering its course," he said. "Yes, the gale's moving northward. We might be spared yet. The main district might not be lost entirely. The next hour will tell." He looked around. Unbelievably, some citizens still refused to help fight fire unless their own places were on fire. As a team of horses galloped by dragging their harness, he saw a man weeping uncontrollably before his flaming store. The merchant, previously burned out in each of the other fires, trembled, wrung his hands, and wept. He leaped past the firemen pumping water and pulling down walls and, howling, ran headlong toward the flames, arms open to embrace them. The volunteers tried to block him, but he dodged past and in a flash of red was vaporized.

The men heard a heartless chuckle. Turning, they saw a man who resembled the fugitive Ben Lewis. The laughter continued. "This man absolutely bricked us up," [silenced them] a volunteer said later. "Stop laughing!" another volunteer screamed. "For the love of God, a man has died." The stranger went on roaring. He graveled, provoked them. Uneven teeth shone in the firelight as he laughed louder. A few onlookers had tears in their eyes. Were they gazing upon the Lightkeeper or his partner who had burned down their city six times? Who else could be so cruel? All the official and civilian firefighters ceased work. "Out of respect, stop," one called, recalling Captain Vincente and all the casualties who had died at the arsonist's hands, recalling his family that had been lost. Finally a few men threw down their buckets and axes and advanced on the laughing man. Amid the horror, his joviality was monstrous.

"By God," said a neighbor. "By God!" The stranger only hooked his thumbs in his belt, spread his legs, drew back his head, and laughed his loudest. The fire was closer. Flames sang on the roofs. A black curtain of cinders and sparks blew over the scene. Crashing timbers and whirling fire rose up at the far end of the alley. The fire had reached them. "Do for him!" said a man, "if nothing less." In an instant several neighbors and volunteers sprang upon the laughing man—kicking, punching, and slapping him. The stranger, rocked off his feet, only grinned up from the ground. A trickle of blood coursed down his chin. A firefighter kicked him and turned away disgusted. Another did the same. The volunteers heard a tremendous creaking and groaning, a low rumble and a crack like thunder. The wall behind pitched forward and hundreds of bricks dropped right where they had left the supine man, bleeding and moaning. Fire swept over the bricks. No one helped. Everyone had gone back to fighting flames and saving the lives that could still be saved. Where the arsonist had been only a moment before was nothing but rubble.

Eventually this last conflagration burned itself out—thanks to the torch boys who nailed stores of blankets to the front of Barny and Patten's building on the southeast corner of Sansome and Pacific streets and kept them saturated with water. The fire, moving east, ran up against the blankets like a wave and died. On Montgomery Street, sheet iron in the windows and doors of Howard and Green's basement halted the flames there.

Farther along Montgomery, gratings and solid iron doors melted and ran off in blazing streams, and streets glowed like the inside of a smelter. Burning skeletons of men, horses, and mules crumbled to powder in the wind. A waxworks dissolved, leaving behind a foot-deep walk of colored wax with bits of costume jewelry congealed inside. Jones's Hotel at the foot of California Street survived, protected by a brick building on one side and an unoccupied iron house on the other side. A lucky alteration of the wind's course toward Sydney Town kept the fire from crossing Sansome to the south of California Street and spared the Happy Valley and great stores of lumber. After igniting upper Washington, the flames had burned all the houses around the square and any areas that had survived the May anniversary fire. Kearny and Sansome streets burned, as did the entire district between Pacific and Cunningham's Wharf between Green and Vallejo. The inferno destroyed ten blocks fronted by Broadway, Powell, and Sansome streets and incinerated the last traces of Colonial San Francisco of just two years earlier. Ghost Fleet ships that had transported hordes of forty-niners burned to their keels.

This time the fire had destroyed the previously untouched northwestern quarter of the city—ten to fifteen blocks bounded by Sansome, Mason, Washington, and Broadway streets and all the buildings between Clay and Powell. Nearly all the northern portion had been incinerated. The foothills were untouched and, after some rains, would be denser than before. Though the sky was still tinted with a lurid glow, the last vestige of the blaze on the other side of the city burned itself out against a barren hillside.

"Just think," said Sawyer. "Five hundred more buildings—gone!"

Stillness fell over the city. Hundreds removed their possessions to the Square and guarded them throughout the night. Piled goods made impressive bonfires. Men rich only a few hours earlier wept and ran their fingers through ashes that had once been splendid fortunes. Women collapsed on steps that led up to only rubble. Others drank from simple tin cups and blankly pondered on fate that had turned the wind at one point and punished the gangs behind the arsons in Sydney Town. Steam condensed and rained over acres of blackened shells. The City Hospital burned and ninety patients were carried to a vacant lot. On the hills at the head of Kearny and Dupont streets, thousands shivered amid chaparral and the few household goods they had saved. Many lives had been lost: A man burned to death on Jackson Street and another perished trying to save his storeroom. Three people in the Square died from flames, the police shot two looters, and four or five other pillagers perished at the hands of outraged citizens, including the unknown man buried by bricks. Sawyer liked to think there had been some justice at the end and never found out anything different. That was good enough for him.

He passed the rubble of a brick warehouse and a melted iron building. He pawed through the ruins of a brick warehouse, examining the flaws that had allowed air to spread the fire into the interior. Last, he trudged to the empty, jack-legged house on Pacific where the fire had originated. Though the abandoned home had been the catalyst for widespread destruction, it had survived with only two walls gone. As wind cut though the shell making an eerie howl, Sawyer could almost hear the mirthless laugh of Ben Lewis. Possibly the arsonist had surrounded himself with fire to warm a cold heart. At least the devil had returned to the flames and he was not going to look for him any further. As in the anniversary fire, the fire was doubtless the work of an incendiary. No fire had been used about the empty, makeshift house for any purpose whatsoever. Sawyer wondered what they would find when they removed the pile of charred rubble by the merchant's store. Would the arsonist still be there or had his body vanished into the warm earth? Was it even him? Perhaps he had escaped to burn again. "Ben Lewis," he thought, "the man who burned San Francisco to the ground." The Lightkeeper was dead, if not at the hands of an infuriated mob then as a casualty of his own blaze. The fires should now be at an end. He had only walked a few feet when he halted. "If Ben Lewis was the Lightkeeper," he asked

himself, "then who had started the second blaze that had simultaneously erupted on the outskirts of town?" Lewis could not have been in
two places at once. The Lightkeeper had to have a secret partner, and
he was still out there.

The June 22 fire reawakened arson fears. Four days after the Vigilance Committee advertised a reward for "the capture and conviction
of anyone guilty of such a crime." At one time, a strong suspicion of
arson rested upon a black man known as Ben Robinson. In spite of an
antislavery clause in the state constitution, he lived in abject subjection
to a depraved white woman, Margaret Robinson, who habitually beat
him if he disregarded her wishes. When police arrested him on suspicion of starting the fire, he confessed he had done so in obedience to
Mrs. Robinson, who had a grudge against the man in whose house the
fire originated. With unusual negligence, officers allowed him to escape,
but vigilantes immediately seized him and took him to headquarters on
June 30, when he repeated the same story. Mr. and Mrs. Robinson were
arrested the same night; thereupon Ben withdrew his whole confession
and accused a cop of bribing him to tell the story. Uncharacteristically
the Committee unraveled a plot to incite the vigilantes to take action
against Mrs. Robinson, "whose evil life made credible any tale that
might be told about her." The Robinsons were discharged on July 12.

According to the *Annals,* four of the conflagrations had been started
by gangs of former convicts from Australia led by Ben Lewis and his
partner. Further proof the arsons were organized came from two more
feeble attempts. A man tried to fire the Pacific Street Wharf and was
arrested. Someone set fire to the rear of Marvin & Hitchcock's building
but was foiled. Police discovered where the arsonist had broken a glass
pane in the door sash leading into the yard and had set fire to the window curtain. The match was still on the floor. "More than ever," wrote
the *Alta,* "we are convinced by this there is in this city an organized
band sworn to destroy it."

Kohler had had enough. "We should abandon this site and find a
place that won't burn down with such damnable regularity," he said
passionately. "Perhaps Benicia or Sacramento." "Will these fires never
end?" other townsfolk lamented. "We can take no more." Hundreds of
San Franciscans loaded their goods into wagons and ferried them to
the East Bay, where their only neighbors were the Gonzales Ranch, a
sprinkling of Spanish ranches, the tiny town of Oakland, a wilderness
stretching all the way to the Benicia settlement, and an army garrison

at the far eastern end of the bay. In the emptying streets the preachers bellowed that the city was a Sodom and Gomorrah, referring to wicked cities reviled in the Bible and destroyed by fire from heaven. "These six horrendous disasters are God's great retribution to an evil city," the local prophets said. The churches filled and people begged for forgiveness. Perhaps the chastened multitude was heard at last. After June 1851 there were no more city-destroying fires. The persistent volunteers and their valiant torch boys had won.

Between December 24, 1849, and June 22, 1851, San Francisco had been completely burned six times (seven times if one counted the December 14 fire, which Kohler did), with three thousand structures lost. The mayor estimated that a total of $25 million of uninsured real estate had been lost in the eighteen months through the fires. He estimated that San Franciscans had lost $44 million of personal valuables, including great quantities of gold and jewels. Unlike four of the previous conflagrations, which had burned out residents, gamblers, and merchants, and the anniversary fire, which had burned out the business section, the June 22 inferno was the "poor man's fire," which hurt the common laborer with a loss of $3 million.

With the mines playing out and the multimillion-dollar loss of the sixth fire, the future looked bleak. The mayor could not go to the City Hall at Kearny and Pacific streets. That was gone. The prison was transferred to Sheriff "Coffee Jack" Hays's jail, and he packed eight or nine more men into each of the already crowded cells. So far only seven new cells and a keeper room had been completed. He had no idea how to finish the expansion project. There was a mortgage of $4,000 and a lien of $2,250. An honorable man, the sheriff paid most of it out of his own pocket.

So much of the city had burned that finding a place to suit Martha Hitchcock's aristocratic pretensions was difficult. The winds of Rincon Hill where her family took temporary refuge disturbed her. So did the neighborhood's constant gunfire. Eventually Lillie and her parents moved into the new hotel on Market Street, at Bush and Battery streets. Martha liked the beautiful exterior with its broad verandahs, but because the hotel was built out over the bay, she had to tiptoe across narrow planks to the entrance. The makeshift interior was furnished with French antiques from the William Leidesdorff estate, but the glare of astral lights revealed scurrying rats. Upstairs flammable cotton ceilings stretched above the bedrooms. All over the city tons of scrap metal protruded from the rubble—safes, tools, metal warehouses, and stoves. Workers spent three weeks cutting up the twisted remnants of Howard and Green's melted warehouse at Clay and Leidesdorff. It cost more than $9,000 to cart it away. All that metal created a new industry. Cheap recovered iron made foundries the city's newest and biggest industry. From the melted wealth came more wealth as brick and iron replaced the flimsy, comparatively worthless lumber flooding San Francisco. San Franciscans were proud of their fires—grand fires, heroic fires, the greatest ever seen—because they had fire in their veins. They thrived on the blazes because each brought a new and finer city.

On July 9, Dutch Charley and Broderick spoke at an antivigilance meeting in the St. Francis Hook and Ladder firehouse. On July 21, Lewis's trial for arson began in the district court. The next day Sawyer heard that he was convicted in absentia and sentenced to two years. Lewis was nowhere in sight. Juror and Vigilance Committee prosecutor and recorder George Schenck speculated in his trial notes that the arsonist had escaped and traveled to New York, where he murdered Dr. Harvey Burdell, a dentist, and killed a second man in New Jersey in 1857. Dr. Burdell, though, had been strangled and stabbed by the mistress of his Bond Street house, Emma Cunningham, and one of her borders, a man named John Eckel. Unless Lewis was Eckel, Schenck was wrong. If Lewis was still alive, he was a very lucky man. Two days after his conviction, a new state statute made arson punishable by death.

On July 21, Ira Cole reported that Dutch Charley was drinking more liquor in one day than he used to drink in a week. Yet his love of fighting fire, an admirable quality, might yet save him. Who could not admire the dedication and single-mindedness of any man who raged against those who interfered with the honest occupation of firefighting and dealt out dreadful punishment to those who disrespected the volunteers? In spite of his furious tantrums and bullying, he was a fireman at heart, possibly the bravest of all. Always first on the front lines, he was cited numerous times for heroism at the scene of a blaze. He was a bad man to have against you and a good man to have with you. When mobs began to lynch men in the streets, Dutch Charley would stand almost alone against the thousands for the rights of a few. He was especially needed in the worsening rivalry between the volunteer companies that had toiled for the public good so long without reward.

On October 4, just as Zeke Wilson erected Wilson's Exchange, the first five-story on the Pacific Coast, Sawyer finally shipped out for the first time as a coal pusher on the ill-fated *Independence* under the colorful Captain Wakeman. It was only the second visit of the new steamer to San Francisco. That same day the tireless promoter Tom Maguire reopened his latest Jenny Lind Theatre on the same site where his earlier Jenny Lind Theatres had been destroyed by fire. Poor Tom Maguire. He had opened one of the city's first theaters above his saloon only to see it burned in the anniversary fire, worked hard to raise another $100,000 to rebuild, even labored as a bartender to earn money. He reopened his Jenny Lind Theatre at Kearny and Washington streets on June 12, and by June 22 it was ashes. "The next Jenny Lind," he vowed, "would be of fireproof brick, yellow-toned sandstone facings shipped from Australia, grander with gilded trim, an orchestra pit and a dress circle." He kept his promise. The handsome new three-story neoclassical structure, shipped in sections around the Horn, had a gorgeous gold and pink interior capable of seating two thousand people that rivaled the best theaters in the Atlantic states. Sadly, the sorely put upon entrepreneur had built too well. The Council cast its coveting eyes on the palace and demanded it as a replacement for the destroyed City Hall. In August, Maguire sold it to them for $200,000, an exorbitant price brokered by his friend Broderick. The cash was diverting but hardly fulfilled the thwarted promoter, who would rather have had his beloved theater. If Maguire could not win on land, then he would triumph on water. He would outfit a floating "Jenny Lind at Sea" from a rebuilt stern-wheel steamer. Within two years the seaborne theater would be throbbing past Pulgas Ranch off San Francisquito Creek when her boiler steam pipes would burst, explode through the dining room bulkhead, and kill thirty-one aboard. Scalded passengers leaped over the side as flames enveloped the *Jenny Lind,* which drifted onto the riverbank and sank. Tom Maguire would die a pauper.

On October 21, Dutch Charley led his men to the St. Francis Hotel fire on Dupont and Clay streets. Seeing the upper two stories in flame, he ran hoses through the ground-floor doors to fight the fire from the inside, an efficient, effective way to fight fire. The flames were out in twenty minutes. The *Alta* wrote, "Mr. Duane . . . regardless of the flames, heat and danger, placed himself in the second story of the frame building using his energy and brawn to save it." His redemption was happening just as Sawyer had predicted. On December 5, Pacific Eight helped reelect him as the volunteer companies' chief engineer.

Dutch Charley, reformed and reforming, enforced the ban on hazardous stored explosives by going from house to house enforcing the "powder ordinance" by seizing kegs of explosives and arresting the owners. One day he came to a small, empty shack in the Mission, saw an unsafe stovepipe encased in wood on its roof, entered and discovered a trap-door in the floor. Prying it up, he located a stamping machine, a press, tools, coins, and dies—a counterfeiting operation. Police confiscated the equipment but not the counterfeiters. He never retired before the first light of dawn. "I told Mr. Yale [who needed his aid] that I made it a rule since the firemen of the city had so honored me with the highest position in their gift never to go out of hearing of the fire alarm bell. The city had been burned to the ground and had been almost wholly destroyed nearly every time there was a fire before I was elected Chief Engineer and I did not propose to let such a catastrophe occur through any neglect of mine."

On Tuesday, November 9, a small fire broke out near the Square. When the flames butted up against a hard brick wall at Washington and Montgomery streets, they went out. The value of the new brick buildings was proved again when a fire on Merchant and Clay streets was restricted to the loss of thirty wooden buildings. Five days later San Francisco adopted a new seal, a large bird with red and gold feathers, rainbow-hued wings, and scarlet feet: a Phoenix, a fabled creature that rose from its ashes after setting itself ablaze on a pyre of cinnamon branches and myrrh. Broderick thought the image far more fitting for a great American city than the odious third eye of the cowardly vigilantes who had dishonored the volunteers by their use of the Monumental fire bell to call forth bloody deeds and bloodier hands.

Merchants begged the Council not to pass a proposed ordinance restricting building of frame houses within fire limits. "Such a measure," they argued, "might drive away many who are now hesitating to risk another trial of their fortune in the city." The Council, convinced of the need for fireproof buildings, passed the measure on December 6, forbidding the future erection of any frame houses within dense areas of the town, prohibiting rags within the fire limits, and mandating slate, tile, or other fire-resistant roofs. New city ordinances demanded that *all* downtown commercial structures were to be either stone or brick. The three-story Custom House at Battery, Washington, and Jackson, under construction to house federal departments and the post office, had deep-set windows like a fortress. The new cast-iron buildings had their own peculiar beauty—stamped ornamental motifs and caryatids, iron floral friezes, and painted glass. Within two years, 626 brick or stone buildings would stand within the limits of Broadway and Bush streets, Stockton Street, and the waterfront. Three hundred and fifty of the buildings were two stories high, 154 were three stories, 34 were four stories, and 3 were five stories. Impressive brick and stone hotels, shops, theaters, and banks began to fill downtown as Montgomery Street became lined with durable structures of granite block.

Senator Broderick had been behind a recent water lot grab involving the former head of the City Hospital, Dr. Smith. In such an imperfect city, but one filled with such promise, Broderick's little faults seemed minor. In such a metropolis of cruel men and arsonists, kindness and goodness were relative things. As the new year was rung in, Broderick continued pursuing his ethic that the end justifies the means. So far his strategy had worked to good ends, but he had made political enemies who were out to kill him and do it legally.

On December 12, George Oakes suddenly died.

By now the foot of broad California Street had been substantially planked, the city's first horse-drawn streetcar line was operating, and the California Street Wharf was being extended farther into the cove. Grading and planking stretched from the junction of Battery and Market streets diagonally to Sacramento and Dupont streets, and from Dupont and Broadway to the bay. A flight of planking nullified the steep pitch of the grade leading to Vallejo Street, and a three-mile-long plank road out Folsom Street was built. With planking almost universal, the job of the volunteers and torch boys became much easier. The Council ripped down the last canvas buildings, improved the fire watch at the new City Hall, mandated the placement of more water tanks, and ordained a fire-free zone, bounded by Union, Powell, Post, and Second and Folsom streets. Within this area vacant lots and open fires were forbidden and laborers had to use enclosed lanterns around hay. The city tore down the last wall of the white adobe relic, rooted up the foundation, and graded the site level with the street. The previous winter's rains had affected its stability and it was feared it might "suddenly fall and overwhelm the neighbors in its ruins." The Casa Grande had seen San Francisco rise from a few fishing hamlets to a city of great commercial wealth and seen the greater portion of it in ashes six times and as often rebuilt with renewed grandeur. "The day of the gay and merry fandan-

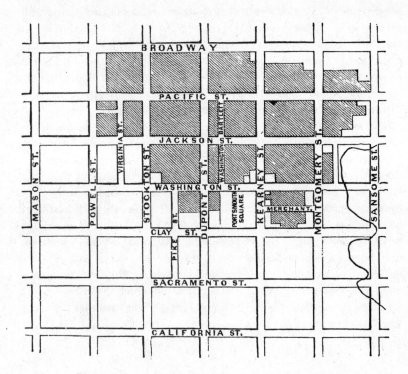

THE BURNED DISTRICT FROM THE JUNE 22, 1851, FIRE

gos is over," the *Alta* reported, "the music that once resounded through its halls is hushed." The city filled in the tidelands between the shores and piers with sand removed from towering dunes downtown. Gradually the crescent-shaped cove, with all its secrets, was plowed over. They filled in the land between the piers and the piers became streets stretching to the waterfront, and upon them homes began to rise.

"It now came out," said George E. Schenck, record keeper for the Vigilantes, "that [English Jim] Stuart was a leader of a gang of nine, who had been concerned in various robberies and assaults, composed of T. Belcher Kay, who was port warden at the time, John Morris Morgan, [Sam] Whittaker, [Robert] McKensie, Jack Edwards, Jim Stuart, Benjamin Lewis, Jemmy-from-Town and one other." English Jim's gang agreed that if their men were hung, "which we expected they would be," Sam Whittaker said, "we would fire the town on Sunday night in several places." He had heard that another member of their gang, "Billy Sweetcheese, whose real name is [Billy] Shears," had assisted in setting the United States Gambling Exchange on fire on the Square "at the time it was vacant." Thus two men had accomplished the May 1850 fire that destroyed San Francisco. Of T. Belcher Kay, historian H. H. Bancroft wrote, "He is said to have been the instigator of the great fire of the 22nd of June." Kay's assistants in the June fire were Whittaker, Jemmy-from-Town, and George Adams. English Jim Stuart, Sam Whittaker, and McKensie were lynched in July 1851. Kay escaped to South America.

Sawyer finally learned the name of Ben Lewis's confederate: Jack Edwards, another Duck, a member of English Jim Stuart's gang, and leader of a gang who robbed and assaulted people on the outskirts of town. Edwards was also the man seen on the staircase with Ben Lewis when he torched his Collier House room. When Edwards was brought to trial after a long delay, like Lewis he was freed by venal judges under the sway of politicians in the Ducks' pocket. When Edwards was searched, police found in his belongings what could have been a small lamp scorched almost beyond recognition but which made Sawyer certain that Edwards had been the second Lightkeeper and that the horror was finally over.

PART III

STEAMING WITH TWAIN AND SAWYER

May 26, 1863–December 16, 1866

Billy Mulligan

TWAIN AND HARTE PROWL THE SAN FRANCISCO DOCKS

Investigations showed clearly that at least four of the conflagrations had been started by a gang of firebugs led by two former convicts from Australia—Jack Edwards and Ben Lewis.

—Herbert Asbury, *The Barbary Coast*

CHAPTER TEN

Steamers

Subsequent confessions of criminals on the eve of execution, implicated a considerable number of people in various high and low departments of the executive.

—Frank Soule, *The Annals of San Francisco*

More than a decade later, in clouds of rolling steam, Mark Twain studied Tom Sawyer, foreman of Liberty Hose and the new San Francisco customs inspector. Sawyer reminded him of the rugged platoon of volunteer smoke eaters, mostly New Yorkers, in the Bowery B'hoy tradition in Virginia City. Virginia, as he called the Nevada town where he currently worked as a reporter, was only a small town, about three times as large as Hannibal, Missouri, his hometown since age four. He visualized their foreman, Big Jack Perry, leaning against the six-foot-high wheels of the town's hand-drawn fire cart and concluded that Sawyer compared favorably. Later he patterned Buck Fanshaw in *Roughing It* on Perry.

Twain, Sawyer, and Ed Stahle, the proprietor of the Turkish baths at 722 and 724 Montgomery, played cards, drank cold bottled beer, and listened to the rain pounding on the street outside. It was May 5, 1863, and Twain was three days into his first visit to San Francisco to "wildcat on Montgomery." He had learned that Sawyer was a former policeman, Fire Corporation yard keeper, and Liberty Hose's foreman. Twain luxuriated in the hot mist and surveyed his cards. The poker deck displayed full-length, single-ended court figures but no numbers. All three men loved to steam, Twain most of all. Stahle's Turkish baths had been part of the Montgomery Block at the intersection of Montgomery and Washington streets for a decade. The ground floor on the northwest corner housed the Bank Exchange saloon (home of Pisco Punch), where Twain and Sawyer had met—drinking, of course. Twain had liked him immensely. Almost everyone did. Bret Harte, a frequent visitor to the bar, wrote "The Luck of Roaring Camp" in the Montgomery Block, the most important literary site of the nineteenth- and early-twentieth-century American West. It was a hub of creative expression that magnetically attracted talent. Former torch boy Charles Dormon Robinson (later called the dean of San Francisco artists) worked out of his upstairs painting studio opposite Ambrose Bierce's old apartment. Robinson and his fellow artists frequented the Occidental Hotel. Jack London, Rudyard Kipling, Gelett Burgess, Frank Norris, George Sterling, Joaquin Miller, Robert Louis Stevenson, and Ralph Stackpole, who would paint murals within Coit Tower, kept their offices there. Sun Yat-sen wrote the first Chinese constitution there.

Steam baths had been a fixture in the area long before the Gold Rush. Two blocks away, on the southwest corner of Montgomery and Sacramento streets, an Indian sweat house had once stood. The *temascal*, a combination hot-air bath and place of spiritual purification, was merely a six-foot-deep hole in the ground tightly covered with brush. A hole in the center allowed smoke to exit from the fire within. A narrow stream, now gone, coursed east down Sacramento Street to form a small freshwater pool known as Laguna Dulce (Sweet Water). After a half hour of steaming, the Native Americans, dripping with sweat, plunged into this chilly slough and emerged physically refreshed and spiritually revived, the same way the sauna affected Twain.

He and reporter Clement T. Rice, affectionately dubbed "the Unreliable" during their mock reportorial feud, were living high in a prestigious new four-story hotel on Montgomery, at Bush, and had grown accustomed to dining on salmon and cold fowl. "I live at the Occidental House," he bragged, "and that is Heaven on the half-shell. . . . In a word, I kept the due state of a man worth a hundred thousand dollars." Sawyer envied him. He lived frugally while saving to buy a saloon on Mission Street. He and Twain discussed steamboats that they had in common. On February 28, 1857, Twain departed from Cincinnati for New Orleans as a passenger aboard the steamboat *Paul Jones*. "One of the pilots," he recalled, "was Horace Bixby. Little by little I got acquainted with him and pretty soon I was doing a lot of steering for him in his daylight watches." Twain got his pilot's license in September 1859 and worked the Mississippi until April 1861, when the Civil War disrupted river traffic and the Confederates purposely sank the first steamboat he ever piloted as a blockade at Big Black River. Piloting was the realization of one of Twain's two powerful ambitions in life. His unrealized goal was to be a minister of the Gospel. Unfortunately, he lacked the necessary stock-in-trade: religion. He found it remarkable that his older, luckless brother, Orion (accent on the *O*), unmistakably heard the voice of God thundering in his ears yet aspired to be a lawyer. "It is human nature," Twain said, "to yearn to be what we were never intended for."

"He was about twenty years old when he went on the Mississippi as a pilot," Twain's invalid mother recalled. "I gave up on him then, for I always thought steamboating was a wicked business, and was sure he would meet some bad associates." When he was a cub in the pilothouse of the *Aleck Scott*, freighting cotton from Memphis to New Orleans, the first engineer had gotten even with Twain (then Sam Clemens) for his practical jokes. "After working Sam to a nervous state about fire," the engineer recalled with glee, "I waited until he was alone in the pilothouse and then set fire to a little wad of cotton, stuffed it into the speaking tube [running from the engine room to the pilothouse] and the smell came out right under his nose . . . hair on end, his face like a corpse's, and his eyes sticking out so far you could have knocked them off with a stick, he danced around the pilothouse . . . pulled every bell, turned the boat's nose for the bank and yelled, 'FIRE!'"

As Twain heard Sawyer's story of saving the passengers on the burning steamer *Independence*, in which hundreds were scalded to death by steam, his eyes grew wide. He had a deathly fear of exploding steamers and felt responsible for his brother's death aboard one. His mother had asked him to kneel and swear on the Bible that he would look out for his slender, bookish, and frail younger brother, Henry. He had agreed.

In early 1858, he had a nightmare in which he saw his brother Henry's corpse in a metal coffin resting on two chairs in his sister's sitting room. A bouquet of white flowers, a single red rose in the center, lay on his chest. "In the morning when I awoke," he wrote, "I had been dreaming, and the dream was so vivid, so like reality, that it deceived me, and I thought it *was* real." Convinced Henry was dead, he walked one-half block up Locust Street toward Fourteenth when he realized it had only been a nightmare. He ran back and rushed into the sitting room. "And I was made glad again," he said, "for there was no casket there." A few weeks later Henry did die, in a boiler explosion onboard a steamer. Twain had gotten Henry the job that killed him, an unpaid post on the New Orleans and St. Louis steam packet *Pennsylvania*. "He obtained for his brother Henry a place on the same boat as clerk," his mother said, her voice trembling and eyes filling with tears, "and soon after Sam left the river Henry was blown up with the boat by an explosion and killed." On the steamer Henry served as a mud clerk, a junior purser who checked freight at landings and often returned aboard from the riverbank with muddy feet. Twain's own job as second clerk was to watch the freight piles from 7:00 P.M. until 7:00 A.M. for three nights every thirty-five days. Henry always joined his brother's watch at 9:00 P.M. to walk his rounds with him and chat for hours. Their first voyage together was uneventful until Tom Brown, the *Pennsylvania*'s pilot, unjustly tried to strike Henry with a ten-pound lump of coal. Twain let go the wheel, picked up a heavy stool, and hit Brown "a good honest blow which stretched him out." Captain John Klinefelter, mightily impressed, offered Twain Brown's job, but he declined and decided to depart the steamer at New Orleans and leave Henry behind.

The night before he left, he sat with Henry on a freight pile on the levee and talked till midnight of steamboat disasters. "In case of disaster to the boat," Twain advised, "don't lose your head—leave that to the passengers." He ordered Henry to rush for the hurricane deck and astern to the lifeboats lashed aft at the wheelhouse and obey the mate's orders. "Thus, you will be useful," he said, adding that the river is only a mile wide and he could swim that easily. At 6:00 A.M., June 13, a full week after Twain deserted the *Pennsylvania*, the steamer, under a half head of steam, exploded sixty miles below Memphis at the foot of Old Bordeaux Chute and four miles ahead of Ship Island. Four of the eight boilers blew up the forward third of the boat. Beefy Captain Klinefelter had been preparing to be shaved when the explosion left the barber's chair with him in it overhanging a gaping chasm. "Everything forward of it, floor and all," Twain recalled, "had disappeared." The ship's carpenter, asleep on his mattress, was hoisted into the sky by the blast and struck the water seventy-five feet away. Shrieks and groans filled the air. Many were burned to the bone or crippled. The detonation drove an iron crowbar though one man's body. After the explosion, Brown, the pilot, and George Clark, the chief, were never seen again. Twain, following on the *A. T. Lacey* from Greenville, had the full story by the time he reached Memphis.

"Henry was asleep," Twain said, "blown up—then fell back on

the hot boilers." A reporter wrote that Twain was "almost crazed with grief" at the sight of Henry's burned form on a mattress surrounded by thirty-two parboiled and mangled victims on pallets. His head was shapelessly swathed in a wad of loose raw cotton. "His feelings so much overcame him, at the scalded and emaciated form before him, that he sank to the floor overpowered." Henry had inhaled the lethal steam. His entire body was badly scalded, but he helped passengers evacuate before he lay on the riverbank under a burning sun for eight hours. Dr. Peyton, an old physician, took charge of Henry and at 11:00 P.M. told Twain that Henry was out of danger. "On the evening of the sixth day, [Henry's] wandering mind busied itself with matters far away and his nerveless fingers picked at his coverlet," Twain recalled. Every day doctors removed the doomed to a partitioned chamber adjoining the recovery room so other patients might not be affected by seeing the dying moments. Twain watched the "death-room" fill with bodies as one victim after another succumbed. "[Henry] lingered in fearful agony seven days and a half during which time he had full possession of his senses . . . and then but for a few moments at a time. His brain was injured by the concussion, and from that moment his great intellect was a ruin."

Dr. Peyton asked the young, barely trained doctors on watch to give Henry an eighth of a grain of morphine if he showed signs of being disturbed by the screams of the wounded. Because the neophyte physicians had no way to measure an eighth of a grain of morphine, they heaped a quantity on the tip of a knife blade and administered that to Henry. When one of his frenzies seized him, he tore off handfuls of cotton and exposed his cooked flesh. Three times Henry was covered and brought to the death-room and three times brought back to the recovery room. He died close to dawn. "His hour had struck; we bore him to the death-room, poor boy. . . . For forty-eight hours I labored at the bedside of my poor burned and bruised, but uncomplaining brother and then the star of my hope went out and left me in the gloom of despair. . . . O, God! This is hard to bear." They placed Henry in an unpainted white pine coffin and Twain went away to a nearby house to sleep. In his absence, some Memphis ladies bought a metallic coffin for Henry, who had been a great favorite of theirs. When Twain returned to the death-room to pay his respects, he found his brother dressed in a suit of Twain's clothing and laid out in a metallic coffin exactly as in his dream. All that was missing was the unique bouquet. "I recognized instantly that my dream of several weeks before was here exactly reproduced, so far as these details went—and I think I missed one detail, but that one was immediately supplied, for just then an elderly lady entered the place with a large bouquet consisting mainly of white roses, and in the center of it was a red rose, and she laid it on his breast." After Henry and 150 other human beings perished, Twain blamed himself and was still working the problem over in his mind by day and in vivid dreams at night. "My nightmares to this day," he said, "take the form of my dead brother and of running down into an overshadowing bluff, with a steamboat—showing that my earliest dread made the strongest impression on me." Twain left the steam baths determined to find a subject for his first novel that matched the rousing excitement of Sawyer's real-life recounting of an exploding steamer. Always on the lookout for a young hero, he filed the story away. He had yet to hear of the six great fires that had destroyed San Francisco and to learn that Sawyer, too, was plagued by nightmares of exploding steamboats.

While in San Francisco, Twain tried to arrange employment as the Nevada correspondent for the *Daily Morning Call*. He picked up news wherever he could: the docks, the firehouse, the police station, the Bank Exchange cigar kiosk, and the Montgomery Street Turkish Baths. "Your deal, Sam," Stahle said the next day. Neither Ed Stahle nor Sawyer called the red-haired journalist Twain. They called him Sam Clemens. "Mark Twain" was only one of dozens of playful pen names the writer had used since he was teenaged Samuel Langhorne Clemens. "W. Epaminondas Adrastus Perkins" was another. He had recently adopted his most famous sobriquet on the third of February and used it again on the fifth and the eighth in a letter from Carson City to the *Enterprise* while reporting legislative proceedings. *Twain* was river jargon for two fathoms (twelve feet) of water under the keel, the shallowest depth a steamboat could safely negotiate a river like the Mississippi. A half twain is fifteen feet. Captain Josiah Sellers, a masterful river pilot of greater navigational talent than the comparatively inept boatman Sam Clemens, supposedly had the nom de plume first while writing river news for the *New Orleans Daily Picayune*. He apparently thought nothing of appropriating Sellers's name. "I laid violent hands upon [his signature] without asking permission of the prophet's remains," he drawled. "Captain Sellers did me the honor to profoundly detest me from that day forth." With Sellers's death a year earlier, the name was solely Twain's. The truth was that Sellers had never used that pseudonym and Sam had perversely launched the self-deprecating myth himself.

His sojourn in San Francisco was profitable. "Ma," he wrote, "I have got five twenty-dollar greenbacks—the first kind of money I ever had. I'll send them to you—one at a time, so that if one or two get lost, it will not amount to anything." Yes, these were rosy times. During his newspapering days in Nevada, he had gotten some free mining stocks as kickbacks for favorable mentions in the *Territorial Enterprise*. His Gould and Curry stock was soaring. He had bought fifty shares of Hale and Norcross silver stocks on margin that he still had not sold and the share price was now a thousand dollars. "I hesitated, calculated the chances, and then concluded not to sell. Stocks went on rising; speculation went mad; bankers, merchants, lawyers, doctors, mechanics, laborers, even the very washer women and servant girls were putting their earnings on silver stocks, and every sun that rose in the morning went down on paupers enriched and rich men beggared. What a gambling carnival it was! I'm close to selling and am anxious to embark upon a life of ease. My ambition is to become a millionaire in a day or two."

On May 16, he and Rice moved out of the Occidental a block up Montgomery into a newer, more sumptuous hotel. The palatial Lick House at the corner of Sutter Street had flagged marble floors and a banquet hall that is a perfect replica of the Palace of Versailles. At the Lick House he "lived like a lord" in room number 165, "a pleasant room at the head of a long hall." He wrote his mother and sister that "the Unreliable and myself are still here and still enjoying ourselves. We go to sleep without rocking, every night. We dine out, and we lunch out, and we eat, drink and are happy—as it were . . . I am going the Dickens mighty fast." His only exercise was sleeping and resting, generally waking at 11:00 A.M. because he was "naturally lazy." When the proprietors sent him and Rice bottles of champagne and claret at dinner, they put on "the most disgusting airs." Twain bought two new suits, put $1,200 in his bank account, attended private parties in sumptuous evening dress, and simpered and displayed his "graces like a born beau." After breakfast, he often did not see the hotel again until after midnight. He took trips across the bay to Oakland, up to Benicia, and down to Alameda and out to the Willows and Fort Point. He and Rice sailed on the fastest yacht on the Pacific coast.

Twain took a carriage out to the Ocean House, south of the Cliff House, to hear the surf crash and sea lions roar. Standing ankle deep in the surf, he studied the wide expanse of the bay. In the distance fleecy white clouds massed and a flock of gulls blackened the mudflats to the north. Returning to Montgomery Street, he realized that the old-fashioned architecture that appeared so stately and handsome from a distance was really made up of "decaying, smoke-grimed, wooden houses." He temporarily left his good life and went back to Virginia City. He had mined a few months in Washoe, the popular name for Nevada, and on the Stanislaus River across the California border, and served a venue as a wandering printer before becoming a Virginia City reporter. He made plans to return to San Francisco in June and wrote Sawyer.

"When I had come back from a trip," Sawyer said, "Sam wrote, asking me to pay him a visit. Well, I was pretty well-heeled—had eight hundred dollars in my inside pocket and since there was nothing much doing in Frisco, I went." Sawyer rocked on the rugged stagecoach ride there, jolting over the mountain roads and feeling sick to his stomach. Warily he studied the chasms on both sides. San Francisco considered Virginia City its lucrative mining suburb, though it presented a tiresome and dangerous mountainous commute of two hundred miles across the Sierra. Wells Fargo's express stage rode with the stages of the Pioneer Stage Line from San Francisco to Virginia City. On Sawyer's journey to visit Twain, Hank Monk, "the Prince of Stage Divers," laid down a blue streak of profanity and "gid-daps" as he lashed his six-horse team through the Sierras. Monk wore the same battered hat and brown corduroy suit he had mended with copper rivets. He handled the ribbons over his teams' backs expertly, though to Sawyer it seemed in slow motion. The trip came complete with road agents. "No driver ever gave a stage robber away," Monk said with a shake of his shoulder-length hair. "He'd get shot if he even showed he recognized the bandit. Later, they would even introduce themselves and have a drink together." When Sawyer reached the silver town after a breakneck descent and put his feet on solid ground, he was glad he had accepted Twain's invitation. During his visit Sawyer provided the most popular origin of Sam's pen name: "It happened at Tom Peasley's Saloon near morning in Nevada City," he said. "Larry Ryan was tending bar."

"Give us two cocktails, Larry, and such cocktails as them were!" Twain sang out. "Twain used to take two horns, one right after the other, and take them on tick," Sawyer said, smacking his lips. "Um, I can taste them yet. Larry mixed 'em and handed 'em over the bar expecting Sam to ante up. Instead, he stood there, held up two fingers and, pointing to the slate, sang out: 'Larry, mark twain.' Larry, who carried a lump of chalk in his weskit pocket to keep score, added two drinks to Sam's account. The barkeep told Peasley of it in the morning, and Peasley thought it such a good joke that he told all the boys. And so it was, d'ye see, that he come to be called Twain." Twain continued the same practice at Johnny Doyle's, but this was one of Sawyer's stories that did not hold water. Twain had used the pen name nearly five months earlier and would use the signature "Mark" in a letter to his mother and sister on July 18.

Sawyer had an exciting few nights with his pal Sam and his friends. He drank and gambled with him and high rollers like Pat Lynch, Sam Davis, Holland of the *Enterprise,* Tom Fox, and Doc Cole. "In four days I found myself busted, without a cent," Sawyer said later. "Where under the sun he got it has always been a mystery, but that morning Sam walked in with two hundred dollars in his pocket, gave me fifty, and put me on the stage for California, saying that he guessed his Virginia City friends was too speedy for me."

After Sawyer left, Twain's luck went bad. He moved into a suite of rooms in the new White House Hotel on North B Street. When it caught fire on July 26, most of his possessions and all his mining stocks were burned to ash. In print, he fictionalized the reason for his sudden poverty. "All of sudden," he lamented, "out went the bottom and everything and everybody went to ruin and destruction! The bubble scarcely left a microscopic moisture behind it. I was an early beggar and a thorough one. My hoarded stocks were not worth the paper they were printed on. I threw them all away." The swagger had gone out of his step. In early September 1863, he dragged himself back to San Francisco and retired to the Lick House to nurse his wounds. He rallied his flagging spirits by submitting his first article to Colonel Lawrence's weekly *Golden Era* at 723 Montgomery Street. The proximity to 722 Montgomery put him back at the steam baths when he most needed them to ease a troublesome cold. He had not felt this poorly since July. Usually he was writing intently, legs tucked up to his chin, fitted into the window of his room. He had all kinds of vivid dreams but suffered most from recurrent nightmares of his brother's corpse. Some cards, some stories, some beer, good company—that was the thing. By the time he sought Sawyer out at the Bank Exchange saloon, he was ashen faced and trembling, having fallen into a bleak, almost suicidal depression, the one constant about his life. He saw the round-faced young man across the room and hailed him. Twain brightened immediately, sat down, and began to hold court.

"Sam was a dandy, he was," Sawyer said later. "He could drink more and talk more than any feller I ever seen. He'd set down and take a drink and then he'd begin to tell us some joke or another. And then when somebody'd buy him another drink, he'd keep her up all day. Once he got started he'd set there till morning telling yarns, provided someone would throw a bowl at him every few minutes."

Sawyer, a fair amateur psychologist, had recognized Twain's competitive nature from the first. After all, he had the same qualities in himself. Sawyer was almost his equal in talking but often had to throw in the towel. "He beat the record for lyin'—nobody was in the race with him there," Sawyer said, "though I myself was considered a pretty good disciple of Ananias [an early Christian who lied to God and died on the spot]. He never had a cent. His clothes were always ragged and he never had his hair cut or a shave in them days. I should say he hasn't had his hair cut since '60. I used to give him half my wages and then he'd borrow from the other half, but a jollier companion and better mate I would never want. He was a prince among men, you can bet, though I'll allow he was the darndest homeliest man I ever set eyes on, Sam was."

The next day Sawyer was fighting fire and Twain had to content himself with exchanging stories with Stahle in the basement cloud land. He left within the hour. He saw Sawyer the next time. It was a stormy day. Rain beat against the Montgomery Block, especially loud in the basement steam room. Nostalgically, Twain recalled for Sawyer and Stahle his own boyhood. "I remember the raging of the rain on that roof, summer nights," he said, leaning back contentedly in the waves of steam and feeling the sweat drip off his arms, "and how pleasant it was to lie and listen to it and enjoy the white splendor of the lightning and the majestic booming and crashing of the thunder." There was rarely thunder or lightning in San Francisco.

On January 31, 1864, Volunteer Billy Mulligan—angry, afraid, trigger finger itching, and a little insane—returned to San Francisco. Haunted by the fear that the vigilantes, who had sworn his death years earlier, were coming for him, he lost himself in extended drinking sprees. After the vigilantes deported him and the rest of Broderick's men during the San Francisco insurrection in 1856, he settled in New York City, where a newspaper described him as a "refined savage" and "a pugilist of the lowest sort." Within a year, he attempted to shoot the owner of a Manhattan gambling house, and after refusing to participate in a forgery conspiracy of his friend Senator Broderick's will, was sentenced to two years in Sing Sing Prison. Pardoned after three months, he returned to California. One night a saloonkeeper bludgeoned him with a champagne bottle and left him delusional. He recovered from his concussion and for several years was a familiar figure drinking brandy in the saloons and gambling dens of San Francisco. The *Sacramento Union* said of him, "No man was big enough to make him tamely submit to an insult offered either to himself, a friend or even a defenseless stranger. He was an active politician and trained with a class of men who in more recent years have been known as 'Stalwarts' or 'machine men'—those who pat up conventions and manipulate primary elections, but he was gentlemanly in his intercourse with his fellow men, exquisite in the matter of dress, and as brave a little man as ever walked. Those who knew him best have only good words to say of Billy Mulligan." The *Alta* said, "Mulligan was one of the best of his kind. Though considered a 'roach' he was never a robber." Yet Mulligan had grafted a fortune as tax collector for the San Francisco County treasurer.

On April 20, 1864, he challenged Tom Coleman to a duel for six o'clock the next morning. Their first shots fell short. With his second shot Mulligan broke the second finger of Coleman's right hand. Coleman's fourth shot went off prematurely. Mulligan's fifth shot hit the fleshy part of Coleman's thigh. Six days later, he was wounded again, this time as a bystander. Once, in less than a week, Mulligan was shot five times by three different men.

Meanwhile, Twain briefly returned to Nevada City, where he was warned he was liable to arrest for demanding a duel with rival reporter and editor James L. Laird. This news sent him rumbling back to San Francisco by a fast stage on May 29. "I left Nevada in 1864 to avoid a term penitentiary," Twain said proudly. Steve Gillis, news editor of the *Enterprise* and a close friend, and Joseph T. Goodman, proprietor of the paper, accompanied him. According to the *Gold Hill Evening News,* Nevada City was delighted to see Twain depart and mentioned his "idiosyncratic eccentricities of an erratic mind. . . . His face is black before the people of Washoe. The indignation aroused by his enormities has been too crushing to be borne by living man . . . in short he has vamoosed." Twain had no overcoat and huddled morose and shivering behind the stage driver during the long ride over the mountains from Virginia City to Carson. Carpenter & Hoog's stage was "a cradle on wheels." Twain advised an outside seat if you prepared for it "with two days sleep so you would not fall asleep on the box." He would have gone to sleep and plunged overboard if the driver of the Concord-type coach had not "enlivened the dreary hours with his conversation." Whenever Twain got to pitching in his direction, the cigar-chomping driver asked if he was asleep. Upon receiving a negative grunt, the driver related cheerful stories of passengers who had got to nodding by his side and fallen off and broken their necks on the narrow winding road. Cracking his whip over the lead horses, he said he could see those fellows now, "all jammed, bloody and quivering in death's agony," and urged his team at a furious speed into deep bends in the black road. Twain knew of a driver sound asleep on the box whose mules galloped unchecked at their usual breakneck speed along the dangerous route and arrived unharmed at the lower elevation. "I intended to go only a little way out on the Geiger Grade," Goodman said cheerfully, "but the company was too good and I kept clear on to San Francisco." The trio went the rest of the way by the Pioneer Line to Folsom and Sacramento. In San Francisco, Twain and Gillis settled into the Occidental Hotel. Twain had fallen in love with "the most cordial and sociable city in the Union. After the sagebrush and alkali deserts of Washoe, San Francisco was Paradise to me . . . the liveliest, heartiest community on our continent."

Around June 6, the two flat-busted writers began working on the *Morning Call,* a newspaper known as "the washerwoman's paper." Housed in a new brick building at 612 Commercial, the *Call,* a single sheet folded in half to create four printed pages, sold for a "bit" (twelve and a half cents) every day but Monday. Gillis labored during the day as a printing room compositor, while Twain, an unreliable and generally untruthful reporter, wore all the other hats for forty dollars per week. By ten o'clock each morning, the paper's sole reporter was at his desk gathering local gossip, and in his silk hat and frock-coated black suit, doing general assignment, rewriting and scanning the blotter at police court before moving on to the higher courts. Twain spent all his evenings at the six theaters where he stayed just long enough to gather enough information to write a review of the rapid-fire plays being produced every day. Coroner Sheldon held his inquests at night. He had to attend those. Afterward he returned to the *Call* to write up his copy for the 2:00 A.M. deadline, put the paper to bed, and then turned in. Every day Twain craved at least twenty-five licorice-flavored cigars, an amalgam of firecracker paper, sawdust, and "who knew what else," selling in bundles of one hundred for two dollars.

He made it a strict rule never to smoke more than one at a time and never while asleep.

"Sam and me was the greatest chums," Sawyer continued, "and Sam and me used to meet at the Blue Wing, kept by Dan Driscoll." The Blue Wing Saloon stood next to the Russ House, which, while only a year old, occupied the entire block on Montgomery between Pine and Bush streets. Gambler Charles Cora had been drinking there minutes before he murdered U.S. Marshal General William Richardson for an imagined slight against his whore, Belle Cora, and outraged all of San Francisco in 1856. "Many a night we'd sit there telling stories till the stars went out and the sun was staring down in our faces.

"Sam was workin' on the *Call* in those days." *Call* stories were not signed and few knew he worked there. "They'd send him out down at the paper to write something up and he'd go into the Blue Wing [or the Hays Saloon, the Cosmopolitan, the Capitol, or the Bank Exchange] and sit around telling stories and drinking all day." It was heaven. The rowdy saloons had "purer liquors, better segars, and prettier courtezans" than anyplace else. While Twain was at the Occidental, hotel bartender Jerry Thomas invented the first martini. "Then he'd go back to the office and write up something. Many times it was all wrong, but it was mighty entertaining, anyhow. Sam came near getting fired two or three times and then he'd brace up for a day or so and square himself with the fellers that run the paper." As the paper's only beat reporter, he raked the town from end to end, prowling the Police Court and the bleak line of cells beneath City Hall on Kearny and intimately inspecting the county prison on Broadway. Twain described the Police Court space as a twenty-four-by-forty-foot room blocked on all sides by brick walls. It is "the infernalest smelling den on earth," he reported. "Once you enter the Police Court, you get yourself saturated with the fearful combination of miraculous stenches that infect its atmosphere. . . . You cannot imagine what a horrible hole that Police Court is. If there is anything more absurd than the general average of Police Court testimony, we do not know what it is. Witnesses stand up here, every day, and swear to the most extravagant propositions with an easy indifference to consequences in the next world that is altogether refreshing." The evening of July 7, Twain, bones aching and fingers ink stained, finished up at the odoriferous booking desk with little to write. The previous night Coroner Sheldon had held an inquest into the death of John McGowan, an ex-cabdriver shot to death in a cellar saloon by a soldier named John Barrett. As Twain deciphered his notes (he made his lowercase *e*'s like uppercase *E*'s), he steeled himself to make the theater rounds.

At the steam baths the next day, he was miserable with a cold, sneezing and snuffling. Sawyer entered, smoked black and fire scorched, returning from Liberty Hose's engine house, a two-story frame building on the east side of Fourth Street at number 24. He looked as beat as Twain felt. As they played cards, Twain admitted how much he loathed his job at the *Call* and detested its editor, George Barnes, even more. He wanted to quit, but because of considerable debt, had vowed to keep dragging himself in to work and be pleasant to Barnes. "It was awful drudgery for a lazy man," he explained, "and I was born lazy. I raked the town from end to end and if there were no fires to report, I started some." There was only one perk. "Reporting is the best school in the world to get a knowledge of human beings, human nature, and human ways. No other occupation brings a man into such familiar sociable relations with all grades and classes of people."

The *Call*'s offices were on the second floor of the United States Mint Annex. One floor above, author Bret Harte, a former Wells Fargo station messenger, worked as a secretary to the superintendent of the Mint. His literary patrons, Jessie Benton Fremont and Unitarian clergyman Thomas Starr King, had introduced him to Robert B. Swain, superintendent of the local U.S. Mint. As Swain's private secretary, a nontaxing administrative post, Harte received $200 a month and had little to do but play croquet and write. Not so for Twain, whose long hours at the *Call* had grown so tedious that he gladly took a $15 salary cut to work in the daylight hours. Occasionally he tramped upstairs to pass the time with Harte, who, with his groomed sideburns, curly dark hair, and white eyes, dressed fashionably in plaid trousers and velveteen coats. Harte judged Twain's dress "careless," his manner supremely indifferent to his surroundings, and admired his "slow, rather satirical drawl which was in itself irresistible." "My sole occupation now, Bret," Twain said, lazily rolling his head back as if napping, "is avoiding acquaintances." He had become adept at slinking down alleys to outwit his creditors, going out only at night with Gillis, or drinking at the Blue Wing with Sawyer and fingering his last dime till it was worn thin. "I slunk from back street to back street, I slunk away from approaching faces that looked familiar. I slunk to my meals . . . I slunk to my bed. I felt meaner and lowlier and more despicable than the worms." The *Golden Era* published Harte's short stories, so Twain listened attentively as the little man patiently "trimmed, trained and schooled" him and changed him "from an awkward writer of coarse grotesqueness, to writer of paragraphs and chapters that have found a certain favor in the eyes of even some of the very decentest people in the land."

CHAPTER ELEVEN

The Fire Girl

Out by the ocean a vivacious young woman raced her team of horses down an almost perpendicular bluff above the Cliff House. She had run her yellow-wheeled, four-horse rockaway carriage to Ocean Beach at top speed, challenging her friends to follow her twists, turns, and breakneck shortcuts and daring a suitor to follow her straight down the precipice. He rolled and crashed at the bottom but survived. The extraordinary Lillie Hitchcock wore trousers, a gun, and holster; rode bareback; and once dressed as a boy to win a race. An avid hunter and excellent rifle shot, she scored medals for her marksmanship, beating out the keen-eyed sharpshooters of Broderick One, the best shots in California. She sailed, fished, swam, and played poker better than most men and could outbox many. She smoked cigars, drank Kentucky bourbon, made late-night visits to men-only clubs, took in a cockfight near Washerwoman's Lagoon, and placed bets at Pioneer Park, winning almost every time. Whenever she dyed her hair and grew bored with the new color, she shaved her head and wore black or red wigs until her hair grew back.

Although Lillie did not resemble Twain's ideal woman, they were attracted to each other. He first met her at the Occidental, with its ankle-deep carpets, where the Hitchcocks took a suite of rooms. When the Civil War broke out, her father, Dr. Charles Hitchcock, a pro-Union West Point surgeon and son of a wealthy Southern family, became fearful of

Bret Harte

reprisals (they had family property in the South). Ironically, during the Mexican War, he had saved the leg of Colonel Jefferson Davis through a magnificent piece of surgery. Hitchcock had resigned his army commission to tend the sick in San Francisco as the Pacific coast medical director. In 1860 he insisted that Martha and Lillie, who shared her mother's Southern leanings, leave the United States. When Lillie left for Paris, the men of Five saw her off at the dock. "Goodbye, Dear Number Five. I'll die game," she told them. At the court of Napoléon III, where she was a favorite for her rebellious and rambunctious ways, she translated Confederate reports into French and smuggled secret documents for the rebel cause. In 1862 she became the "lady correspondent" of the *San Francisco Evening Bulletin*. Her detailed "Letter from Paris" became an anticipated weekly feature in the city. On October 3, 1863, Lillie, now twenty years old, returned to San Francisco to wild applause. At the pier, Five gave her a gold fire helmet with a diamond set in its shield, a gold badge, and an honorary certificate of full-fledged membership. Lillie had become the first and only woman member of a U.S. fire department. Whenever she attended their annual banquet, she wore a red woolen blouse over a black silk skirt, a white mackintosh, and a large-buckled firefighter's belt with the number 5 in imitation of the volunteers' uniform. When she wore her exquisite Paris gowns, her mother hid the number 5 among the ruffles and embroidered all of her undergarments with 5s. At parties Lillie waved fans with Fives on them, even signed her name "Lillie Hitchcock 5." In all parades and festivities she rode next to the driver on top of Engine Five, surrounded by flowers, flags. Five's sweetheart was so vivacious and charming, San Francisco loved her. "Everybody loves Miss Lil," it was said of her. "She has 'to-wardliness.'" "Just as generous and warmhearted girl as you ever saw," Twain wrote. "And her mother is such a rare gem of a woman. The family are old, old friends of mine and I think ever so much of them. That girl, many and many and many a time, has waited till nearly noon to breakfast with me, and when we all lived at the Occidental Hotel and I was on a morning paper and could not go to bed till two or three. She is a brilliant talker. They live half of every year in Paris. It always seemed funny to me that she and I could be friends, but we were—I suppose because under all her wild foolery, that warm heart of hers would always show. I thought of her as stored to the eyelids with energy and enthusiasm, her mind, hands, feet, and body in a state of tireless activity, not unlike mine."

Bret Harte had met Lillie nine years earlier while trying to eke out a living writing poetry. Martha Hitchcock, who found him an endlessly fascinating conversationalist, entrusted the penniless writer to teach her and her daughter conversational writing. Infatuated, he dined with them in sumptuous restaurants while his own family endured a meager life. Soon Martha, one of his strongest benefactors, was writing so well she was being published in the *Golden Era* as often as he. Lillie showed promise, too. Harte drew Twain into the enclave of the local Southern aristocracy through Martha, who found in Twain and Harte the answer to improving Lillie's journalistic style. "An earlier flippant tone in her writings disappeared," Lillie's biographer Helen Holdredge wrote, "cheery praise from the editor of the *Bulletin,* who said her articles were 'bright and sparkling.'" Twain and Harte often joined Martha and her daughter for dinner. Lillie, rebellious and possessed of boundless energy, interested Twain for another reason. In this irrepressible girl, so full of brightness and fun, he found the grist of a first novel, which he called *Shirley Tempest.* Why," Twain wondered, "had her fortunes become inextricably intertwined with those of Knickerbocker Five?" It took Sawyer to explain how Five's volunteer John Boynton had saved her from a burning building.

Meanwhile, Twain and Gillis moved into a succession of hotels, private homes, and rooming houses, each of descending value. Twain unwound at the baths, in the bars, and sometimes in his room. On July 12, as he and Gillis were carrying on with some "roughs," the French landlady ordered her husband upstairs to complain. Gillis reacted by leveling a pistol at him and telling him, "Take your head out of the door because I want to shoot in that direction. Get scarce!" "Oh, I never saw such creatures," the landlady fumed. "One of them always went to bed at dark and got up at sunrise, and the other went to bed at sunrise and got up at dark. . . . They used to bring loads of beer bottles up at midnight, and get drunk, and shout and throw their empties out of the window at the Chinamen below: You'd hear them count 'One—two—three—fire!' . . . They always had women running to their room—sometimes in broad daylight—bless you, THEY didn't care. They had no respect for God, man or the devil!"

"When Sam's father died," Twain's mother said, "which occurred when Sam was eleven years of age, I thought that then, if ever, was the proper time to make a lasting impression on the boy and work a change in him, so I took him by the hand and went with him into the room where the coffin was in that his father lay, and with it between Sam and me I said to him in this presence I had some serious requests to make of him, and I knew his word once given was never broken. For Sam never told a falsehood. He turned his streaming eyes upon me and cried out, 'Oh, mother, I will do anything, anything you ask of me except go to school. I can't do that!' . . . That was the very request I was going to make. . . . [Then] I asked him if he would promise on the Bible not to touch intoxicating liquors, nor swear, and he said: 'Yes, mother I will.' He repeated the words after me with my hand and his clasped on the Holy Book, and I believe he kept that promise."

"I am not adverse to social drinking," Twain, one of the great drinkers in San Francisco, said modestly. On July 15, he and Gillis moved for the fourth time. "Yes, sir, they are gone," said the French landlady, "and the good God was kind to me when He sent them away!" Gillis went to stay with his younger brother on Brannan Street between Seventh and Eighth streets. Their father, Angus, a one-eyed war vet of William Walker's filibustering expedition to Nicaragua, had a "dry, unsmiling way" of recounting a funny story that Twain enjoyed. Twain moved to 32 Minna Street, one of the narrow little alleys paralleling Market Street between Mission and Howard streets. Rows of frame cottages with gardens were set close to sidewalks on what he called the "quiet little street." He enjoyed the babble of many languages, the smell of factory and gashouse smoke, and the fragrance of the bakery down the street. A week later, on July 22, a quake made his new lodgings "waltz from side to side with a quick motion" like the "suggestive of sifting corn meal through a sieve; afterward it rocked grandly to and fro like a prodigious cradle."

Sawyer lived a scant three blocks away just off the same quiet, narrow street at the southwest corner of Mary Street, number 18, near Fifth Street. He had fallen in love with young Mary Bridget. Her sparkling eyes, lilting smile, and brunette curls had enraptured him. After they were married, the couple moved into a two-story at 935 Mission Street. Sawyer set up housekeeping on the top floor while he converted the ground floor into a saloon.

By the afternoon of July 25, Twain was steaming and playing a few hands of poker, pleased that Sawyer was more himself again. His spirits had been lifted by fighting a fire that had broken out at 2:00 A.M. in the Arcade Restaurant on Market between Third and Fourth. His nearby Liberty Hose Company had gotten to the blaze just as it spread to the Apollo Baths and Saloon. "We saved them!" Sawyer said. A grin lit up his face, then faded. Antonio Silva, the restaurant owner, and his cooks, William Bell and John Marx, had been sleeping inside and died in the flames before they reached the scene. Sawyer fought fire the rest of the summer. September, the hottest month, began with the burning of the Winfield Scott Saloon at the corner of Howard and Stewart. Sawyer talked about February 1850, when he first set foot in San Francisco. The city was still rebuilding after the city-destroying Christmas Eve fire. Twain puffed on his Wheeler's long nine, its smoke mingling with clouds of steam and enveloping both men. Contented, he paid strict attention as Sawyer told him of the Lightkeeper and the six great fires. In the murk, Twain's mind filled with exciting ideas. He circled in clouds of steam, cracking his towel and endlessly talking, talking, talking. Finally he stopped. He still had to make the rounds of the courts. He took a cold plunge, dressed, and got back to the *Call* while Sawyer returned to his engine house to prepare for any alarms. As foreman, a post he had worked his way up to after fourteen years fighting fire as a torch boy and volunteer at various houses, he was always needed if only to oversee maintenance of their ancient manual pumper. Today he was thinking about startling new developments in firefighting in the East. Such new technology threatened to do away with the volunteers.

Nearby at Big Six, Big George Hossefross was doing all he could to bring the new engines to San Francisco. Over at Social Three, so was former New York volunteer David D. Hayes, inventor of the Hayes truck. He ordered five new 1863 Amoskeag steamers. The first arrived just as a grocery store caught fire in the wholesale district. Hayes and his men scrambled to their new steam engine and dragged it into the street. Their stoker, Godfrey Fisher, laid the boiler fire with dry shavings, well-tarred wood, and knobs of coal, but hesitated starting the boiler. Leaks might occur if he started the engine too suddenly and with too much steam. Sparks from the engine's furnace might cause secondary fires as they rumbled to the scene. An unsecured hose leaking at the joints could draw in air or suck up stones that might jam the valves or crack the pistons. Condensed water could collect in the cylinder. Ten minutes from the fire, Fisher wiped the sweat from his brow and, taking a match and a pint of camphine, ignited the shavings. The coals began to glow. As the engine rattled along, he heard the boiler's gratifying hiss and gurgle but worried whether he had enough fuel to keep the fire going. Social Three reached the scene at the same time as a manual pumper from a competing company. Fisher flung wide the valves and to his relief Three's pumper effortlessly threw four streams of water to the two thrown by the rival hand engine and their sweating volunteers. As the boiler began to cool, Fisher looked around frantically for more fuel. At last his eyes rested on the burning grocery store. Throwing a box of hams into the firebox, he kept the boiler to a hundred degrees and extinguished the blaze. Steam had won its first West Coast victory against hand pumping.

At once a harsh rivalry developed between the traditional manual pumpers and the newfangled "smoke bottle" steam engines. The hand pumpers felt steam heralded a loss of prestige and romance. "Why the machine does all the work!" they sniffed. "Boys," replied Sawyer—as a veteran fireman and cofounder of Liberty Hose, his words carried weight—"the towns are gettin' too big for the crude methods we've been using. These modern, efficient machines will give your outfits a chance to put out fires." The hand pumpers replied that human brawn was more effective, and other companies would have to be convinced. To decide, a number of public trials reminiscent of John Henry's steel-driving contest against a machine were scheduled during 1864. At first the more seasoned, disciplined veterans with their manual machines prevailed, beating their challengers to fires, extinguishing them first, and disgorging longer streams of water. But the men soon exhausted themselves pumping the brakes while steam-driven pumps kept going. Worse for the old-timers, the new steam machines required a new kind of volunteer and only fourteen men instead of the sixty needed for a manual pumper. Fewer well-trained professionals made more effective firefighters and the complex new machines demanded skilled mechanics, not rough street brawlers. Because no single unit could afford to maintain a steam machine, all the companies would have to contribute to its upkeep. Ultimately, this would lead to consolidation of departments, municipal financing of the firefighters, and the end of the volunteers and their wild and romantic ways.

At 10:00 A.M. on September 7, Twain's memories of his brother Henry, scalded to death onboard a steamship, were reawakened by a story he had to cover for the *Call*. "Terrible Calamity," he scrawled with a trembling hand. "Explosion of the steamer *Washoe*'s boilers—supposed killed, one hundred." The detonation occurred just above Hog's Back, ten miles above Rio Vista on the *Washoe*'s up trip. A rusted boiler, at twenty-five pounds pressure with two cocks of solid water, collapsed a flue, exploded, shattered the upper works of the aft section, and set the *Washoe* afire in three places. When he closed his eyes that night, his slender brother Henry's image floated before him, alive again in clouds of steam. Smoking until dawn, he went sleepless.

The next day or two he perched in his window seat to work. Outside, the rain had let up and evening was falling. He tried again to work on his book about Lillie, whom he had renamed Rachel. In this draft the fire department made Rachel an honorary member with an official belt and helmet, just as Knickerbocker Five had made Lillie a member. "In another dramatic scene," he reported, "in the midst of smoke billows and leaping flames, I showed her climbing over the roof of a house to rescue its inhabitants." In another draft, he named her Rachel "Hellfire" Hotchkiss and set the action in Dawson's Landing. He portrayed her galloping bareback on her black horse to rescue a boy named Oscar Carpenter (based on his brother Orion) stranded on a cake of ice in the Mississippi. He could not get the character to work and abandoned his firegirl book for good. As he lolled in Stahle's steam room, feeling a continuous flow of hot, dry air around him, he again contemplated his first novel. The Chinese as a subject had crossed his mind. He felt guilty about his earlier harsh treatment of them. Months earlier he had considered basing a character on his beloved brother, Henry, then discounted it. Twain splashed his face with water in the hot room to cool down, but his mind was already aflame with ideas.

On September 28, Sawyer and Twain went on a momentous bender. "Me and Jack Mannix, who was afterwards bailiff in Judge Levi's court, was walkin' down Montgomery Street," Sawyer recalled in an interview. John E. Mannix lived at 829 Mission Street, near Fifth Street close to Sawyer at 935 Mission Street. "We drifted into the Capitol saloon [at 220 Mongomery Street] where the Mills building now stands and Mark caught sight of us from a window across the street in the Russ House."

"Tom," Twain cried, "up here. Wait for me. I'll be right down."

As Sawyer waited, he wondered what Twain was doing at the Russ House, because he was presently lodging in a private family home and preparing to take rooms farther along Minna Street to within two blocks of Sawyer's. It turned out that Twain's close buddy and comrade for two years, Steve Gillis, was getting hitched to Emeline Russ, a pretty young woman worth $130,000 in her own right and the daughter of the late Christian Russ, who had owned the most real estate in San Francisco. Twain considered Emeline a "good sensible girl" who would make Steve an excellent wife. As far as marriage for himself, Twain was "resolved on that or suicide—perhaps." The wedding was set for October 24 and he was going to stand up for his friend at the nuptials as "chief mourner" and take a "bridal tour of a week's duration."

"Well, as soon as he seen us he come down," Sawyer continued, "we all went in [to the Capitol Saloon] and had a few jolts together." The bartender who prepared their drinks was dressed as most of his brethren in striped trousers and a brocaded waistcoat studded with a diamond. The brandy vanished. "The result was, to be plain with you, we got full. Mark was as much sprung as I was, and in a short time we owned the City, cobblestones and all." Laughing and singing, they made the rounds of the Montgomery Street saloons, growing more expansive as they spent most of the night drinking brandy at the Blue Wing and the Capitol Saloon. "Toward mornin' Mark sobered up a bit and we all got to tellin' yarns," Sawyer said. "I dished up a few, Mark dished up a few, but

Mannix was speechless." Twain had never heard anything before like Sawyer's stories of an entire city waiting to be burned and listened with fascination. Somewhere along the line, they lost Mannix. The sun was up by the time Sawyer and Twain called it a night.

"The next day I met Mark down by the old *Call* office. He walks up to me and puts both hands on my shoulders. 'Tom,' he says, 'I'm going to write a book about a boy and the kind I have in mind was just about the toughest boy in the world. Tom, he was just such a boy as you must have been. . . . How many copies will you take, Tom, half cash?"

Sawyer did not take him seriously. He got to the firehouse on Fourth Street and tried to sleep off his hangover in a back room. Twain went home, slept, and then wrote his sister about the Gillis nuptials. "As soon as this wedding business is over," he wrote, "I believe I will send you the files, & begin on my book (mind you this is a secret and must not be mentioned)." He had already spoken of his ambitious literary plan to write a novel to his brother Orion, cautioning him to say nothing of it. Twain told him he would like to begin right away and asked him to send him his Nevada "files" and any scrapbooks he had kept of his newspaper articles. Meanwhile, Gillis's love affair, house-building plans, wedding arrangements, and a dozen other events kept Twain so busy it would be six years before he got back to his secret project. In the meantime, things went terribly wrong for Gillis: Emeline Russ did not marry him. Instead she married Frederick Gutzkow on December 28, 1867. On the rebound, Gillis married Kate Robinson.

In the steam room Twain and Sawyer discussed Yankee Sullivan, whom Sawyer had known. Everyone was aware of Twain's sojourn as a river pilot. Few knew of his aspirations to be a boxer. He had once hired the best boxing coaches, but they had never seen any man of such little account as a boxer as Twain. Once, he entered the ring in a loose woolen shirt that concealed his muscular deficiencies, and when his sparring partner gave him a light slap under the ear, Twain threw a double somersault, fell on the back of his neck, and stretched full length on the canvas. "Shall I send for a doctor for you?" Denis McCarthy asked. "Send for an undertaker," Twain gasped.

In October some Irish hoodlums stoning a Chinese laundryman awakened Twain's long-slumbering moral conscience and he wrote the only article he mustered any real enthusiasm for in the four months he had been at the *Call*. On October 10, he eagerly scanned the morning edition. His piece was not there. He found the metal type buried under some condemned matter on the standing galley in the composing room. Gillis said Barnes had pulled the story. Twain stormed into his cubicle. "What's this about!" he thundered. Barnes fixed him with a cold eye and asked, "Who are the *Call's* readers?" "The Irish working class, I guess." "Yes, the Irish," editor George Barnes said. "The *Call* is the paper of the poor. The *Call* gathers its livelihood from the poor and therefore must respect their prejudices or perish. The Irish are the poor . . . and they hate the Chinamen." He paused. "Do you know what I think of you as a local reporter? You're out of your element. I believe you are unsuited to it. Besides, you're obviously capable of greater things in literature." "You mean to say that I don't suit you." "That's exactly what I mean." The mild firing so frightened Twain that he referred to his discharge throughout his lifetime and contemplated revenge. In 1906 he said that the San Francisco earthquake and fire had been God's retribution on the *Call* for his firing.

That October, Sawyer and his men were exceptionally busy. The entire city seemed ready to burst into flame again. On October 18, a Brannan Street stable was destroyed and Peter Reynolds was burned to death in the straw among the rearing horses. The next day Maurice Doyle's house on Jones Street caught fire. Liberty Hose got their new four-wheel hose carriage to the scene immediately, but two children were lost. Sawyer returned slowly to his engine house, vowing to do better. Fresh from battling another fire, he entered the steam room with a towel around his waist. He and Twain talked over cards and afterward at the Blue Wing over drinks. Sawyer regaled him with his adventures fighting black fire, the worst kind; all the bad things come together at once. Twain listened attentively. Sawyer's speaking voice was melodic and he had a beautiful singing voice. He sang Irish ballads at the bar for the rest of the night.

Again Twain tried to tackle his first novel and again it was Steve Gillis who derailed him. On December 4, Gillis got into trouble with the San Francisco police for whipping a bullying bartender. Twain, who was in trouble with the cops, too, hustled down to the smelly courtroom and signed a $500 straw bond for Gillis. Sawyer was not surprised that the police were out to get Twain. "He and I used to play pranks," he said in an interview with the *Call*. "And the narrow escapes we had from the police . . ." He rolled his eyes. "I am sober enough to tell it, I guess. It was great sport in those days to bait the police. We just escaped getting locked up many a night. Guess Sam hasn't forgotten how we used to go around to the dance halls and scatter cayenne pepper on the seats and get all the girls crying."

Twain intended to even the score with the police by writing some scathing critiques when he and Gillis returned from the played-out goldfields of the Sierra Nevada and Tuolumne, one hundred miles east of San Francisco. He still had $300 in his pocket from the sale of his last two shares of plummeting Hale and Norcross silver stock. "The Hale & Norcross officers decide to sink a shaft," the *Call* reported that week (December 4, 1851), telling how their shareholders were being victimized. "They levy $40,000. Next month they have a mighty good notion to go lower, and they levy a $20,000 assessment. . . . Thus it goes on for months and months, but the Hale & Norcross sends us no bullion."

By January 1865, they were in Angel's Camp in Calaveras County linking up with Steve's brothers, Jim and William, who were pocket miners on the hill. Steve returned to Virginia City and left Twain with them. It was the rainy season and his most frequent journal entries were "rain," "beans," and "dishwater." Twain, trapped indoors hearing the recycled tales of the miners, listened to pocket miner Ben Coon's recitation about a celebrated jumping frog, a story first mined by the Greeks two thousand years earlier. He made an entry: "Coleman with his jumping frog—bet stranger $50—stranger had no frog, & C got him one—in the meantime stranger filled C's frog full of shot & he couldn't jump—the stranger's frog won." He turned the tale into a story. On January 20, he wrote his mother and sister he longed to be back piloting up and down the river again. "Verily, all is vanity and little worth—save piloting. To think that after writing many an article a man might be excused for thinking tolerable good, those New York people should single out a villainous sketch to complement [*sic*] me on!—'Jim Smiley & His Jumping Frog,' a squib which would never have been written but to please Artemus Ward."

In late February, Twain, blue with cold, returned to San Francisco. No Occidental Hotel for him this time, only the inexpensive family rooming house managed by Margaret Gillis at 44 Minna Street. He sometimes saw Sawyer, helmet tucked under his arm, dashing to Liberty Hose's firehouse on the east side of Fourth Street about four blocks from the boardinghouse. His company of twenty-four smoke eaters often awakened Twain as they responded to a blaze, but returned quietly on one night, slinking back to the engine house after having lost more lives. Sawyer's men needed better equipment.

In March, a week after her return from another trip to Paris, Lillie joined her "Dear Number Five" at a blaze and rode with the engine driver. "There's Lillie. There she is!" shouted spectators as she passed. The fire lasted all night. When it was over, she treated her handsome men in their tight black leggings to a feast at the little two-story Ivy Green Restaurant. "The City had not been the same without Lillie," wrote the *Call*. Now she was the belle of San Francisco society with a considerable circle of suitors (she had already been engaged fifteen times). Her mother said that in Paris, Lillie was "knee-deep in men." With her "brilliant accomplishments and personal graces," a contemporary reported, "she would entertain at one time a circle of twenty gentlemen." She had never seen Lillie enter a ballroom. "I would see a crowd of men walking into the room and another following; then you knew Lillie Hitchcock was in the center." The Hitchcocks moved to the new Cosmopolitan Hotel modeled in the French style with a château roof, iron fencing on the topmost story, and frescoed rooms filled with carved rosewood furniture. In Lillie's room crimson velvet drapes encircled a huge wardrobe for her Paris gowns. Her mother forced a maid on her, the better to keep an eye on Lillie's rebellious ways. In retaliation Lillie began singing outrageous and filthy songs from her balcony to medical students passing below. She invited Twain to dinner with her mother to brighten his spirits and her mother invited Harte to brighten hers. All four headed to the Cosmopolitan Restaurant.

Chief Davey "the Prince of Rogues" Scannell, who lived nearby in room 11 of a hotel on the northeast corner of Montgomery and Jackson, was eating one of his marathon dinners there. With age his lean face had grown plump and pink, but in his younger years he had been fair, tall, straight, and compact of frame, with light blue eyes and a droopy blond mustache and goatee. "[He had] solid powerful arms and legs like a horse," Big Six torch boy Charlie Robinson, one of the great marine artists of San Francisco Bay, described him: "His head rose large and full in the back like General Grant's, showing great bravery and determination. He was lacking in the great thought processes of the General, as indicated in the lessened prominence of the forehead. And now I will tell you something of Scannell that I have never known of any other human being in the world. The first thing on coming down in the morning, he would take a dinner goblet of half-absinthe and half-whiskey. I have seen him often at the Commercial bar. How much is a dinner goblet? Just measure one out and see. You should have seen him in the early

'50s. He was a dandy, a wit and a municipal character in an age of notable individualists . . . and everybody's darling."

Scannell still looked dashing but had not changed his diet since 1850. He scanned the Cosmopolitan menu listing wild game and fowl of every variety. The surrounding hills offered elk, deer, turtle, hare, antelope, and beef. He ran his finger along the list—oxtail soup, baked trout with anchovy sauce—and came to rest, then went on, searching . . . roast stuffed lamb, roast pork with applesauce, baked mutton with caper sauce, corned beef and cabbage. A pause. He licked his lips. He liked them all. Scannell's finger was moving to the next page when a friend pointed out Lillie, Martha, Twain, and Harte sauntering in the door and sitting down at a table. Scannell did not look up, only lifted the menu to cover his face. "Why there's Miss Lil, our lady fireman," his friend exclaimed, grasping his arm. "You don't need to tell me who she is!" Scannell snapped and slapped the menu down. He made a practice of never mentioning Lillie in his many newspaper interviews. His head was by now inflated to immense proportions. Across the dining room, Twain saw him and waved, chuckling and calling out his name loudly. "The Chief does look younger than his years," Harte said. In spite of his gluttonous past, he still cut a fine figure in his pure white foreman's coat, helmet ornamented with gold and silver lettering, and bright silver trumpet slung over his shoulder. Right now his speaking tube hung on the back of his diner chair.

An inspiring leader, Scannell managed his men skillfully and they admired his reckless courage. He had, while fighting fire, broken his arm three times, cracked two ribs, and fractured his collarbone. When Scannell served at Broderick One, the air was always blue with his oaths. He was prone to more cussing than all One's Bully B'hoys combined. Broderick had explained away Davey's profanity as "merely his rough manner of expression when moved." Scannell had come west to fight with Colonel Jonathan Stevenson's regiment during the Mexican War and stormed the heights of Chalpultepec shouting, "Go in there, boys." As a war hero, he reached San Francisco onboard the *Gold Hunter*. Scannell had heard Lillie was not going to run with Five anymore. Her decision had puzzled her parents, who believed the firehouse to be the most important thing in her life. Scannell was delighted, though, and bent to his food with renewed vigor. His fork flashed in the candlelight. "Naturally she has to suffer the penalties," he said as if she were being punished. "Lillie has to pay her fines for being absent."

The morning of the May firemen's parade, the harbor was trimmed with flags. At daybreak fire bells began to ring. Thirteen guns in the Square saluted. Firehouses swung open. Engines were pushed and dragged to California Street by men in skintight breeches and high boots. As Scannell donned his white helmet and slicker, he was perturbed. Any firefighter in town who eclipsed his own popularity always inflamed him. The most popular volunteers in town were Curly Jack Carroll of Five, a fine singer who now owned a barbershop and was another of Lillie's favorite firemen, and Crooked Con Mooney and Cockeyed Frank Atkinson of Number Ten. "The most romantic rival of Scannell was Sawyer of Liberty Hose," Helen Holdredge wrote. This day, though, the celebrated smoke eater, whose past was so romantic and future so bright, was not the star. That was Lillie, resplendent in her red shirt, black skirt, a parade helmet with her initials, and a formal parade belt from the Veteran Firemen's Association. Scannell was vexed that she would ride Five's flower-bedecked engine after resolving to no longer fight fire. It seemed dishonest. Lillie climbed over the oversize front wheels and confidently took her place atop the engine's wash box amid wreaths, garlands, and bouquets of flowers. Seven years earlier she had ridden on top of the same first-class, hand-pumped $5,000 engine. Five's engine had two ten-inch cylinders, the longest pumping bars ever built on a side-stroke machine, and in full operation, powered by a pumping crew of sixty, it could throw a stream of water more than 250 feet. Lillie waved. The yells of "Tiger, Tiger!" in return were deafening. As the roar of cheers and hand clapping for Lillie rose, Scannell sank lower in his seat, his mouth a thin line. Twain, in the crowd of cheering San Franciscans, studied the petite Lillie, smiled, and went to look for Sawyer.

CHAPTER TWELVE

Let Us Build a City

Peter Donahue, owner of the Union Iron Works, south of Market, had heard about the new, improved steam fire engines from New York, Philadelphia, and Baltimore. He enumerated Moses Latta and Abel Shawk's Uncle Joe Ross, a 22,000-pound steam horse-drawn wagon, the Old Rock; Hunsworth, Eakins & Co.'s Independent; and Reaney & Naafie's Mechanic, the Hibernia, and the Good Intent, which had taken part in the Philadelphia steam engine trials of 1859. Lee & Larned exhibited their Elephant, the first practical mobile steam fire engine, at the International Exhibition at London's Hyde Park and afterward presented to Manhattan Engine Company Eight. Donahue decided to buy his own steam engine. The High-toned Twelve learned of his mission and ordered their own steam engine shipped by way of the Isthmus. Simultaneously Big Six foreman George Hossefross dispatched his own order by Pony Express to have a steamer quickly sent around the Horn. Big George bet $500 with Twelve's foreman that Six would have a steamer in their engine house before Twelve hauled theirs from the ship's hold. He won, but his express freight charges equaled exactly the amount of his winnings.

On July 3, Billy Mulligan was arrested for assault with a knife against Walter McGairy in a Clay Street cellar. Three nights later, two veteran firefighters, Con Mooney and Jack McNabb, saw him throwing money around Ten Engine House on Kearny Street. "He's suffering

from delirium tremens," McNabb realized. At 1:30 A.M., they fetched a
dose of valerian to steady his nerves. He pushed aside the bottle and
rushed out into the street to beg the police to lock him in a cell for his
own protection. "They are after me," he cried. "I feel like I'm going to die
tonight." Released in the late morning, he bought a gun at a pawnbro-
ker's shop. The next day Sawyer heard that brewer Tony Durkin had
fallen under Number Two's engine while running to a fire and crushed
his arm so badly it had to be amputated. Sawyer himself was prone to
accidents. On July 7, Mulligan barricaded himself in his San Francisco
Hotel room and began sniping from his second-story window at passing
pedestrians below. Across the street on the corner of Dupont and Clay,
a Chinese laundryman ducked as a bullet crashed through his window.
McNabb went to calm Mulligan. Carrying another glass of valerian, he
knocked gently on his friend's door. Believing McNabb to be one of the
vigilantes come to deport him again, Billy shot twice through the door.
One ball hit McNabb in his right breast near the armpit. He tumbled

downstairs and was dead within a half hour. Next, Con Mooney tried to reason with Billy. "Con, if you come another step," Mulligan said, cracking the door, "I'll shoot you." Mooney backed down the stairs and went for help.

Mulligan returned to his window and continued firing at the second-story houses across the street. The police surrounded the hotel just as Eureka Hose Number Four foreman John Hart was passing on his way to a neighboring engine house to return a borrowed trumpet. Mulligan was aiming at the cops but instead gunned down Hart with a single shot to the heart, killing him on the spot. Shortly after 4:00 P.M. he climbed out on the balcony, pistol in hand, and took a turn along the ledge on the Dupont Street side as if out for a stroll. He reentered the hotel by climbing through a window on the upper Clay Street side overlooking the Square. Police distracted him with a gunnysack and straw dummy they swung in front of Billy's window. Mulligan opened the swinging window sash and leaned out to shoot "the man." As his attention wavered, police marksman Mortimer "Johnny" Hopkins, in a room directly across the street, took a bead and fired. A single shot from his mini rifle tore through the pane and brought Billy down for good. Hopkins, the partner of Crescent Ten's "Mountain Buck" McGreevy, was another friend of Sawyer's and a special policeman, as he had been. "Billy Mulligan was a desperate man," a reporter said, "but not as black as he has been painted. His life, however, is to be regarded far more as a warning than as an example in any, and he met his fate as most of his kind meet their fate—with his boots on. It is a bad way to die."

When Twain visited his friend Dr. Stephen Harris, the coroner, he saw two policemen lay a corpse on a board. He lifted the bloodstained sheet and saw the body of a short man in a tidy black suit with a shot in the forehead. Huge muttonchop whiskers surrounded a savage, pinched face. He had been shot in the late afternoon after inexplicably firing on a number of citizens and killing two firemen and one of his close friends. Harris told him the deceased was Billy Mulligan, a famous gunfighter, a dangerous man in any segment of life, and an old firefighting friend of Sawyer's. Twain listed Billy Mulligan among such "long-tailed heroes of the revolver" as Sam Brown, Pock Marked Jake, El Dorado Johnny, Sugarfoot Mike, Six-fingered Pete, and Jack McNabb. More than a dozen years earlier, he and fifty or sixty other misfits had saved San Francisco. In return most had been deported or murdered. "Why," Twain wondered, "had these flawed heroes come to such inglorious ends?"

On May 31, 1856, Yankee Sullivan had awakened bewildered, shivering, and clad only in pantaloons and a shirt. From his cot he could see the windows where the vigilantes had hanged ex-fireman James Casey for shooting down King of William in front of Stahle's steam baths. A large cell in the northwest corner held Rube Maloney and adjoined Yankee's cell, the largest, the eighth, for important prisoners. Around the center of the west wall a platform had been erected across the passageway to the Executive Committee rooms. Inside were several long tables, cases filled with papers, and the president's seat at the north wall. Behind was a rack filled with muskets. Yankee shrieked for his jailer. "Could I have a drink of water," he said. "I just had a terrible nightmare. I thought I had been condemned to die, the last rites had been performed, and I had been seized and my arms pinioned behind me. They took me from my cell and led me to the window. The rope was adjusted around my neck and then I was marched to the window and placed on the platform before the jeering crowd. The trap was sprung and I was launched into space. I could feel the agony as I awoke." "There's no danger of you being hanged," the guard said. "At the worst you will only be expelled from the country." "Expelled from America?" "In another land you could reform and lead a life of virtuous industry." "Leave the United States?" Yankee took a cup of water from the guard. His hand was shaking. The guard returned two hours later with breakfast. Yankee was lying on his back on the floor of his cell—jaws locked, lips bloodless. Just above and inside his left elbow the guard saw a large, ragged "frightful" wound. Nearby in a pool of blood was the dull case knife Yankee had used to cut his food. The former champ had killed himself rather than suffer the indignity of deportation. Poor faithful Yankee. His name and the flag he wore in the ring were more than window dressing. He truly loved the United States. As he lay in the cell, his red blood leaking away, the bars from the window fell over him like the bars of Old Glory. In his hand he clinched his handkerchief with the star-spangled U.S. flag painted upon it.

Shortly after, the vigilantes deported Dutch Charley aboard the steamer *Golden Age*. "Captain," he begged, "let me go back. I will pay my fare. I will give myself up to the Vigilance Committee immediately on landing, let them do with me as they please. I cannot go elsewhere and hold up my head." "But they will hang you high," the captain said. "Captain, I would rather die in California without touching ground with my feet than live a Prince in any other country!"

Senator Broderick's enemies in the proslavery faction next held a caucus to decide how to permanently remove him from the political scene. As his executioner they selected hot-tempered Judge David Terry, who was skilled in pistol dueling while Broderick, a famously poor shot, was not. Terry supplied the pistols: two Belgian-made eight-inch single-ball dueling pistols. On September 12, 1859, the two challengers met in a small gully to the east of the southernmost extremity of Laguna de la Merced, ten miles south of San Francisco. The predawn was cold and gray. Several times the convoy of twenty buggies lost their way in the fog. Finally the seventy-eight witnesses and officials crossed over the county line to the farm adjoining the Lake House Ranch. The sun rose thin and raw along the lonely shore as they drew up to a rail fence, the boundaries of Davis's milk ranch, and went down into the valley. Broderick occupied his side of the field. Terry did the same. Armorer Bernard Lagoards said loudly as he loaded Broderick's pistol, "The hair triggers might be so finely set that the breath of a strong-lunged man would discharge them. That used by Broderick carries the lightest bullet." In his earlier duel with Caleb Smith, Broderick's life had been spared when a bullet glanced off his heavy gold presentation watch. He still carried the timepiece as a lucky talisman but now was forced to relinquish it.

Broderick heard birds hopping in the underbrush. The sun was fighting through. Clouds were racing north and then south over their heads. The gun in his broad palm felt wrong. Terry smiled, took deliberate aim, and fired before the word *two* was completed. *Crack!* A puff of dust showed on Broderick's right lapel. He winced, and clapped his left hand to the upper-right side of his breast. "Hard hit!" his friends said. Broderick's half-raised right arm slowly stretched to full length. He swayed, fought to stay erect, and raised both arms over his head. His body shuddered. His right arm, still holding the pistol, contracted. His left knee gave way, then his right, and he half fell still clasping his pistol. Forty-five minutes later a dozen men gently carried Broderick to a spring wagon, laid him on a mattress in its bed, and drove him twelve miles north to Leonidas Haskell's house at Black Point, where he lingered for the next three days. "They have killed me," he murmured. "I die because I was opposed to the extension of slavery and a corrupt administration." His breath was labored through the rent in his chest. Broderick died at age thirty-nine. "I die—protect my honor," were his last words. Tears coursed down the cheeks of men in the streets. Crowds stood in stricken silence. Businesses closed. Funeral blinds were pulled. Buildings were draped in black. Dueling had been made illegal five years earlier, thus Terry tried to flee the state but was arrested as he neared the Nevada border. "Broderick is dead," the *Sacramento Union* editorialized. "He died by the trickery of a mutually arranged occasion." Rumors flew that the gunsmith Natchez had set the triggers of the guns so delicately that the sudden raising of one would cause it to go off and had made Terry aware of this fact. A. A. Selover, an observer, examined the pistols and discovered that "the triggers were set so fine a strong puff of wind would prove sufficient to spring and discharge them."

Thousands filed past Broderick's bier. Sawyer, in the city hall tower, rang the bell joylessly. Soon the bells of all the firehouses joined in until an enormous tolling resounded over the entire city, not the busy call of volunteers but slow and funereal. In death Broderick triumphed as he never had in life. As a martyr in the cause of freedom, his death persuaded California to cast its allegiance to the antislavery faction of the Union.

On July 8, Sawyer heard about Billy Mulligan's death and realized that those great and glorious days of firefighting were gone forever, as were his heroic friends. In just a dozen years the volunteers had shrunk. Broderick One now had only fifty-two full-time members, down by more than half. Sadly he went to view Mulligan's body laid out in an expensive rosewood coffin in the Broderick One firehouse. On August 31, the Niantic Hotel at Clay and Sansome streets, another link with the past, caught fire. Big Six answered the alarm first, but as their brakeless engine rushed from its housing on the hill at Brenham Place, it reeled out of control down the steep Washington Street hill. Careening from side to side, the huge steamer shook off clinging firemen like fleas from a dog. James Washington and Foreman Walter Bohen were thrown under the boiler that kept punching down upon them as the engine ran away. Big George rushed to the still figures, but both had been crushed to death. Charles Rhoades composed a song, "Our Engine on the Hill," to commemorate them and Big Six sang it at the top of their lungs to the next fire.

At noon on Sunday, October 8, Twain rose in his bed at the Gillis family rooming house on Minna Street and decided to visit the *Dramatic Chronicle* (its first issue had only been in January) and get some paying work. He reached the corner of Minna and Third streets, where William Love's Bakery stood, admired the sign, and then turned right. In the distance a horse-drawn streetcar clopped along Mission Street. Crowds of people passed. As he ambled down Third Street he was shaken off his feet. "The entire front of a tall four-story brick building in Third Street sprung outward like a door," he wrote, "and fell sprawling across the street. . . . A lady sitting in her rocking chair and quaking parlor saw the wall part at the ceiling, open and shut twice, like a mouth, and then drop the end of a brick on the floor like a tooth. She was a woman easily disgusted with foolishness, and she arose and went out of there." Blocks away some of Sawyer's antique firefighting memorabilia was smashed. As he swept up the shards, he realized he had not seen Twain recently. The writer had tried to borrow money but could not arrange it even though Gillis's brother was a moneylender. Ten days after the quake Twain had reached a momentous decision. "I have a call to literature of a low order—i.e. humorous," he wrote Orion and his wife, Molly. "It is nothing to be proud of but it is my strongest suit." He turned "to seriously scribbling to excite the laughter of God's creatures. Poor, pitiful business!"

At 328 Montgomery Street, Harte was editing a new literary weekly, Charles Henry Webb's *Californian.* When he arranged for Twain to write four signed articles a month at $50 apiece, equal to the $12.50 per article he received from the *Golden Era* and the *Sacramento Union,* Twain quit the *Golden Era.* "It wasn't high toned enough," he explained. Soon after Joe Goodman of the *Territorial Enterprise* offered him a contract to write a letter a day for $100 each. Things were looking up. "The *Dramatic Chronicle* pays me," he said, "or rather will begin to pay me next week—$40 a month for dramatic criticisms. Same wages I got on the *Call,* and more agreeable and less laborious work." He freelanced for the *Dramatic Chronicle* and hung around their office with other Bohemian writers until the paper tired of him and he of them. Because the *Chronicle* consistently neglected to pay Twain or Harte, it was no great loss.

After the Civil War ended in April 1865, tempers were raw. Sawyer commonly heard stories of volunteer firemen back east fighting for possession of a hydrant while buildings burned to the ground around them. The last five years had been the most divisive and explosive in the Republic's history: battles at Antietam, Gettysburg, and Shiloh; the surrender at Appomattox on April 9; and Lincoln's assassination five days later. The New York City volunteers had fallen under the sway of politicians who promoted the intercompany rivalries that got in the way of honest firefighting. The volunteers cut one another's towropes, jammed carriage wheels, stole valuable equipment, and laid ambushes for their competitors along the route to the fire. Sawyer's old volunteer company, New York Number Fourteen, was disbanded for fighting. Company Two's long, colorful career ended when its steam engine was transferred to Engine Eleven of the new paid New York Fire Department and they were disbanded. Would the San Francisco volunteers meet a similar fate? All fourteen San Francisco volunteer fire companies held divergent views. The regional, ethnic, and national difference of the strikingly disparate companies caused friction. Three in particular held strongly divergent views—Knickerbocker Five embraced all things Northern, Social Three supported all things Bostonian, and Big Six embraced all that was Southern, especially politics and slavery. In fifteen years, discord among the volunteers had grown worse and only escalated after the Civil War. A battle was building between them.

Tensions as furious as those back east exploded into bloodshed in San Francisco toward the end of 1865. Always competitive, the local volunteers' races took on a new seriousness in the war's heated aftermath. On Sunday afternoon, December 17, an alarm sounded for a fire from a box at Fourth and Mission streets. A heated race between Big Six, Knickerbocker Five, and Social Three began. Three, with 35 to 40 volunteers running on the rope, rumbled along Sansome Street at a fast clip, turned onto Market and Second streets, and saw Five gaining. Fearful of an oncoming fight, the extra men dropped off and gave a slack rope as Three turned onto narrow Jessie Street, made narrower by wagons and carts lining both sides. Five, 125 strong, attempted to run Three's engine onto the sidewalk and capsize it. Two of Three's men jumped on top of their engine and, armed with nozzles, successively fought off Five as Three's engine turned onto Third Street. They made up time on the steep downhill grade toward Mission Street. Reaching Mission, Three drew their rope across the street to keep Five from passing, but they beat their way through and dashed along Mission. As Five passed them they jeered, "A nice lot of fellows you are!" and rumbled toward Fourth Street with Six right on their tail. Five passed between Six and Three in the direction of the alarm and now all three engines were running neck and neck.

They all collided at the corner and quit their engines with cries of "Johnny Reb," "Billy Yank," and "Blue Belly." Dropping their ropes, Six and Three jumped on top of their engines and attacked Five with crowbars, spanners, and blunderbusses. A crowd gathered. Five fled, leaving behind their engine and a few officers. The remaining volunteers beat one another with ax handles, billets of wood, and stones. Pistol shots rang out. Ed Flaherty, Five's assistant foreman, was shot in the head and back. Six's George Stanton was wounded. Twenty-eight men were shot. Many others had broken bones, blackened eyes, and bloodied noses. As the volunteers battled, the blaze died out and the building collapsed in ashes around them. Three of the twenty-five policemen watching arrested Stanton of the Monumentals; Charles McMann, Knickerbocker assistant foreman; and two of Five's men. The winning unit celebrated joylessly amid smoldering ruins and bloodied bodies as in the distance the fire bell tolled. It was the volunteers' death knell. The battle between Three, Five, and Six concluded the crucial period of the volunteer firemen who had served so bravely and now ended so tragically.

On December 30, the *Californian* announced Harte's withdrawal. Twain quit, too, after producing only eight pieces for them, and returned to slinking from creditors. Angered by Twain's unrelenting criticism of their brutality and racism, the police wanted to arrest him. He grew morose in the damp. It had rained from December 11 through December 16, then intermittent showers continued to the end of the year. "One hundred and twenty days in varying succession of rain is the norm," he wrote. "If it is Winter it will *rain*—and if it is Summer, it *won't* rain." He slumped in his window box, smoked his long nines, and watched the rain streak down his window and citizens slog through the mud outside. What was the point of it all? It seemed so hopeless. The new year was no better. Twenty days into 1866, he informed his mother and sister he would write for the New York *Weekly Review* and possibly for the *Saturday Press*. "I am too lazy to write oftener than once a month, though I sent a sketch by yesterday's steamer which will probably appear in the *Review* along about the middle part of February."

One night in the first days of 1866 he got out his pistol, put it to his head, and slowly began to tighten the trigger. Sweat beaded on his forehead. He gritted his teeth and grimaced. He shook all over. Finally he put the gun down. He did not know why. "Many times I have been sorry I did not succeed," he wrote of the attempt, "but I was never ashamed of having tried. Suicide is really the only sane thing the young or old do in this life." He had not shaken the idea, though, and wrote Orion, "If I do not get out of debt in three months—pistols or poison for one—exit me."

He laid out a text for a sermon called "Self Murder." "Twain later said he never saw a dead man whom he did not envy 'for having had it over and done with it.'"

By January 20, he was no longer disposed to commit suicide but enthusiastically laying out long-term literary projects and wishing he were back piloting up and down the river again. He loved piloting more than writing. He held those old river friends above all others. In "genuine manliness," he wrote, "they assay away above the common multitude, the only unfettered and entirely independent human being that lived on earth . . . all men—kings and serfs alike—are slaves to men, save, alone, the pilot—who comes at no man's beck or call, obeys no man's orders and scorns all men's suggestions." The papers got wind that he was working on his first book, "a pet notion of his of about three hundred pages, probably about the river," but they were only guessing. "Nobody knows what [the novel] is going to be about but just myself," he said. "I am slow and lazy and the bulk of it will not be finished under a year. . . . If I do not write it to suit me at first I will have to write it all over again, and so, who knows? I may be an old man before I finish it. I have not written a line in it for three weeks, and may not for three more. I shall only write when the spirit moves me. I am the Genius of Indolence." In February, his public feud with Colonel Albert S. Evans, a city editor for the *Daily Alta California,* bore poisoned fruit. Twain had fired the first verbal shot. Evans, in the *Gold Hill Evening News,* called him "a bail-jumping, alcoholic deadbeat who rolled in whorehouses and probably had a venereal disease." Next, the *Chronicle* reported that Colonel Evans was making "physical threats against Twain." "I have but one definite purpose in view," Twain replied seriously, "that is, to make enough money to insure me a fair trial, and then go and kill Colonel Evans." Because the *Chronicle* had advised that he leave the state, he decided to travel to the Sandwich Islands [Hawaii] to file some stories as a freelancer. He would miss Sawyer's stories of fighting fire but had already heard most of them in the Turkish bath, the Blue Wing Saloon, or at the Bank Exchange Bar. So he steamed and played cards, crammed his pipe with Bull Durham, or smoked one of his lethal cigars, and passed the time planning his novel. As he listened to more of Sawyer's youthful adventures with the first volunteers, he began to construct a more ambitious work than one based on Lillie's life as a torch girl. God, he enjoyed the firefighter spinning stories as steam drifted around them like a five-alarm fire. Gradually the mist blotted out everything but their cards, and it was as if he were there in the heat with Sawyer and the oddest assortment of rogues and heroes who ever lived, fighting fire against a deadly arsonist.

He loved the San Francisco climate, but if folks were out to kill or jail him, he didn't love it that much. Before Twain left for a five-month trip to the Sandwich Islands, he thought about the volunteers' inglorious ends. Fifteen years earlier San Francisco had trembled daily on the edge of destruction. These brave men had been the only obstacles fending off complete destruction, yet they had been murdered, crippled, run out of the state, and shot down in the streets. Many factors had contributed to the final cataclysmic result. Not one would have happened without the other. In mid-February 1866, he ambled over to Stahle's for a steam and a few hands of poker. He hoped to break his writer's block with some stimulating conversation. He marveled at what a talker Sawyer was, gesturing with his hands and arms as he spun his history of the last of six great fires. On March 5 he wrote his mother and sister that he was to depart for the Sandwich Islands in two days. "We shall arrive there in about twelve days. I am to remain there a month and ransack the islands, the great cataracts and the volcanoes completely and write twenty or thirty letters for the *Union* for which they pay me as much money as if I stayed at home. Goodbye for the present." He left San Francisco onboard the *Ajax,* the newest, fastest ocean steamer in America, the first regular steamship service between the Islands and the United States. While there, Twain produced twenty-five letters on trade prospects in the Islands. By April 3 he had ridden horseback all over Oahu, visited ancient battlefields, and enjoyed a five-course banquet. On July 19, he steamed back to California and reached San Francisco on August 13. He stayed again at the Occidental Hotel, encumbered by work on a book revising his Sandwich Island letters to the *Union* that might prove both a literary and a pecuniary success. Orion and his wife were in the city and he visited them. After they sailed for the East Coast, he decided to join the lucrative lecture circuit. On October 2, he presented a comic lecture on the great volcano of Kilauea at Maguire's Academy of Music on Pine Street, near his old Montgomery Street stomping grounds.

"The doors," he advertised, "open at 7:00 P.M. The trouble to begin at 8:00 P.M." The trouble began the instant he set foot on stage. He suffered an attack of stage fright so intense that he felt he "saw the face of death." Gradually he realized that he could make the audience laugh and control them. Before their eyes he gained confidence. He revealed that the object of his talk was to obtain funds to publish a book on the Islands with illustrations by local French artist Ed Jump. The Islands book was doomed from the beginning, so to clear his mind he visited the Turkish baths to see Sawyer. As he sweated his worries away, he studied the round-faced young firefighter. This exceptional young man had found happiness, married, and with a prosperous, popular bar, was still fighting, saving lives, and helping build a great city.

Twain puffed his cheap cigar and settled back as Sawyer related how most of the heroic volunteers came to tragic ends. The steam in the Turkish bath gathered until they were sitting in a country of the clouds, cigar smoke and water vapor lifting them up. Twain left the baths refreshed, inspired, and thinking over the tragic story as he prepared for his lecture tour. His comic timing grew masterful as he toured in Sacramento, Marysville, Grass Valley, Red Dog, and You Bet in California. In Arizona he repeated his success in Carson City, Gold City, and (most triumphantly) in Virginia City, where no one shot at him. He returned to the Golden State and lectured in San Jose; in Oakland on November 27; and finally in December, in San Francisco, which was changing before his eyes. Fifteen years earlier San Francisco, thirsting for fresh spring water, had contracted with Arzo Merrifield's Mountain Lake Water Company to lay pipes to the city. Merrifield put down a $50,000 bond to ensure the works would be completed by January 1853. They were not. Drinkable water finally became available from a lake, supplied by drainage and several springs, three and a half miles west. The city installed thirty-eight cisterns at every major intersection to guard the flourishing boat, flour, and saw mills, following the New York plan of more than a decade earlier. By spring, San Francisco's first serious depression was on the horizon. The post–Gold Rush letdown emotionally affected everyone because the mines had not made everyone rich, as had been expected. Buying power plummeted and merchants' warehouses bulged with surplus commodities. Over the next year, one-third of the city's thousand shops would lie vacant and two hundred men would go bankrupt. If the city's economy was to be improved, San Francisco needed better roads for commerce and fire protection, a serious problem from the beginning. Only Battery Street really connected the central business district with warehouses at the north end of the city.

With the economy in free fall, San Francisco fell back on its old, indifferent, indolent ways. Streets in the city—worn, pitted, and rutted from iron wheels and horseshoes—were not repaired, so the volunteers could no longer roll their engines below Davis Street. Cisterns built five years earlier had not been maintained. Half, filled by dray and hose with salt water from the bay, became cracked or leaky, though the city now had 175 windmill-driven artesian wells. During a small fire a volunteer was asked if there was any water in the cistern. "It's full at the bottom," he said, "but there isn't any at the top." There were still only thirteen engines and three hook and ladder companies with 950 certificate members. Many engine houses were inconvenient to fighting fire. Almost all were within one area—bounded by Broadway, Bush, Stockton, and Front streets. Only two companies lay south of Market or in the distant countryside near Mission Dolores. Homes burned long before the volunteers reached them. One day a fire broke out at a suburban slaughterhouse near California and Larkin streets. The nearest fire company was on the other side of Nob Hill. The alarm sounded and the intrepid volunteers set off at a dead run, dragging their massive engine up the California Street hill. The steep incline down to Larkin Street so exhausted the men that the engine, weighing several tons, whipped away and thundered downhill, firemen clutching at the tail rope. Hitting a bump, the machine rolled over, injuring several men, and tumbled to the bottom of Larkin Street. The race had been for nothing: The slaughterhouse burned to ashes. Hand-operated fire engines constructed in New York, Rhode Island, and Baltimore began to be shipped to the West. In San Francisco a yearlong economy drive reduced the volunteers' effectiveness. Company Five and Company Three were given defective replacements for their worn-out hoses and were temporarily evicted from their firehouses.

Sixteen years earlier J.B.M. Crooks, a whale oil dealer, had been awarded a lucrative contract to light the blocks bounded by Battery, Kearny, Jackson, and California streets with oil lamps. The few light posts he erected were too dim to see by. "Crooks only accomplished a way to render darkness visible, having gone about his work in true San Francisco style," the press reported. Now the city manufactured gas inside brick structures at the corner of First and Howard streets for its own limited-area lighting system. At midnight on February 11, 1854, the gas had officially been turned on and eighty-four gas lamps mounted along Montgomery, Bush, Jackson, Sacramento, Kearny, Dupont, Commercial, and Washington streets flickered with a feeble light. A glow lit Dupont Street to the water and from Jackson to California Street. Down

Washington Street a line of Chinese shops, restaurants, and saloons were drenched in green light. To Kearny and north to Broadway beamed a cheerful light. The city kept the lights lit until 2:00 A.M., even on bright moonlit nights or sometimes only part of the night or not lit at all. When gaslight finally extended to unhappy Happy Valley in 1856, the usefulness of the torch boys was ended.

On December 1, 1866, the California State Legislature passed a measure creating a paid fire department for San Francisco. As Twain lolled in his window box, writing, midnight tolled the end of the volunteers. The next afternoon, Broderick One marched to Lone Mountain Cemetery to unveil a statue of Senator and Chief David Colbert Broderick. The next day, less than a year after the lethal battle between the companies, the volunteer companies disbanded and handed over the protection of San Francisco to a paid fire brigade. Organized under Chief Frank Whitney, the 148-member paid department was sworn in and operating within hours. At 3:00 A.M., a fruit store fire at Second and Folsom streets initiated the new professional department. When Liberty Hose Company conducted a mock funeral of a stuffed figure in a fireman's uniform representing the defunct department, Tom Sawyer saved the hose carriage from burning by carting it to the Corporation Yard.

Because Five's engine house was in terrible disrepair, the legislature authorized an appropriation for a new one. Presently Lillie's favorite firemen were using a borrowed Jeffers engine manufactured in Pawtucket, Rhode Island. They had sold their ancient third-class James Smith engine to the Virginia City volunteers, whom Twain so admired. The next day Five's volunteers, led by Bill Fairman and Lillie Hitchcock, rode to the Nevada town to personally deliver the engine. The trek required several stagecoaches, relays, and lodgings. Lillie expertly drove Hank Monk's team of six horses up the narrow grade on the mountain as Monk drawled his stories. After Lillie delivered the engine, Virginia City celebrated with a banquet. While in town, she helped extinguish a burning miner's shack just to keep her dainty hand in.

Twain saw Sawyer, "beaming with smiles and good nature," coming down Montgomery Street. He had been drinking and told Twain how much he wanted to hear his last San Francisco lecture. "If you knew how bad I want to laugh," Sawyer said, "you'd give me a ticket." "Is your laugh hung on a hair-trigger?" Twain asked him, "That is, is it critical, or can you get it off *easy*?" "He laughed a specimen or two that struck me as being about the article I wanted and I gave him a ticket, and appointed him to sit in the second row, in the center, and be responsible for that division of the house. I gave him minute instructions about how to detect indistinct jokes, and then went away, and left him chuckling placidly over the novelty of the idea." On December 10, nine days after the initiation of a paid fire department, a crowd, including California governor Frederick Low and Nevada governor Henry Blasdel, gathered in front of Congress Hall on Bush Street just above Montgomery to hear Twain repeat his popular Sandwich Island talk. He intended to alter only one portion and to give an uncharacteristic speech at the end summing up San Francisco, what it had been and what it would be. He would speak of its destiny. Now there were twenty blocks, 1,500 new homes and offices, fireproof buildings. "Think of it! San Francisco is here to stay." That would be the crux of Twain's farewell speech. Waiting for his lecture to begin, Twain said he was "quaking in every limb with a terror that seemed like to take my life away. The tumult in my heart and brain and legs continued a full minute before I could gain any command over myself." Tom Sawyer wriggled in his seat next to Mary Bridget, his mind occupied by the $183 he owed in delinquent property taxes. At 8:00 P.M. the gaslights dimmed. Twain shuffled to the podium dressed in a claw-hammer coat, looking much as he had months before, steaming, laughing, and telling jokes and stories, though perhaps a little more rumpled. Solemn faced, he shuffled a stack of ragged pages, dropping them in feigned confusion until he had the crowd laughing. "And whenever a joke did fall," he wrote in *Roughing It,* a semiautobiographical adventure story and his first solo effort, "and their faces did split from ear to ear, Sawyer, whose hearty countenance was seen looming redly in the center of the second row, took it up, and the house was carried handsomely. The explosion that followed was the triumph of the evening. I thought that honest man Sawyer would choke himself."

Twain had delivered his lecture in his attenuated delivery (his father had been a man of precise, grammatical manner) and now spoke solemnly. "My Friends and Fellow-Citizens—I read the signs of the times," he said, looking out over the audience of dignitaries and his many friends. He told them he could behold the things that are in store for them. "Over slumbering California is stealing the dawn of a radiant future!" he said, dropping his comic stance. "This straggling town shall be a vast metropolis: this sparsely populated land shall become a crowded hive of busy men: Your waste places blossom like the rose and your deserted hills and valleys shall yield bread and wine for unnumbered thousands: railroads shall be spread hither and thither and carry the invigorating blood of commerce to regions that are languishing now: mills and workshops, yea, and factories shall spring up everywhere, and mines that have neither name nor place today shall dazzle the world with their affluence." He half-unconsciously lapsed into a lazy tone and manner.

He seemed to be speaking directly to Sawyer when he said that the time was drawing near when the dark clouds would pass away and prosperity lay upon the land. "I am bidding the old city and my old friends a kind, but not a sad farewell, for I know that when I see this home again, the changes that will have been wrought upon it will suggest no sentiment of sadness; its estate will be brighter, happier and prouder a hundred fold than it is this day. This is its destiny!"

Twain spoke of the forty-niners, the volunteers, San Francisco's great men, asking, Where are they now? "Scattered to the ends of the earth, or prematurely aged and decrepit, or shot or stabbed in street affrays—or dead of disappointed hope and broken hearts—all gone, or nearly all. . . . It is pitiful to think upon." He was speaking, too, of Billy Mulligan, David Broderick, George Oakes, James Casey, Yankee Sullivan, and all the other volunteers who had met such tragic fates. Ringing in Sawyer's ears were Twain's two questions: "Has any other State so brilliant a future? Has any other city a future like San Francisco?" No, Sawyer thought, there were none. The city bid farewell to Twain, who had just turned thirty-one. Enthusiastically, Sawyer pumped his hand, hugged him good-bye, and was gone. They would never meet again. William Dean Howells, who had known all the great writers, wrote, "They were like one another and like other literary men, but Clemens was incomparable. [He was] the Lincoln of our literature."

On December 16, Twain left aboard the Opposition Line steamer *America*, leaving behind more friends than any newspaperman who had ever sailed out of the Golden Gate. The fabulous pirate Ned Wakeman, a seven-foot-long gold chain wrapped several times around his neck, was the skipper. As they sailed for Nicaragua and San Juan, Twain jotted down his stories of a snake as long as a ship's mainmast and rats as big as greyhounds. Twain considered him one of the "most winning and delightful" people he had ever met. "I'd rather travel with that old portly, hearty, jolly, boisterous, good-natured sailor . . . than any other man I've ever come across," he later wrote of him in *Roughing It*. He never forgot his old friends and always included them in his books. He crossed Central America by way of Nicaragua and headed toward fame.

Twain visited Lillie in Paris on July 11, 1867. "I should think you would feel mighty rascally now to let me go away without that picture," he wrote her from Marseille. "All right my dear. I am coming back to Paris before long and when I do the Grand Hotel du Louvre will not be big enough to hold both of us. We had a gorgeous time in Paris. It isn't any use to say anything about it—I am only writing to let you know I am well." Then Lille shocked him when she abruptly married a San Francisco firefighter. "Poor Lillie Hitchcock!" Twain wrote. "She who they talk about her in print . . . the hearts that rascal has broken on both sides of the water! When I saw the family in Paris, Lillie had just delivered the mitten to a wealthy Italian Count, at her mother's request (Mrs. H. said Lillie loved him)—but ah me!—worse to jilt anybody to marry Howard Coit . . . a dissipated spendthrift, son of a deceased, wealthy eminent physician, a most worthy man. Until that moment I said the whole affair must be untrue, because as detestable as some of Lillie's freaks were, she could not be capable of deceiving her mother and father marrying secretly. And to tell the plain truth I don't really believe it yet. She is an awful girl, but she is not that awful. But remember there was never so much as a whisper against her good name. I am so sorry for that girl and so very, very sorry for her good kind mother. I hold both of them in happy remembrance always—for they were your brave, outspoken sort of friends and just as loyal to you behind your back as before your face." Just over a year later, Twain got married himself. Lillie Hitchcock left one third of her estate to the city with the request that they should "expend it in an appropriate manner for the purpose of adding to the beauty of San Francisco which I have always loved." Her friends and the firemen of the city gathered to dedicate a 210-foot-high white granite tower on top of Telegraph Hill where she had so often played to the memory of one *they* had always loved. To them the tower resembled a fire hose nozzle. By 1866, fifteen U.S. cities had adopted steam. A decade later, 275 departments were using fire to fight fire, lighting the boiler fires of steam engines. Thus steam had replaced hand pumpers, horses had replaced men to haul the heavy engine, and a telegraph alarm had replaced the bell Sawyer once rang to alert the firefighters. Better streets and widespread gas lighting replaced the torch boys who grew up and were forgotten. On April 23, 1869, Sawyer was seriously injured when Liberty Hose's engine and hose cart overturned. He had inspected the harness and found it sound that morning, but the strain of two jerking fire horses excited by the frenzied clanging of the fire bell snapped it as they dashed from the station. He convalesced at home with Mary Bridget and their three boys—Joseph, Thomas junior, and William—now able to pay more attention to his saloon on the southwest corner of Mission and Fifth streets.

On May 26, 1870, the cornerstone for the huge new U.S. Mint was laid across the street at Fifth and Mission streets. "At two o'clock that afternoon," Jack O'Brien wrote, "waiting crowds heard band music in the distance and out Mission Street from the Masonic Temple at Montgomery and Post Streets came a dazzling procession. . . . The throng cheered. A woman fainted. Out of Tom Sawyer's Saloon across the street [where the Chronicle Building now stands] stumbled a score of amiable drunks, who, once they had recovered from the blast of the fresh air, supported the marchers with unruly applause." Sawyer stood at the door of his tavern and surveyed the concrete and granite Greek Revival monolith that would soon house one-third of the nation's gold reserves.

Sam Brannan returned to San Francisco in the early 1870s, and came into Charlie Robinson's painting studio in the Montgomery Block on a rainy day, wet, bedraggled, and liquored up. They talked together of the old happy days. "At the same time," Robinson said, "he paid a visit to Pioneer Hall and saw on the wall his own photograph, showing him as a tall, handsome man, with large beautiful eyes, and richly attired. Tears rolled down his cheeks." Robinson lost his paintings by fire in 1906 and 1921. The dapper, engaging Brannan, once the state's first millionaire and its wealthiest man, had thrown his money away "like wheat before chickens." He never recovered from a costly divorce settlement that drained most of his capital. He gave up being a Mormon, began to drink, and went bankrupt building the Calistoga summer resort and the Napa Valley Railroad. Historian H. H. Bancroft knew him personally and disliked him. Brannan moved to Mexico to realize the Yaqui land grants the Mexican government had given him in exchange for arms and money, but the Yaquis never let him take possession. May 5, 1889, when he was just over seventy, he died alone in Escondido. His body was held in a San Diego receiving vault of Mount Hope Cemetery for sixteen months awaiting funds for burial.

On April 4, 1871, Scannell was made chief engineer of the new paid fire department—twenty-three companies of firemen—the city's most picturesque and beloved chief. He never married or had a sweetheart.

The department was his mistress. He still ate those fabulous marathon dinners on the cuff and devoted the rest of his life to the San Francisco Fire Department, and to Broderick One in particular. Broderick had used the fire station's influence to put him and his friends politically in power in almost every aspect of San Francisco government for years—from San Francisco's first appointed sheriff to chief engineer of the volunteer fire department. He was removed from office in 1874 over a squabble between fire commissioners, but when the Veteran Firemen's Association was organized in 1888, Sawyer helped name the firemen's medal of bravery after him. By then there were fire escapes, extension ladders, fire poles, good roads, alarm systems, fire codes, effective lighting, and water towers. When Scannell died, still in harness, fire department bells all over San Francisco tapped once for each of his seventy-three years. He had not a bone in his body that had not been fractured at some time during his battles with fires and men. He had given his heart to the San Francisco Fire Department. In return, San Franciscans had given him theirs. The overwhelming applause he had so long desired was finally his.

Ed Stahle closed his steam baths after Twain left San Francisco in 1866 to refit them "in a style worthy the prestige and reputation of this celebrated institution for bathing, hair cutting, shampooing, hair dying, etc. . . ." With his new partner, George Held, he reopened the Montgomery Baths on August 22, 1867. On January 1, 1870, he dissolved the copartnership by mutual consent and carried on the business alone.

In 1876, Twain published *The Adventures of Tom Sawyer* in his friend's image and name. Thirty-seven when he began writing it, he wrote one hundred pages in longhand in 1873, but composed the rest of his famous novel in the summer of 1874 and of 1875, when his friend William Dean Howells read a draft. For the character of Sawyer, Twain would only say he had drawn upon the characteristics of three different living boys. Albert Bigelow Paine, Twain's approved biographer, in his 1923 introduction to Twain's "What Is Man?" named the three boys as John B. Briggs (who died in 1907), William Bowen (who died in 1893), and Twain himself. In 1907, in an unguarded moment, Twain revealed himself as the primary model for Sawyer. In a note to a young girl he wrote, "I have always concealed it, but now I am *compelled* to confess that *I* am Tom Sawyer!" But he would not have said it was a "living boy he had known" if he had not meant a third person. "'Sawyer' was not the real name . . . of any person I ever knew, *so far as I can remem-*

ber. . . ." he said slyly. The great appropriator liked to pretend his characters sprang fully grown from his fertile mind. Twain, as Sawyer had reported, took ideas from anywhere he might find them and claimed them as his own. Sawyer had no doubts *he* was the inspiration for the name of Tom Sawyer. His claim was widely published in 1900, when those in San Francisco who knew them both could have challenged the assertion. No one, including Twain, ever did.

"You want to know how I come to figure in his books, do you?" Sawyer told *Call* reporter Viola Rodgers. He turned on his stool, acknowledged the reporter, raised his brandy, and took a sip. "Well, as I said, we both was fond of telling stories and spinning yarns. Sam, he was mighty fond of children's doings and whenever he'd see any little fellers a-fighting on the street, he always stop and watch 'em and then he'd come up to the Blue Wing and describe the whole doings and then I'd try and beat his yarn by telling him of the antics I used to play when I was a kid and say, 'I don't believe there ever was such another little devil ever lived as I was.' Sam, he would listen to these pranks of mine with great interest and he occasionally take 'em down in his notebook. One day he says to me: 'I am going to put you between the covers of a book some of these days, Tom.' 'Go ahead, Sam,' I said, 'but don't disgrace my name.'"

In *Mark Twain's San Francisco*, Bernard Taper wrote, "All sorts of characters swim into Twain's ken—miners, millionaires, actors, bill collectors, notables, bums. He is on easy terms with them all. In the Turkish bath in the Montgomery Block he even meets a man named Tom Sawyer, with whom he likes playing penny ante. Long afterward this man enjoyed the conviction that it was he who had inspired Twain's famous book, and outside of a tavern he acquired . . . he proudly hung the sign: ALE AND SPIRITS! THE ORIGINAL TOM SAWYER: PROP." Idwal Jones wrote, "His belief that the tale was dedicated to him grew, as also grew the number of tales involving himself and 'my friend Sam Clemens,' going back not only to Sam's Washoe period but also his unrecorded infancy. The sign swung profitably in the wind." Twain's old bathhouse crony ran the most popular watering hole in town, and in 1876 he was still an extra man with Engine Six on the east side of Sixth Street and corporation yard manager for the entire fire department. In 1884, he retired from public life as inspector of the Custom House, a job he had held for twenty-one years. After helping organize the Liberty Hose, he was elected its foreman for three terms and a member of the Board of Delegates. Four years later he was elected vice president of the Veteran

Firemen's Association along with Crooked Con Mooney, Singing Jack Carroll, and Cockeyed Frank Atkinson. On January 3, 1888, four hundred veteran firemen who had run with the first engines and worked the brakes long before met at the Pioneer Building on Fourth Street to relieve those early days. On July 4, he marched in a huge parade.

On October 13, 1890, Sawyer organized a society to call for passage of a bill to make the city fire department a metropolitan one with a fully paid force. In the preceding twenty-five years, 1,200 men had been removed or forced to resign from the fire department, and Sawyer intended to lobby the next legislature. On July 17, the discharged firemen met at his saloon. "The fire department is badly managed," he told them, "and many of the engines in the corporation yard could be repaired at little expense and would do good service for many years." He complained that many cisterns downtown had not been cleaned for years and caused much of the disease prevalent in the downtown area. "In old times," he said, "when the Volunteer department was in existence, they were cleaned every three months." On August 17, his name was suggested as the new fire commissioner. On September 16, 1891, the Veteran Firemen Association made him first vice president of both the Vets and the Manhattans. "Sawyer hails from New York where he did his first fire duty," the *Call* noted, calling him "Hale and hearty, ever genial and courteous." "That big engine—just think of it," W.D.L. Hall, a veteran, recalled. "How we ever got that over the sand, mud, and planks with her in the early days, and the service we did. It's simply astonishing to think of it. Newcomers can hardly realize it, but it was so all the same."

On June 17, 1894, Sawyer and the other vets who ran with the hose in the fifties told what it was like as they "battled with the flames which destroyed the tumble-down landmarks of a boom town. There was something to being a Volunteer fireman in those good old days when heads were cracked and human claret flowed to taps. There were no nickle-plated steamers or water towers in those days." That afternoon, a race for fat veterans over sixty years old was held. A one-eyed whiskered gent not "a day under ninety ran like a chief and won a prize of a case of champagne which he fled with." Sawyer came in fourth and was presented with a bootjack by his large group of lady friends. In mid-March 1895, as president of the Society of Old Friends, he celebrated with the veterans at Sutro Baths by roasting three oxen and a number of sheep and hogs. In May he performed an overture and a vocal solo at a Jolly Ladies' High Jinks Night at Liberty Hose. The old volunteers told stories, sang, and danced until midnight. In January 1896, Thomas L. Adington, an elderly bartender, swallowed a big dose of morphine in his Ninth Avenue room and left behind a stamped, unsealed letter: "If anything happens to me, I wish you would see Mr. Tom Sawyer, 935 Mission Street and ask him to intercede to have me buried in the Old Friends' plot . . . I cannot live this way any longer, and I hope he will forgive me. So goodbye and God bless everybody. PS Friend Tom, Do what you can. I think I am going crazy."

On October 20, 1897, the *Call* wrote, "The surviving eighteen members of the old Volunteer Fire Company, Knickerbocker Five, met and celebrated the forty-seventh anniversary of their organization. Present were Thomas Sawyer and his wife." Sawyer had briefly served on Lillie's favorite fire company. On October 23, 1898, Viola Rodgers of the *Call* decided to interview him. She was intrigued by what Twain had written in postscript to *Tom Sawyer:* "Most of the characters that perform in this book still live and are prosperous and happy. Some day it may seem worthwhile to take up the story of the younger ones and see what sort of men and women they turned out to be; therefore it will be wisest not to reveal any of that part of their lives at present." She reached the old-fashioned Mission Street saloon just to the east side of the Mint. "Over the front door hangs a sign 'The Gotham—Sawyer Proprietor,'" she wrote. "To a casual observer that name means no more than if it were 'Brown' or 'Tom Jones,' but to Twain it meant the inspiration for his most famous work. For the jolly old fireman sitting in there in an old fashioned haircloth chair is the original Sawyer and it was from him that Twain gathered material for his two greatest works, *Sawyer* and *Huckleberry Finn.* This real-life, up-to-date Sawyer spends his time telling stories of former days while he occasionally mixes a brandy and soda or a cocktail." The walls were completely covered with helmets, belts, election tickets, badges, hooks, bugles, nozzles, mementos, and other firefighting paraphernalia. A huge frame containing small photos of a hundred firemen hung on the south wall. A mounted stag's head looked on impassively. "He prides himself on being a member of the first volunteer fire company ever formed in California," she wrote. "One knows intuitively he is a character the moment one sees him." He wore a navy-blue cap and on his vest he had pinned an electric diamond that glittered alongside badges of the orders of volunteer firemen. "Next to his badges of his fire company, Sawyer values his friendship with

Twain, and he will sit for hours recalling the jolly nights and days he used to spend with Twain." Sawyer's parrot, whose companionship he enjoyed for eighteen years, had just died. His voice got shaky and he got teary when he spoke of "old Pol's" demise, but he soon regained his jolly attitude. Mary Bridget was busy cooking dinner in the rooms above his saloon where they have lived for thirty-seven years. One of his sons, Thomas junior, a former secretary of the Veteran Firemen's Association, was behind the bar as his father's full-time bartender.

"Well, when *Tom Sawyer* was published Sam sent me a copy," Sawyer said. "It was as if I was reading my own diary." His shining morning face lit up. He looked not a day over fifty. Being good-natured kept him young. "Sam got me down to a science, I tell you. He also used some of the things I told him in *Huckleberry Finn*." Sawyer told how Twain used to listen to tales of his youthful antics. "Sam, he would listen and occasionally take them down in his notebook. 'He was just such a boy as you must have been,' he told me. 'I believe I'll call the book *Tom Sawyer.*' That's the way it came about, and you can bet when Mark shows up here in August he'll bear me out. Have a drink?

"But he's coming out here some day, and I am saving up for him. When he does come there'll be some fun, for if he gives a lecture I intend coming right in on the platform and have a few old time sallies with him. I'll just ask him right in meeting about a few of those things when he comes to Frisco." Rodgers ended her full-page interview: "And so Tom Sawyer, who gave Mark Twain the impetus for his famous book, now stands at the bar giving other things to other people." Another interviewer wrote how Sawyer spoke of Twain "with that feeling which signifies the invisible bond between the old timers and their comrades."

On January 26, 1899, Sawyer sang "On the Rocky Road to Dublin" at the volunteers' banquet and all one hundred guests drank a toast to "our departed members and sang, 'Auld Lang Syne.'" Sawyer had little money, only a building lot at Douglass and Duncan streets, but he had lived a rich, full life. During the Veteran Firemen's Association's second annual picnic on June 23, 1901, Sawyer bested Con Mooney in a tree-climbing contest. On December 15, 1905, "Tom Sawyer's" cave, where Tom and Becky Thatcher were lost, and "Injun Joe" perished, was gone. A manufacturing plant had ground all seven miles into Portland cement.

On October 1, 1906, the *San Francisco Call* headlined "Tom Sawyer, Whose Name Inspired Twain, Dies at Great Age." It continued, "A man whose name is to be found in every worthy library in America died in this city on Friday. . . . He was Sawyer, pioneer, steamboat engineer, veteran volunteer fireman and vigilante, who in the early days was a friend of Twain. So highly did the author appreciate Sawyer that he gave the man's name to his famous boy character. In that way the man who died Friday is godfather, so to speak, of one of the most enjoyable books ever written. He was one of the organizers of the volunteer fire department and later was a member of the regular department."

The original Tom Sawyer's Saloon was destroyed that same year—by fire. The memory of the fleet brave lads had always remained in Sawyer's mind. In the middle of the night, surrounded by mementos of his adventurous past, he frequently returned to memories of those early days when he'd heard the *slap, slap, slap* of bare feet racing through the mud as a contingent of boys sprinted ahead of the volunteers' hand-drawn engines. They bore flaming torches over the pitch-black and hazardously pitted roadways of Old San Francisco, lighting the way for the salvation of a great city. The torch boys carried fire to the fire—a very poetic occupation.

SOURCES AND ACKNOWLEDGMENTS

The initial spark for *Black Fire* was Matthew Brady's October 29, 1990, *San Francisco Independent* column, "The Torch Boys." Unfortunately, only the names of a few had survived, and what records the conflagrations of 1850–51 did not destroy, the great quake and fire of 1906 did. A year later I read in Rand Richards's *Historic San Francisco*, "It was in the basement steam baths in fact that Twain met a fireman named Sawyer. Twain used the name for his famous novel, and Sawyer, who later opened a saloon on Mission Street . . . capitalized on his immortality by advertising his tavern as 'the Original Tom Sawyer's.'" Then I discovered a number of interviews Sawyer had given the press. "He prides himself upon being a member of the first volunteer fire company ever formed in California [Broderick One]," Sawyer said on October 23, 1898. Sawyer was already a hero and worthy of a book when he returned from the sea in 1859. Proof of his earlier experience fighting fire in San Francisco between February 1850 and June 1851 was that upon his return he was appointed fire corporation yard keeper and fire bell ringer in the City Hall Tower, coveted positions held by seasoned firefighters. Articles about the Veteran Firemen's Association of California prominently highlighted Sawyer in a drawing. As he told his stories of fighting fire and running for the volunteers in front of the firefighters of 1850, he was never contradicted.

I relied upon the original hardcover 1850–51 volumes from my personal library, including *The Works of Hubert Howe Bancroft: History of California, 1849–1859*, volumes 4 and 23, with two foldout maps and diagrams of the vigilante cells in proximity to the cage holding Yankee Sullivan. Bancroft's volume 37, *Popular Tribunals*, discusses Billy Mulligan on pages 604–8, and on page 7 it is the primary source for

Sullivan's invention of the false-bottom ballot box. Of equal importance is Frank Soule, John H. Gihon, and James Nisbet's *The Annals of San Francisco,* which mentions on page 244 the muddy streets and children who ran with the fire engines.

Mary Floyd Williams's *History of the San Francisco Committee of Vigilance of 1851,* volume 12, lists minutes of the Executive Committee for July 21, 1851, and comments by George E. Schenck on the apparent fate of Ben Lewis. I relied upon the June 3, 1851, handwritten depositions given by the residents of the Collier House to the police in *The People v. Ben Lewis.* These documents are part of the H. H. Bancroft Collection, Bancroft Library, University of California at Berkeley. Captain George B. Coffin's *A Pioneer Voyage to California and Around the World, 1849–1852* provided firsthand accounts of the great fires. The San Francisco Fire Department's *Historical Review,* with résumés of its personnel, was written while Tom Sawyer was still alive. Pages 100–101 include his biography as a volunteer firefighter. "He arrived in San Francisco Bay in February, 1850 . . . and immediately went to steam shipping, running as a fireman between this port and San Juan and Panama. He continued at this occupation for some years during which time his vessel, the steamer *Independence,* was wrecked on a reef off the Southern coast and burned to the water line and sunk." The piece implies that Sawyer left for the sea immediately, but the *Independence* was not launched in New York until Christmas Day, 1850, and did not reach San Francisco Bay for the first time until September 17, 1851, three months after the great fires ended. Sawyer may have done some sporadic work on the Sacramento River or on a freighter between fires, but he remained in San Francisco, with its clogged harbor, and used his fleetness to save a great city.

The *Fire Department History* states of Sawyer: "Through his ingenuity and heroism he saved the lives of ninety people aboard. . . . When nearly exhausted with the great task of swimming ashore with each passenger on his back, his great mind came to his rescue. By putting the rest of them in life preservers he towed them ashore and landed in the boiling surf safe and sound." The history includes a Lillie Hitchcock piece by Frederick J. Bowlen, battalion chief, San Francisco Fire Department. I consulted period newspaper accounts of the fires and central figures in Sawyer's story from the San Francisco Library microfilm collection and the California Digital Newspaper Collection, a repository of digitized California newspapers from 1846 to the present, including the *Daily Morning Call*, 1863–64; the *Californian*, 1864–67; *San Francisco Dramatic Chronicle*, 1865–66; *Sacramento Daily Union*, 1865–66; *Daily Hawaiian Herald*, 1866; *San Francisco Bulletin*, 1866; and the *Daily Alta California*, 1867–69.

Sources for Henry Clemens's death in an explosion in 1858 onboard the steamer *Pennsylvania* are a *Memphis Eagle and Enquirer* article, June 16, 1858, on the arrival of Twain at his dying brother's bed. *Sunday* magazine, March 19, 1908, printed an illustrated article on Mark and Henry. Twain's precognition of Henry's death appeared in his *Notebooks and Journals, volume 2, Notebook #20*. Margaret Sanborn's *Mark Twain: The Batchelor Years* relates Twain's dream of his brother Henry in his casket on pages 124–29. Twain in his autobiography and in his *Mississippi Writings*, chapter 20, "A Catastrophe," writes of his brother Henry's death and the fatal steamboat explosion.

I reviewed the San Francisco Fire Department Museum for lists of SFFD firehouses, volunteer companies of 1850–66, and notable people; consulted 1850s diaries and letters, birth and death records, coroner's reports, and census reports of 1856–66; looked at city maps of 1852, 1853, 1873, 1896, early city views of 1837–55, city directories for 1850, 1852–53, 1863, 1864, city street guides for 1861 and 1882; and read weather reports, San Francisco County voting records, ward maps and the voter register for 1867, fire insurance maps, ships' passenger lists, descriptions of arrivals, marriages at sea, and shipwrecks; and studied fleets lists, pictures, journals, immigration reports, and the San Francisco Delinquent Tax List, 1867. I used the San Francisco History Center, the San Francisco Public Library, the Historical Abstract of San Francisco for 1897, Vigilance Committee trial transcripts, hundreds of books on the Gold Rush and the adventurers who sailed to San Francisco, tide and wind charts, survivors' accounts of the *Independence* sinking, and San Francisco and Bay Area histories. As a longtime San Francisco resident, I walked all the sites over many years. In 1968–69, as the *San Francisco Chronicle*'s political cartoonist, I sat at my desk during reconstruction on the southwest corner of Mission and Mary streets, directly above the site of Sawyer's saloon at 935 Mission.

At every opportunity I tested the validity of Sawyer's claims. He recalled in an interview that on September 28, 1864, he and Twain went on a bender. "Me and Jack Mannix, who was afterwards bailiff in Judge Levy's court, was walkin' down Montgomery Street." A man named John E. Mannix lived at 829 Mission Street close to Sawyer at 935

Mission. "Mark caught sight of us from a window across the street in the Russ House." Twain should not have been at the Russ House. During that time he was one of two lodgers with a well-to-do private family on Minna Street and preparing to take rooms farther along Minna only two blocks from Sawyer. But I learned that three days earlier, Twain had written his mother and sister that his comrade of two years, Steve Gillis, was getting hitched to Emeline Russ, daughter of the late Christian Russ, who owned the Russ House. Twain was going to stand up for his friend at the nuptials. Sawyer was correct and there was no other way he could have known this. The same day as their bender, September 28, 1864, Twain wrote Orion and Mollie Clemens to say, "I *would* commence on my book, but (mind, this is a secret, & must not be mentioned), Steve & I are getting ready for his wedding, which will take place on the 24th Oct. He will marry Miss Emmelina [sic] Russ." So Sawyer's mention of a book on that day and Twain's presence at the Russ House was not only true but a secret.

"The next day I met Mark down by the old *Call* office," Sawyer continued. That Twain worked at the *Call* was not known, because his articles were not signed. He was later fired from the *Call,* something he never spoke about, but Sawyer knew. "He walks up to me and puts both hands on my shoulders. 'Tom,' he says, 'I'm going to write a book about a boy and the kind I have in mind was just about the toughest boy in the world. Tom, he was just such a boy as you must have been.'" Twain was working on his first book, "a pet notion" of his of about three hundred pages, probably about the river. "Nobody knows what [the novel] is going to be about but just myself," Twain said.

Twain was more definite about the real-life model for Huckleberry Finn than Tom Sawyer. He admitted he had based *Tom Sawyer*'s Becky Thatcher on Laura Hawkins, who lived opposite the Clemenses on Hill Street and modeled Sid Sawyer, Tom's well-behaved half brother, on his late lamented brother Henry. John Briggs, the Joe Harper of *Tom Sawyer*'s gang, was based on one of Mark's closest boyhood friends. Twain's friends from San Francisco were always on his mind. In *Tom Sawyer,* Injun Joe murders Doctor Robinson, the name of torch boy Charlie Robinson's famous father, Doc. Years later, Twain and Harte in their disastrous play, *Ah Sin,* would name Broderick a villain and use the character Shirley Tempest.

Mark Twain's eighty-one-year-old mother, Jane, might have known who the real Tom Sawyer was. On April 17, 1885, a Chicago reporter decided to ask. She was living with Twain's brother, Orion, and his wife, Mollie, in an unpretentious two-story brick house at the intersection of High and Seventh streets in Keokuk, Iowa. Twain was the sole support of the crippled household: a widowed mother, Jane; a widowed sister, Pamela; and Orion, now a lawyer who still trod a long road of foreclosure and bankruptcy. Nearly deaf, Twain's mother needed an ear trumpet to hear the reporter's questions. She painted Mark as "always a good-hearted boy" who was also very wild and mischievous and often skipped school. "Often his father started him off and in a little while followed him to ascertain his whereabouts," she said. "There was a large stump on the way to the schoolhouse and Sam would take up a position behind that, and as his father went past would gradually circle around in such a way to keep out of sight." He asked if Twain in his boyhood days resembled his Tom Sawyer. Was he the immortal character? "Ah, no!" replied the elderly lady firmly, "he was more like Huckleberry Finn than Tom Sawyer. He was always a great boy for history and could never get tired of that kind of reading, but he hadn't any use for schoolhouses and textbooks. This used to trouble his father and me dreadfully, and we were convinced that he would never amount as much in the world as his brothers because he was not near so steady and sober minded as they were." Molly added that Twain had gotten all his humor and talent from his mother. "Tom Sawyer's 'Aunt Polly' and Mrs. Hawkins in *Gilded Age*," she said, "are direct portraits of his mother." And that's where the matter lay. The reporter did note that the old lady could not discuss the death of her son Henry onboard a steamboat without sobbing uncontrollably.

Curiously, the claim that Twain was supposed to have named his book *Tom Sawyer* after his San Francisco acquaintance was well known in 1900 when all of the principals were alive, including Twain, Sawyer, and probably several hundred San Franciscans who knew them both, and could have authenticated or challenged the claim. No one disputed it in San Francisco. The life of Tom Sawyer is replete with stirring scenes and adventures, and he never doubted that Twain named his first book for his longtime friend who had been the inspiration for his best work.

When I worked as a cartoonist and artist at the Stockton, California, *Record* in 1963, I was told the story of "the man who burned down San Francisco" by a sea captain in his late eighties who called the arsonist the Lightkeeper. He said the firebug was set off by the Lightkeeper's Wind, the gales that propelled fogs through the Golden

Gate and up from Southern California. These gales imperiled shipping and set lonely lighthouse keepers to trimming their wicks and activating their blazing lights. I found this name most evocative and used it. I speculated on the arsonist's death at the hands of irate firemen because many suspected looters and arsonists were beaten to death that night. If Ben Lewis did escape, his ultimate fate remains unknown.

Profound thanks to my agent, Joel Gotler, Jenna Ciongoli, Michael Chernuchin, Dan Gordon, Michael Larkin, Michael Goldstein, Thomas Ellsworth, Darren Hattingh, Ryan Fischer-Harbage, Margot Graysmith, Aaron Smith, David Smith, Melanie Graysmith, Penny Wallace, David Zucker, Jordan Sheehan, Kevin Fagan, Marli Peterson, and Mizuki Osawa. Special thanks to the spirited and always reliable Miriam Chotiner-Gardner, art director Christopher Brand and designer Elina Nudelman, Patricia Shaw, Ellen Folan, and Rachel Meier. I am deeply indebted to Charles Conrad, whose wise guidance, sometimes only a word or two, put me on the right path.

SELECTED BIBLIOGRAPHY

Andrews. Ralph W. *Historic Fires of the West: 1865 to 1915*. New York: Bonanza Books, 1966.

Asbury, Herbert. *The Barbary Coast*. New York: Alfred A. Knopf, Inc., 1937.

Askins, Col. Charles. *Texans, Guns & History*. New York: Winchester Press, 1970.

Bacon, Daniel. *Walking San Francisco on the Barbary Coast Trail*. San Francisco: Quicksilver Press, 1996.

Baldwin, Joseph G. Edited by Richard E. Amacher and George W. Polhemus. *The Flush Times of California*. Athens, Georgia: University of Georgia Press, 1966.

Bancroft, Hubert Howe. *The Works of Hubert Howe Bancroft: History of California, Vols. 4 and 23, 1849–1859*. San Francisco: The History Company, Publishers, 1888. (From the original first edition with two foldout maps and diagrams of the vigilante cells in proximity to the cage holding Yankee Sullivan.)

————. *The Works, Vol. 37, Popular Tribunals*. San Francisco: The History Company, Publishers, 1887. (First edition. Billy Mulligan is discussed on pp. 604–8.)

Barker, Malcolm E. *San Francisco Memoirs 1835–1851: Eyewitness Accounts of the Birth of a City*. San Francisco: Londonborn Publications, 1996.

————. *More San Francisco Memoirs 1852–1899*. San Francisco: Londonborn Publications, 1994.

Beebe, Lucius, and Charles Clegg. *San Francisco's Golden Era: A Picture Story of San Francisco Before the Fire*. Berkeley: Howell-North, 1960.

Bell, Major Horace. *On the Old West Coast*. New York: William Morrow & Company, 1930.

Benemann, William, editor. *A Year of Mud and Gold. San Francisco in Letters and Diaries, 1849–1850*. Lincoln and London: University of Nebraska Press, 1999.

Boessenecker, John. *Against the Vigilantes: The Recollections of Dutch Charley Duane.* Norman: University of Oklahoma Press, 1999. (Duane's memoir was originally printed in the *San Francisco Examiner,* 1881. An excellent history, well written and an important source.)

———. *Gold Dust & Gunsmoke: Tales of Gold Rush Outlaws, Gunfighters, Lawmen, and Vigilantes.* New York: John Wiley & Sons, Inc, 1999. From published edition and advance uncorrected proofs. (This is a valuable source for the stories of Billy Mulligan, Dutch Charley, and Yankee Sullivan.)

Block, Eugene E. *Great Stagecoach Robbers of the West.* Garden City, NY: Doubleday and Company, Inc., 1962. (Great resource for Hank Monk.)

Brands, H. W. *The Age of Gold: The California Gold Rush and the New American Dream.* New York: Anchor Books, 2002.

Browning, Peter. *San Francisco/Yerba Buena.* Lafayette, CA: Great West Books, 1998.

Camp, William Martin. *San Francisco, Port of Gold.* Garden City, NY: Doubleday & Company, 1947.

Carlisle, Henry C. *San Francisco Street Names: Sketches of the Lives of Pioneers for Whom San Francisco Streets Are Named.* San Francisco: The American Trust Company, 1954.

Coffin, George B., and Gorham B. Coffin, editor. *A Pioneer Voyage to California and Round the World, 1849 to 1852.* Chicago: Gorham B. Coffin, 1908. (First-hand accounts of the great fires by an artistic sailor.)

Cole, Tom. *A Short History of San Francisco.* San Francisco: Don't Call It Frisco Press, 1981.

Country Beautiful editors. *Great Fires of America.* Waukesha, Wisconsin: Country Beautiful Publishing, 1973.

DeFord, Miriam Allen. *They Were San Franciscans.* Caldwell, ID: The Caxton Printers, Ltd., 1941.

Delgado, James P. *To California by Sea: A Maritime History of the California Gold Rush.* Columbia, South Carolina: University of South Carolina Press, 1996.

———. *Gold Rush Port: The Maritime Archaeology of San Francisco's Waterfront.* Berkeley, California: University of California Press, 2009. (A treasure trove of valuable archaeological information about Yerba Buena Cove from a leading maritime archaeologist.)

Dickson, Samuel. *Tales of San Francisco.* Stanford, CA: Stanford University Press, 1965.

———. *Tales of Love and Hate in Old San Francisco.* San Francisco: Chronicle Books, 1971.

Dillon, Richard H. *Embarcadero: Being a Chronicle of True Sea Adventures from the Port of San Francisco.* New York: Coward-McCann, Inc., 1959.

————. *Humbugs and Heroes*. Garden City, NY: Doubleday and Company, Inc., 1970.

————. *Shanghaiing Days*. Garden City, NY: Coward-McCann, Inc., 1961.

Dobie, Charles Caldwell. *San Francisco: A Pageant*. New York: D. Appleton-Century Company, 1934.

Dunshee, Kenneth Holcomb. *As You Pass By*. New York: Hastings House, 1952. A major source for information about New York firehouses and volunteers, 1832–66.

Duke, Donald, editor. *Water Trails West: The Western Writers of America*. Garden City, NY: Doubleday & Company, Inc., 1978.

Eldredge, Zoeth Skinner. *The Beginnings of San Francisco, Vol. 1*. New York: John C. Rankin, 1912.

The Exempt Firemen of San Francisco: Their Unique and Gallant Record. Also includes a Résumé of the San Francisco Fire Department and its Personnel. San Francisco: H. C. Pendleton, 1900. (This book was written while Tom Sawyer was still alive. Pp. 100–101 include his biography as a volunteer firefighter and his heroism during the sinking of the steamer *Independence* as well as a long Lilly Hitchcock piece as a torch girl and an honorary fireman by Frederick J. Bowlen, battalion chief, SFFD.)

Fehrenback, T. R. *Lone Star: A History of Texas and the Texans*. New York: Macmillan, 1968. (Coffee "Jack" Hays biography.)

Fishkin, Shelley Fisher, editor. *The Adventures of Tom Sawyer in The Oxford Mark Twain*. New York: Oxford University Press, 1996.

Fracchia, Charles A. *Fire & Gold*. Encinitas, California: Heritage Media, 1996.

Garvey, John. *San Francisco Fire Department*. Charleston: Arcadia Publishing, 2003.

Gilliam, Harold. *San Francisco Bay*. Garden City, NY: Doubleday & Company, Inc., 1957. (A terrific book and one of my all-time favorites.)

Goodenough, Simon. *The Fire Engine, an Illustrated History*. Secaucus, NJ: Chartwell Books, 1978.

Gorn, Elliott J. *The Manly Art: Bare-Knuckle Prize Fighting in America*. Ithaca, NY: Cornell University Press, 1989.

Green, Floride. *Some Personal Recollections of Lillie Hitchcock Coit-5*. San Francisco: Grabhorn Press, Limited Edition of 450 copies, 1935. Includes plates from old photographs of Lillie, her mother and father, and engravings. Illustrator might have been Green herself.

Greer, James Kimmins. *Colonel Jack Hays, Texas Frontier Leader and California Builder*. Texas: Texas A & M University Press, 1987.

Harlan, George. *San Francisco Bay Ferryboats*. San Diego: Howell-North Books, 1967.

Hazen, Robert M., and Margaret Hindle Hazen. *Keepers of the Flame*. Princeton: Princeton University Press, 1992.

Hearn, Michael Patrick, editor. *The Annotated Huckleberry Finn*. New York: W. W. Norton and Company, 2001.

Hoffer, Peter Charles. *Seven Fires*. New York: Public Affairs, 2006.

𝄡 Holdredge, Helen. *Firebelle Lillie*. New York: Meredith Press, 1967. (A very valuable biography of the little torch girl that mentions Tom Sawyer's rivalry with Davey Scannell and Lillie's enduring friendship with Mark Twain.)

Jackson, Donald Dale. *Gold Dust*. New York: Alfred A. Knopf, 1980.

Jackson, Joseph Henry, editor. *The Western Gate, A San Francisco Reader*. New York: Farrar, Straus and Young. (Jackson reprints "The Terry-Broderick Duel," Ben C. Truman, 1859.)

Jacobson, Pauline. *City of the Golden 'Fifties*. Berkeley: University of California Press, 1941. (Tom Sawyer is mentioned on p. 84, Ed Stahle on pp. 80–81. Davey Scannell's marathon eating sessions are covered on pp. 54–55. Charlie Robinson's torch boy story is told on pp. 46–47, and the tale of Curly Jack Carroll's botched wedding is on p. 49.)

Johnson, Kenneth M. *San Francisco As It Is*. Georgetown, CA: The Talisman Press, 1964.

Johnson, Paul C. *Pictorial History of California*. New York: Doubleday & Company, 1970.

Johnson, Paul C., and Richard Reinhardt. *San Francisco As It Is, As It Was*. San Francisco: Doubleday & Company, Inc., 1979.

Johnson, William Weber. *The Forty-Niners*. New York: Time-Life Books, 1974. (On p. 192 Charles Robinson relates how he and two other torch boys fell into a pit leading an engine when he was a torch boy in North Beach, San Francisco.)

Jones, Idwal. *Ark of Empire, San Francisco's Montgomery Block*. Garden City, NY: Doubleday & Company, 1955. (The author discusses Sawyer and Twain steaming together in the baths in the Montgomery Block on p. 200. "It was a fortunate acquaintance for the ex-fireman. . . ." Jones speaks of torch boy Charlie Robinson's upstairs painting studio on p. 236.)

Kaplan, Justin. *Mr. Clemens and Mark Twain: A Biography*. New York: Simon and Schuster, 1966.

Kelly, Joellen L., Robert A. Yatsuk., and J. Gordon Routley. *Firefighters*. New York: Universe Publishers, 2003.

Kemble, John Haskell. *San Francisco Bay, A Pictorial Maritime History*. Cambridge, MD: Cornell Maritime Press, 1957.

Kersey, A.T.J., and William J. Goudie, editors. *Ripper's Heat Engines*. London: Longmans, Green and Co., 1939.

Kowalewski, Michael, editor. *Gold Rush*. Berkeley, California: Heyday Books, 1997.

Levy, Jo Ann. *They Saw the Elephant*. Norman, OK: University of Oklahoma Press, 1992.

Lewis, Oscar. *San Francisco: Mission to Metropolis*. San Diego: Howell-North Books, 1980.

———. *Sea Routes to the Gold Fields*. New York: Alfred A. Knopf, 1949. (The sinking of the *Independence* is presented on pp. 252–53.)

Lewis, Oscar, editor. *This Was San Francisco*. New York: David McKay Company, Inc., 1962.

Lockwood, Charles. *Suddenly San Francisco*. San Francisco: The Hearst Corporation, 1978.

MacMullen, Jerry. *Paddle-Wheel Days in California*. Stanford: Stanford University Press, 1944.

Marryat, Frank. *Mountains and Molehills*. Reprint of 1855 edition. Stanford: Stanford University Press, 1952.

Mayer, Robert, editor and compiler. *San Francisco, A Chronological and Documentary History, 1542–1970*. New York: Oceana Publications, Inc., 1974.

McGloin, John Bernard, S. J. *San Francisco, The Story of A City*. San Rafael, CA: Presidio Press, 1978.

Mee, Bob. *Bare Fists*. Woodstock, NY: Overlook Press, 2001. (Yankee Sullivan fights and background.)

Meltzer, Milton. *Mark Twain Himself: A Pictorial Biography*. New York: Bonanza Books, 1960.

Mullen, Kevin J. *Let Justice Be Done: Crime and Politics in Early San Francisco*. Reno and Las Vegas: University of Nevada Press, 1989. (A scholarly, factually reasoned, and deeply researched study of the police records of Old San Francisco by an ex–deputy police chief with twenty-six years of service with the San Francisco Police Department.)

Muscatine, Doris. *Old San Francisco, the Biography of a City from Early Days to the Earthquake*. New York: G. P. Putnam's Sons, 1975.

Myrick, David F. *San Francisco's Telegraph Hill*. Berkeley: Howell-North Books, 1972.

Neville, Amelia Ransome. *The Fantastic City*. Boston and New York: Houghton Mifflin Company, 1932.

Newell, Gordon. *Paddlewheel Pirate*. New York: E. P. Dutton and Company, Inc., 1959. (A biography of Captain Ned Wakeman that includes Ben Lewis's arrest.)

O'Brien, Robert. *This Is San Francisco*. New York: McGraw-Hill Book Company, Inc., 1948. (Quote about the opening of the Fifth and Mission streets U. S. Mint across from the original Tom Sawyer's Saloon is on p. 273.)

Paine, Albert Bigelow, Introduction to *What Is Man? And Other Essays by Samuel Langhorne Clemens, Vol. 26 of The Writings of Twain*, with the assistance of Mary Jane Jones. *The Works of Twain*. Berkeley: University of California Press, 1923.

Quinn, Arthur. *The Rivals*. Lincoln, NE: University of Nebraska Press, 1994. (Excellent book on Broderick and his courage. It is one of my favorites and a tremendous source.)

Rasmussen, Louis J. *San Francisco Ship Passenger Lists*. Volumes 1, 2, 4. San Francisco.

Rathmell, George. *Realms of Gold*. Berkeley: Creative Arts Book Company, 1998.

Richards, Rand. *Historic San Francisco*. San Francisco: Heritage House Publishers, 1991. (Twain met "a fireman named Tom Sawyer," p. 342.)

Riesenberg, Felix, Jr. *Golden Gate*. New York: Alfred A. Knopf, 1940.

Royce, Josiah. *California*. New York: Alfred A. Knopf, 1948. (Details the burning of the *Alta* office and the sinking of the *Independence*.)

Russ, Carolyn Hale, editor. *The Log of a Forty-Niner* (edited from the original manuscript). Boston, MA: B. J. Brimmer Company, 1923.

San Francisco Fire Department. *History of the Fire Department*. San Francisco: Press of Commercial Publishers Co., 1900.

San Francisco Fire Department, *Historical Review. Part II, the Paid Department*, December 3, 1866. (Tom Sawyer, paid corporation yard keeper, December 3, 1866.)

Sanborn, Margaret. *Mark Twain: The Batchelor Years*. New York: Doubleday Dell Publishing, 1990. (Tells the story of Mark Twain and Lillie Hitchcock, p. 244. Relates Twain's dream about his brother Henry in his casket, pp. 124–29.)

Schultz, Charles R. *Forty-Niners 'Round the Horn*. Columbia, SC: University of South Carolina Press, 1999.

Scott, Mel. *The San Francisco Bay Area*. Berkeley: University of California Press, 1959.

Secrest, William B. *California Badmen*. Sanger, CA: Word Dancer Press, 2007. (Includes Yankee Sullivan's and Billy Mulligan's biographies.)

Senkewicz, Robert M. *Vigilantes in Gold Rush San Francisco*. Stanford, CA: Stanford University Press, 1985.

Soule, Frank, John H. Gihon, and James Nisbet. *The Annals of San Francisco: A Complete History of All the Important Events Connected with Its Great City*. San Francisco: Appleton & Co., 1854. (Mentions children who ran with the fire engines, p. 244.)

Stellman, Louis J. *Sam Brannan, Builder of San Francisco*. Fairfield, CA: James Stevenson Publisher, 1996.

Stewart, George R. *Committee of Vigilance*. Boston: Houghton Mifflin Company, 1964.

Tapper, Bernard, editor. *Mark Twain's San Francisco*. Berkeley: Heyday Books, 1963. ("Over the Mountains," pp. 3–6; "Earthquake Almanac," pp. 124–28; "Mark Twain's Farewell," pp. 261–63.)

Thomas, Lately. *Between Two Empires*. New York: Houghton Mifflin Company, 1969.

Time-Life editors. *The Forty-Niners*. New York: Time Inc., 1974.

Twain, Mark. *Autobiography of Mark Twain*. Vol. 1. Edited by Harriet Elinor Smith. Berkley, CA: University of California Press, 2010.

———. *Mississippi Writings*. Guy Cardwell, editor. New York: Library of America, 1982. (*Life on the Mississippi*. Chapter 22, "A Catastrophe." Twain's brother Henry and a fatal steamboat explosion.)

———. *The Innocents Abroad & Roughing It*. Guy Cardwell, editor. New York: Library of America, 1984. (*Roughing It*, Chapter LIX: "I slunk from back street to back street. I slunk away from approaching faces that looked familiar, I sluck to my meals . . . I felt meaner and lowlier and more despicable than the worms.")

———. *Collected Tales, Sketches, Speeches, and Essays. Vol. 1: 1852–1890*. Lewis Budd, editor. New York: Library of America, 1992.

———. *Collected Tales, Sketches, Speeches, and Essays. Vol. 2: 1891–1910*. Lewis Budd, editor. New York: Library of America, 1992.

Utley, Robert M. *Lone Star Justice*. New York: Berkley Books, 2003.

Walkins, T.H., and R.R. Olmsted. *Mirror of the Dream: An Illustrated History of San Francisco*. San Francisco: Scrimshaw Press, 1976.

Williams, Mary Floyd. *History of the San Francisco Committee of Vigilance of 1851*. Herbert Botton, editor. Vol. 12. (Lists minutes of the Executive Committee for July 21, 1851, and comments by George E. Schenck on the fate of Ben Lewis.)

Newspapers and Periodicals

"Parker House, City Intelligence." *Daily Alta California*, May 4, 1851.

"Terrible Conflagration! Loss About $5,000,000." *Daily Alta California*, May 4, 1851.

"The Conflagration." *Daily Alta California*, May 5, 1851.

"Reflections after the Event." *Daily Alta California*, May 6, 1851.

"The Spirit of Lynch Law." *Daily Alta California*, June 4, 1851. (Mentions Ben Lewis.)

"Another Conflagration!! Ten Squares Burned. Loss Three Millions of Dollars!!" *Daily Alta California,* June 23, 1851.

"The effects of the Conflagration." *Daily Alta California,* June 24, 1851.

"Dinner to Captain Wakeman." *Daily Alta California,* July 27, 1851.

"Resignation of Captain Wakeman." *Daily Alta California,* October 5, 1851.

"The Wakeman Testimonial." *Daily Alta California,* March 9, 1853.

"Natchez." *Sacramento Daily Union,* September 6, 1856, vol. 11, no. 1700.

"Natchez reports theft." *Sacramento Daily Union,* February 19, 1857, vol. 12, no. 1841.

"My Brother, Henry Clemens . . ." *Memphis Eagle and Enquirer,* June 16, 1858.

"Natchez the Pistol Man." *Sacramento Daily Union,* September 25, 1858, vol. 16, no. 2339.

"David C. Broderick Biography." *Sacramento Daily Union,* September 17, 1859, vol. 17, no. 2644.

"Death of Senator Broderick." *Sacramento Daily Union,* September 19, 1859, vol. 18, no. 2645.

Brady, Matthew. "The Torch Boys," October 29, 1990. *San Francisco Independent* column "The Old Town," p. 20.

Mark Twain columns in the *San Francisco Daily Morning Call:* "A Trip to the Cliff House," June 25, 1864; "Police Court," July 12, 1864; "The County Prison," July 17, 1864; "The Police Court Besieged," July 22, 1864; "Fire at Hayes Valley," August 18, 1864.

Mark Twain: "Terrible Calamity, Explosion of the Steamer Washoe's Boilers. One Hundred Wounded," *San Francisco Daily Morning Call,* September 7, 1864.

"Thomas Sawyer was run over by a hook and ladder truck and seriously injured." *San Francisco Call,* April 23, 1869.

"The Coyote Hill Duel," reporter James O'Meara's eyewitness account of Billy Mulligan and Jimmy Douglass's shoot-out. *San Francisco Call,* December 25, 1881.

Moulder, A. J. "Broderick's Moral Courage." *Argonaut 3,* no. 24 (1878): 9–12. "Worked the Brakes, Some of the Old Boys Who Ran With 'the Machine' in Days Long Ago." *San Francisco Call,* January 3, 1888. (Includes drawing of Tom Sawyer in fire helmet as the first vice president.)

"Tom Sawyer organizes a society for passage of bill to make the City Force a metropolitan one with a fully paid force." *San Francisco Call,* October 13, 1890.

"Tom Sawyer described as over 60 years old, hale and hardy, hails from New York." *San Francisco Call,* September 16, 1890.

"Sawyer comes to aid of recently discharged fireman." *San Francisco Call*, October 13, 1890, vol. 67, no. 135.

"Discharged Firemen. Tom Sawyer was not in a position to lose by the new movement." *Daily Alta California*, October 17, 1890, vol. 83, no. 109.

"The History of a Pistol." *Daily Alta California*, April 21, 1891, vol. 84, no. 111.

"Among Firemen. Tom Sawyer seeks job of Fire Commissioner." *San Francisco Call*, August 17, 1891, vol. 70, no. 78. (Includes ink drawing of Chief Scannell.)

"Old-Time Firemen, Pioneer Firefighters Meeting, Tom Sawyer, corporation-yard keeper." *San Francisco Call*, August 31, 1891, vol. 70, no. 92.

"Veteran Firemen Association." *San Francisco Call*, September 16, 1891.

"Supervisors petitioned to make Sawyer Fire Commissioner." *San Francisco Call*, November 8, 1891.

"Our Firemen. Tom Sawyer sings. Celebrates Tom Sawyer's Birthday." *San Francisco Call*, January 2, 1892, vol. 71, no. 32.

"Vet's Election." *San Francisco Call*, January 18, 1892, vol. 71, no. 49. (Tom Sawyer, Jr., the ex-secretary speaks.)

"The Veteran Firemen's Association of California," *Sacramento Daily Union*, September 20, 1893, vol. 86, no. 26.

"Veteran Firemen. Tom Sawyer runs in race." *San Francisco Call*, June 17, 1894, vol. 76, no. 17.

"Veteran Firemen, Vocal Solo by Tom Sawyer." *San Francisco Call*, May 23, 1895, vol. 77, no. 164.

"The Real Tom Sawyer, Living in This City and Doing Business on Mission Street." *San Francisco Call*, July 14, 1895, vol. 78, no. 44. (Sawyer and his friend Mannix meet Twain coming out of Russ House and spend the night drinking.)

"Billy Mulligan Dies (a review)." *San Francisco Call*, September 30, 1895, vol. 78, no. 122.

"He took morphine, aged bartender asks for Tom Sawyer's help." *San Francisco Call*, January 29, 1896, vol. 79, no. 60.

"Jumped into the Sea, Thomas Sawyer is an old acquaintance of Mark Twain, and it was from him the name of 'Tom Sawyer' was taken." *Sacramento Daily Union*, March 15, 1897, vol. 81, no. 105.

"Old Friends Picnic." *Daily Alta California*, May 31, 1898, vol. 83, no. 183.

Viola Rodgers Interview. "Here is the Original of Mark Twain's Tom Sawyer." *San Francisco Call*, October 23, 1898, vol. 84, no. 145, pp. 25–26 (Long article with drawn illustrations of the literary Tom Sawyer and the original Tom Sawyer. "He prides himself upon being a member of the first volunteer fire company ever formed in California.")

"Old Time Firemen, Tom Sawyer sings 'On the Rocky Road to Dublin.' *San Francisco Call,* January 27, 1899.

New York Herald, "Mark Twain's Reunion," June 15, 1902. (Who is the real Tom Sawyer? "Town's full of 'em," Twain said. "They are not absolute portraits of any one person. Some of the incidents accredited to Tom Sawyer happened to one and some to another and some not at all.")

"Mark Twain interview." *New York American Journal,* March 18, 1906, p. 10. ("There is more than a dozen real Tom Sawyers and Huck Finns have succumbed in the past twenty years.")

"Tom Sawyer, Whose Name Inspired Twain, Dies at Great Age." *San Francisco Call,* October 1, 1906, vol. 100, no. 123, p. 1. (Includes photo of Tom Sawyer.)

"Tom Sawyer's Will Filed." *San Francisco Call,* October 19, 1906, vol. 100, no. 141.

Twain, Mark. "Chapters from my Autobiography" (*North American Review,* October 1907).

"Henry Clemens." *Sunday* magazine, March 29, 1908. (With illustration of Twain at his dying brother's bedside.)

"Illustration of Mark Twain at his dying brother's bedside." *Sunday* magazine, March 29, 1908. (Letters and citations from the Twain Project at the University of California, Berkeley.)

Perrigan, Dana. "Beneath the City." *San Francisco Examiner,* March 16, 1998, p. A-1 and p. A-10.

Bancroft Library, University of California at Berkeley, http://bancroft.berkeley. edu. Guardians of the City, the Firemen's Museum (which now has a Tom Sawyer exhibit): www.guardiansofthecity.org/sffd/companies/volunteer/.

The Mark Twain Project at the University of California at Berkeley is a magnificent depository of everything about Twain, including his letters, manuscripts, and biographical notes: www.marktwainproject.org.

See also the Virtual Museum of the City of San Francisco, "Tom Sawyer," www. theshipslist.com/ships/passengerlists/, and San Francisco: Ships in Port, www.maritimeheritage.org/inport.htm. See San Francisco Fire Department Museum, 655 Presidio Avenue, San Francisco, CA, 9415-2424; the fire engines of 1850–1866 are on display there.